BUDDHISM IN CANADA

Buddhism has become a major religion in Canada over the last half-century. The 'ethnic Buddhism' associated with immigrant Asian peoples is the most important aspect, but there is also a growing constituency of Euro-Canadian Buddhists seriously interested in the faith. This book analyzes the phenomenon of Buddhism in Canada from a regional perspective, providing a review of the history of Buddhism and an analysis of its current situation in the provinces and in three major metropolitan areas. The work provides an important examination of the place of Buddhism in a developed Western country associated with a traditional Judeo-Christian culture, but a country nonetheless undergoing profound sociological transformation due in no small part to large-scale immigration and religio-cultural pluralism.

Bruce Matthews is the Dean of Arts and C. B. Lumsden Professor of Comparative Religion at Acadia University, Nova Scotia, Canada. A former Commonwealth scholar in Buddhist Civilization at the University of Ceylon, Peradeniya (1970–71), he has a long-standing interest in Buddhism and the modern world.

Routledge Critical Studies in Buddhism

General Editors:
Charles S. Prebish and Damien Keown

Routledge Critical Studies in Buddhism is a comprehensive study of the Buddhist tradition. The series explores this complex and extensive tradition from a variety of perspectives, using a range of different methodologies.

The series is diverse in its focus, including historical studies, textual translations and commentaries, sociological investigations, bibliographic studies, and considerations of religious practice as an expression of Buddhism's integral religiosity. It also presents materials on modern intellectual historical studies, including the role of Buddhist thought and scholarship in a contemporary, critical context and in the light of current social issues. The series is expansive and imaginative in scope, spanning more than two and a half millennia of Buddhist history. It is receptive to all research works that inform and advance our knowledge and understanding of the Buddhist tradition.

The following titles are published in association with the *Oxford Centre for Buddhist Studies*

Oxford Centre for Buddhist Studies

a project of The Society for the Wider Understanding of the Buddhist Tradition

The *Oxford Centre for Buddhist Studies* conducts and promotes rigorous teaching and research into all forms of the Buddhist tradition.

EARLY BUDDHIST METAPHYSICS
Noa Ronkin

MIPHAM'S DIALECTICS AND THE DEBATES ON EMPTINESS
Karma Phuntsho

HOW BUDDHISM BEGAN
The conditioned genesis of the early teachings
Richard F. Gombrich

BUDDHISM IN CANADA

Edited by Bruce Matthews

Routledge
Taylor & Francis Group

LONDON AND NEW YORK

First published 2006
by Routledge
2 Park Square, Milton Park, Abingdon, Oxon OX14 4RN

Simultaneously published in the USA and Canada
by Routledge
270 Madison Ave, New York, NY 10016

Routledge is an imprint of the Taylor & Francis Group

Typeset in 10/12pt Times New Roman by Graphicraft Limited, Hong Kong
Printed and bound in Great Britain by Biddles Ltd, Kings Lynn, Norfolk

British Library Cataloguing in Publication Data
A catalogue record for this book is available
from the British Library

Library of Congress Cataloging in Publication Data
Buddhism in Canada / edited by Bruce Matthews.
p. cm. – (Routledge critical studies in Buddhism)
Includes bibliographical references and index.
ISBN 0-415-32279-0 (hardback : alk. paper)
1. Buddhism–Canada. I. Matthews, Bruce, 1941– . II. Series.
BQ742.B83 2005
294.3′0971–dc22
2005018225

ISBN10: 0–415–32279–0
ISBN13: 9–78–0–415–32279–9

CONTENTS

CONTENTS

CONTRIBUTORS

Mathieu Boisvert has been a professor at the Département des sciences religieuses de l'Université du Québec à Montréal (UQÀM) since 1992. He was initially trained in philology (Sanskrit, Pali), but now primarily works in the anthropology of religion. He is one of the founders of the *Groupe de recherches interdisciplinaire sur le Montréal ethno-religieux* (GRIMER), research funded in part by the Social Sciences and Humanities Research Council of Canada.

Paul Bramadat is an associate professor in the Department of Religious Studies at the University of Winnipeg. His research interests include religion and public policy in Canada and the intersection between religious and ethnic modes of identity. His most recent work reconsiders the relationship between religions, Canada's multiculturalism program, and the federal government.

Victor Chan is Executive Director of the Contemporary Tibetan Studies Program, Institute of Asian Research at the University of British Columbia.

Larry DeVries is located in the Pacific Rim Department at Langara College in Vancouver BC and teaches mostly religious studies courses. He holds a MA and PhD in South Asia Studies from the University of Minnesota and has taught at such institutions as the University of Minnesota, the University of Hawaii, and the University of Washington, as well as holding a research position at the University of Chicago under the National Endowment for the Humanities.

Louis-Jacques Dorais graduated in anthropology from Université de Montréal (MSc), and in ethnolinguistics from Université de Paris-III, Sorbonne (Doct.). He has taught since 1972 in the Department of Anthropology, Université Laval, Québec, Canada. Dorais specializes in language and identity among overseas Vietnamese, the Inuit, and French-speaking minorities in North America.

Mavis L. Fenn received her PhD from McMaster University, Hamilton, Ontario, Canada. She teaches Asian Religion at the Department of Religious Studies at St Paul's College (University of Waterloo), Ontario, Canada. Her research interests include women in Buddhism and the adaptation of Buddhism to the West. Her most recent articles are 'The Kutadanta Sutta: Tradition in tension' and 'The Ordination Issue: Where are we now?' (in progress). She is currently working on two projects: 'Buddhism on a Canadian Campus' and 'Buddhist Women in Canada' with Janet McClellan at Wilfrid Laurier University.

Leslie Kawamura is Professor of Buddhist Studies in the Department of Religious Studies, Faculty of Humanities, the University of Calgary. He is currently the Chair of the Asian Studies Group, the Coordinator of the Tri-Faculty East Asian Studies BA Major program (Faculties of Communication and Culture, Humanities, and Social Sciences), and the Coordinator of the East Asian Studies Minor for the Faculty of Communication and Culture. He has written numerous papers as chapters of books or articles in various journals. He has published eight books, including translations of G. M. Nagao's *Māadhyamaka and Yogācāra*, Ye-shes rgyal-mtshan's *Sems dang sems byung (Mind in Buddhist Psychology)*, and *The Bodhisattva Doctrine in Buddhism*. He has read papers at various conferences held in the Netherlands, Hungary, Austria, England, China, Japan, USA, and Canada. His major field of research interest is early Yogācāra in India, using Tibetan, Chinese, Japanese, and English sources.

George Klima graduated from the University of Victoria. Subsequently, he completed a PhD in General Psychology at Queen's University, Kingston. Ontario. After graduation, Klima worked in information technology for twenty years in Montréal and Toronto, particularly with IBM Canada.

Kay Koppedrayer is a full-time faculty member of the Department of Religion and Culture at Wilfrid Laurier University, Waterloo, Ontario, Canada. Her scholarly interests have taken her to places as diverse as Rosebud, South Dakota; the Kingdom of Bhutan; Pawhuska, Oklahoma; Tanjavur (in South India); and Barnet, Vermont. In addition to her work on Hinduism and Buddhism in North America, her academic forays have taken her into the world of expressive culture, in work on performance, sports, ritual activities, and visual display.

Manuel Litalien is a PhD student in political science at Université du Québec à Montréal. His research focuses on the relationship between religion and politics in Southeast Asia, international relations in Pacific Asia, and transnational theologico-political movements.

Bruce Matthews is Dean of the Faculty of Arts and C. B. Lumsden Professor of Comparative Religion, Acadia University, Wolfville, Nova Scotia. He has studied Buddhism and politics in South and Southeast Asia (particularly Sri Lanka and Burma) since 1970. He regularly travels to Asia and in Sri Lanka has developed strong, informative links with both government and civil society. He has written many authoritative articles on conflict and peace processes in Buddhist countries.

Janet McLellan is Assistant Professor in the Religion and Culture Department at Wilfrid Laurier University. She is the author of *Many Petals of the Lotus: Five Asian Buddhist Communities in Toronto*. Her current research involves Cambodian refugees in Ontario and examines the role religion plays in their resettlement and adaptation, in constructing a Khmer Canadian identity, and in the development of transnational networks.

James G. Mullens received his PhD in Religious Studies from McMaster University and is a member of the Department of Religious Studies and Anthropology at the University of Saskatchewan, where he has taught Buddhist Studies and Comparative Religion since 1989. His areas of research specialization are Buddhist monastic history; Buddhism and society; engaged Buddhism; and religion and nonviolence.

James Placzek is the Chair of the Pacific Rim Department at Langara College in Vancouver BC, and an honorary research associate of the Institute of Asian Research, University of British Columbia. He lived for seven years in Thailand, and witnessed the beginnings of the Western branch of the Ajahn Chah lineage, but never ordained. He has degrees in Psychology, Linguistics, and an interdisciplinary PhD in Southeast Asian Cultures and History, all of which he finds relevant in the study of Buddhism in the West.

François Thibeault is currently studying religions at Université du Québec à Montréal, in the MA program of the Département de sciences religieuses. His research focuses primarily on the interpretation and the process of the implantation of Buddhism in the West, particularly in the Province of Québec. His research includes a specific concern for Buddhist ethnic communities and their relationship to the larger Québec society.

Marybeth White completed a double major honors degree in Religious Studies and Philosophy at York University. Her Master of Arts thesis explores Thich Nhat Hanh's and Rita Gross' views of family, community and Buddhist practice, and the validity of parenting as a path toward the Buddhist ideal of enlightenment. Currently, she is a doctoral candidate in the Religion and Culture Department at Wilfrid Laurier University. Her research involves issues of religious identity among second-generation Lao refugees in North America.

FOREWORD

Paul Bramadat

For most of its roughly 2,500 years, Buddhism has been confined to various parts of Asia. However, at least two phenomena have introduced the tradition to a great many people outside Asia. First, of course, the interaction in the past half millennia between European scholars, clerics, merchants, soldiers, and colonizers on the one hand and the inhabitants of predominantly Buddhist (or Buddhist-influenced) regions on the other hand have brought Buddhism into the imaginations of many people in the West. While such forays into the Orient produced highly distorted images of the East that still bedevil us today (Said 1978; Paper, Paper and Lai 2005), these several centuries of interaction did lay the groundwork for the more favourable contemporary reception of Buddhism in the West.

Second, and more recently, a number of changes within the spheres of communication, capitalism, and mass transportation have made it possible for millions of Buddhists to migrate to North America. Such migrations have been occurring for a variety of reasons for over a hundred years (and longer in Europe), but these movements clearly entered an entirely new phase by the 1960s, due to the global reorganization occasioned by World War II. These historical changes in international migration patterns are interesting, but this is not the place to consider them.[1] What is worth noting, though, is that while there have been small Buddhist communities in Canada since the beginning of the twentieth century, the numbers of Buddhists in this country have increased dramatically in roughly the past twenty years. This is partly due to the fact that in the late 1960s, federal policy makers dramatically revised their approaches both to immigration and Canadian culture.

Regarding the question of Canadian culture, most readers will know that Prime Minister Trudeau's 1971 inauguration of the Multiculturalism Policy represented a fairly significant change in the way the Canadian national meta-narrative was to be reconstructed. Although there are still debates about why the policy was launched and whether it was and is effective, public opinion polls consistently show that most Canadians embrace the policy and the progressive ethical ideals on which it is founded.[2]

Regarding the question of immigration, some readers will be unfamiliar with the fact that our immigration policies were once rather unapologetically based on race (or, to put it another way, were generated by racism). After World War II, as racism became increasingly discredited, Canadian and American policy makers and cultural leaders rejected these policies as ineffective means of preparing ourselves for the more multicultural world so many people felt was emerging. The highly problematic 'quota' system that had helped for decades to 'keep Canada white' (a popular slogan in the early part of the twentieth century) finally gave way at the end of the 1960s to the 'point' system. According to this new approach – still in place today, in modified form – immigration candidates are deemed acceptable if they accumulate a certain number of points which are awarded for their education level, family status, occupational experience, proficiency in one of the two official languages, and so on. These policy changes opened the door to many Buddhists, Muslims, Hindus, and Sikhs, and fundamentally altered the nature of Canadian immigration. Moreover, as any study of contemporary Canadian Buddhism will demonstrate, many Buddhists also found their way to Canada as refugees in the wake of the Vietnam War, the Chinese invasion of Tibet, and the Cambodian genocide.

While it is very difficult to determine with much precision the size of what is variously called the non-Asian, white, convert, non-ethnic, or Euro-American Buddhist population, anecdotal evidence suggests that their numbers are significant. Their forms and levels of involvement in Buddhism might be, in historical terms, somewhat unusual,[3] but they are an increasingly important segment of the larger Buddhist community. Although this is not the central concern of these chapters, part of the backdrop of this book is the tension between 'Asian' or 'ethnic' and 'Western' or 'non-Asian' Buddhists. In Canada, even within the same sub-tradition of Buddhism, Asian and non-Asian groups often operate separately, in what Numrich (1996) calls 'parallel congregations.' While some Asians are concerned that Westerners and some 'new agers' are merely dabbling temporarily in a deep and demanding tradition, some non-Asians are concerned that Asian practitioners are perhaps too attached to culture-bound (e.g., strictly Thai or Sinhalese) accretions rather than the strictly religious or spiritual elements of Buddhism.

Although there are Buddhist groups across Canada, it is easy to see why Cambodian and Vietnamese refugees and their children, relatively recent and economically mobile Chinese business class immigrants, third- or fourth-generation overwhelmingly exogamous integrated Japanese, and non-Asian Buddhists, would find it very difficult to work together to build a pan-Buddhist or ecumenical movement in this country. Nevertheless, although the linguistic, cultural, and social class differences between these groups tend to militate against the kinds of institutions that seem to be necessary to ensure the future health of Buddhism, we are presently witnessing the beginnings of some of these structures (most obviously, the Nalanda College of Buddhist Studies, and Buddhismcanada.com).

In short, a variety of forces have combined to greatly increase the Buddhist presence in Canada. At the same time, most Canadians know very little about Buddhism. In his Preface, Bruce Matthews echoes Charles Prebish (1999: 234) by noting that the study of Buddhism in North America is in its infancy. In *Buddhism in Canada*, Matthews and his colleagues have provided readers with an extremely valuable contribution to the public and private conversations many people are having about a tradition that is no longer strictly associated with distant lands and epochs. The question is whether or not non-Buddhist Canadians are prepared to understand this tradition, or to relate constructively with its communities and practitioners. The answer to both questions is, emphatically, no. Research conducted by Chris Klassen (2002) indicates that with a few exceptions (notably, in Québec), most Canadian secondary schools do not consistently offer education about religion to their students; and, when such elective courses are offered, they are rarely promoted. Of course, what Lois Sweet calls our 'religious illiteracy' (1997) is not simply a by-product of an ill-conceived secularization of our schools. In fact, virtually throughout our governments and in most places in our media, religion is treated as either dangerous, doomed to extinction, or at least a strictly private matter. Consequently, we know little about Buddhism or our Buddhist neighbours (not to mention our Christian, Muslim, and Sikh neighbours).

Buddhism in Canada functions first and foremost as a kind of national Buddhist 'map.' In this sense, it is an important step in the study of this tradition in Canada. Clearly, this book will serve as the reference point for future in-depth studies of the temples, traditions, and leaders the authors discuss. Furthermore, as local and national policy makers endeavour to improve the way governments respond to religious – rather than merely ethnic or racial – differences, they will benefit from this book's broad topographical sketch of the tradition. In addition, the book also offers several thick descriptions of particular groups and individuals. Matthews' discussion of Trungpa Rinpoche's time and legacy in Halifax, and White's consideration of the challenges the Lao community faced in Caledon are just two examples of the kinds of portraits that will help to add some ethnographic detail to the map.

There are elements of Canadian institutions, history, and society that are often promoted by our governments as core features of our culture (e.g., hockey, politeness, Medicare), but the inhabitants of this vast geography have never been able to agree upon a single unifying culture, ideology, or identity. Many Canadians are beginning to feel a sense of pride in our much celebrated (and often criticized) willingness to accept the cultural changes and ambiguities that are associated with evolving demographic, moral, and political realities. With this in mind, it is not surprising that Buddhists, whose tradition seeks to illuminate the impermanence at the heart of the universe, would find Canada to be a congenial environment in which to root and recreate their lives and tradition. Those of us interested in Buddhism in Canada will find this book to be a most helpful guide to the new terrain of Canadian religion.

Notes

1 See Ebaugh and Saltzman Chafetz 2002; Haddad, *et al.* 2003; Bramadat and Seljak 2005; *Journal of International Migration and Integration.*
2 However, the xenophobic backlash against Muslims and others in the aftermath of 11 September 2001 indicates that at least some Canadians do not, or do not unequivocally, support all of the goals of the Multiculturalism Policy.
3 In other words, some are 'nightstand' Buddhists, some are 'New Age' Buddhists, some are serious practitioners (who might take vows and become monks or nuns), some are closely associated with a specific, well-defined Asian Buddhist teacher or school of thought, some pick and choose from the various leaders and traditions, some import elements of Buddhist practice or thought into their core Christian or Jewish identities. This is, of course, just a partial list of the various ways a non-Asian might express his or her Buddhism.

Bibliography

Bramadat, Paul and Seljak, David (eds) (2005) *Religion and Ethnicity in Canada.* Toronto, ON: Pearson Education.

Ebaugh, Helen Rose and Chafetz, Janet Saltzman (eds) (2002) *Religion Across Borders: Transnational Immigrant Networks.* Lanham, MD: AltaMira Press.

Haddad, Yvonne Yazbeck, Smith, Jane T. and Esposito, John L. (eds) (2003) *Religion and Immigration: Christian, Jewish, and Muslim Experiences in the United States.* Lanham, MD: AltaMira Press.

Klassen, Chris (2002) "Teaching World Religions in Public Schools Across Canada," Unpublished manuscript. York University, Ontario.

McLellan, Janet and White, Marybeth (2005) "Social Capital and Identity Politics Among Asian Buddhists in Toronto," *Journal of International Migration and Integration,* 6(2): 235–53.

Numrich, Paul David (1996) *Old Wisdom in the New World: Americanization in Two Immigrant Theravada Buddhist Temples.* Knoxville, TN: University of Tennessee Press.

Paper, Jordan, Paper, Li Chuang and Lai, David Chenyuan (2005) "The Chinese in Canada: Their Unrecognized Religion," in P. Bramadat and D. Seljak (eds) *Religion and Ethnicity in Canada.* Toronto, ON: Pearson Education.

Prebish, Charles (1999) *Luminous Passage: The Practice and Study of Buddhism in America.* Berkeley, CA: University of California Press.

Said, Edward (1978) *Orientalism.* London: Routledge and Kegan Paul.

Sweet, Lois (1997) *God in the Classroom.* Toronto, ON: McClelland and Stewart.

PREFACE

Bruce Matthews

Buddhism has a fascinating history in Canada. This book aims to show how the faith has developed in Canada, and something of its present circumstances. The contributors focus on specific geographical regions. The account unfolds from west to east, beginning with a review of Buddhism in British Columbia by James Placzek and Larry DeVries, for the West Coast was the site of the original migration of Asian Buddhists in the mid-nineteenth century and is still a vital centre of Buddhist activity and culture. An addendum to this chapter by Victor Chan on the impact of the visit of the Dalai Lama to Vancouver in the spring of 2004 provides an interesting insight into the importance of Asian Buddhist leadership and image in the Canadian context. Leslie Kawamura sets down the story in Alberta, and James Mullens the two prairie provinces of Saskatchewan and Manitoba. Kay Koppedrayer and Mavis Fenn examine Buddhism in Ontario, and Janet McLellan the city of Toronto, which claims the most diverse number of Buddhist communities in the country. Marybeth White offers a 'thick description' of a unique situation with the Lao Buddhist community in that city, alerting us to several challenges that confront ethnic Buddhist groups in many parts of the nation. Louis-Jacques Dorais provides an analysis of Buddhism in Québec, with special focus on the Vietnamese community. Mathieu Boisvert, Manuel Litalien and François Thibeault have provided a valuable survey of Buddhism in Canada's largest French-speaking city, Montréal. Bruce Matthews shows that the Atlantic provinces may not have significant numbers of Buddhists, but what sects and communities there are give a fascinating glimpse into the spread of the faith into this sparsely populated and traditional region, reminding us that there is not a province or territory in Canada (including Nunuvut in the far north) that does not have some Buddhist outreach or expression. A final appendix by George Klima relates to a vital website that he has carefully constructed of hundreds of Canadian Buddhist organizations, a resource of significance for anyone interested in the enormous diversity of the Buddhist experience in this land. I need as well to thank five others in particular: Paul Bramadat of the University of Winnipeg (and recent editor and author, along with David Seljak, of *Religion and Ethnicity in Canada*)[1] for kindly agreeing to write the Foreword; Robert Florida of the University of Victoria, British Columbia, has helped in editing some of the work in this volume, as has Mrs Herbert (Lee) Lewis of Wolfville. Lindsay Taylor, a graduate student in the Faculty of Education at Acadia University, and Leanna McDonald in my office, have kindly helped guide the manuscript over its entire evolution as a computerized document.

These chapters will largely speak for themselves. Most of the contributors began discussion on the need for such a record at a symposium on 'Buddhism and the Challenge of Religious Pluralism', held at Bishop's University in Lennoxville, Québec, in 1999. Two years before, I had participated as the Canadian contributor at an international conference on 'The State of Buddhist Studies in the World', at Chulalongkorn University in Bangkok. The task of preparation gave me the opportunity to review Canadian scholarly work on Buddhism produced over the last twenty-five years. There was, in fact, a great deal, but only a small sector of that published scholarship dealt directly with the Canadian Buddhist experience, notably work by Roy Amore (1979), Elliot Tepper (1980), Louis-Jacques Dorais (1993) and Janet McLellan (1999).[2] The Lennoxville symposium stimulated a more detailed, published record of Buddhism in our land. In discussing how to 'characterize' the different kinds of Buddhism (to use the language of Jan Nattier), we considered separate reviews of ethnic Buddhism identified with specific cultures or 'vehicles' (*yānas*), Euro-Canadian Buddhism, and a seemingly evolving 'North Americanized' or 'Canadianized' Buddhism.[3] We noted that previous ground-breaking work on Buddhism in the United States by such scholars as Charles Prebish (1979, 1999, with Tanaka 1998), Rick Fields (1981), Paul Numrich (1996) and Kenneth Tanaka (1999) used one or more of these approaches to explore a complex subject. In the end, however, we decided that the best way for us to consider the topic in the Canadian context was from a geographical perspective. In this regard, we are conscious of the limitations such a method imposes. There are a few 'thick descriptions' to be sure, but in general the chapters are deliberately designed to set down in broad terms relevant historical information and reviews of the current state of the religion in Canadian society. As contributors, only two of us (Leslie Kawamura and Victor Chan) come directly from an ethnic Buddhist background. In this regard, we take seriously the caution of E. H. Rick Jarrow when he warns about the danger of 'outsider' research becoming a kind of 'voyeurism . . . the non-involved gaze that may theorize without the risk of contact . . . a disembodied objectivity' (Hori 2002: 108). Hopefully our chapters go beyond this dismal prospect, and offer informative and empathetic accounts of this great global religion in the contemporary Canadian circumstance.

By way of background, I turn now to offer some general observations on the subject of Buddhism in Canada. The Canadian federal census (Statistics Canada 2001) indicates that just over 300,000 people specify a Buddhist affiliation (1 per cent of the total population), though official statistics do not likely tell the whole story.[4] The question of who is a Buddhist has always been at the forefront of any inquiry such as this. The two most widely cited groupings are ethnic and so-called Euro-Canadian Buddhists, though because there will be adherents who do not fit either of these categories, some argue that such characterization needs to be fine-tuned (e.g., a specifically 'Canadian' Buddhism may be emerging as a third category).

Ethnic Buddhism is perhaps easier to identify and define in all regions of Canada (though it is clearly not 'ethnic' to those who practice it). It arrived first as the faith of immigrant Asian peoples on the West Coast in the mid-nineteenth century, almost all of whom worked as labourers in the railway and agricultural industries. Within a half century, a substantial number – or their progeny – had moved east, to the towns and cities of the Prairies, Ontario and Québec. Some ventured further to the Maritimes. They took up different occupations and professions, gradually moving into the middle class. As the generation gap widened for Asian Buddhists (e.g., Japanese Issei, Nisei and Sansei), along with access to the English or French languages, the challenge of assimilation into the world-view and customs of a largely Judeo-Christian and Caucasian majority greatly increased. Notwithstanding this, all our contributors have identified and described numerous ethnic Buddhist groups that are highly successful in promoting their native Asian culture, at the same time as becoming 'Canadian' in every sense of the word.

It is an imperative of our analysis to indicate the impact on Buddhism of several modifications to the Canadian Immigration Act in 1962, 1978 and 1989. The initial legislation was directed towards traditional immigrants, replacing the older selection process based on race with one centered on education and ability. Chinese immigrants in particular benefited from this change. There was the added feature of making family reunification a high priority, and by 1970, the Chinese immigrant population in Canada (which was, incidentally, largely Buddhist) expanded to 120,000. In 1976, largely as a result of the social chaos in Indochina precipitated by the Vietnam War, Canada again adjusted its immigration policy in order to accommodate 60,000 displaced Indochinese (and largely Buddhist) refugees. The number more than doubled with the addition of the Orderly Departure Program, which brought entire extended families to sanctuary in Canada. In 1989, precipitated in part by China's Tiananmen Square incident and its aftermath, and a new Entrepreneur and Investor Class, immigration policy attracted Hong Kong Chinese immigrants and raised the number of Chinese in Canada to over 600,000 by the turn of the millennium. McLellan emphasizes the importance of distinguishing between 'immigrant Buddhist' and 'refugee Buddhist' (1999: 20, 193), and the needs, both cultural and spiritual, that these two quite different communities might have, given the hardships which precipitated their departure. For example, no branch of ethnic Buddhism is without some aspect of an indigenous Little Tradition, the animistic, spirit religion that coexists with Buddhism in all parts of Asia. For 'refugee

Buddhists', the loss of proximity to the homeland, to ancestors and to 'spirits' is especially keen. But Van Esterik (1992: 114) points out how for all ethnic Buddhists, 'recreating Buddhist institutions' in Canada is a special challenge. Ritual corners must be cut, so to speak, to accommodate a new sense of time and place.

Other adjustments for ethnic Buddhism in a strange land include difficulties in establishing an indigenous Canadian monastic order, intermarriage with non-Asians, a less traditional role for women, survival of the cultural basis of the Buddhist faith (especially for Canadian-born generations), and relationships with other Buddhists from differing cultural backgrounds. As Kenneth Tanaka has pointed out,

> Buddhist groups in North America find themselves in an immensely pluralistic religious environment . . . The plurality of religions also characterizes the Buddhist groups as well, for virtually every school of Buddhism has now found a foothold on American soil. These schools now exist side by side, often in the same community – a situation unthinkable in Asia, where they often had no knowledge of each other.
>
> (Prebish and Tanaka 1998: 294)

In Canada, ethnic Buddhism remains for the most part culturally insular, not because a particular group thinks other ethnic Buddhist expressions are less adequate or legitimate, but simply because of the comfort of belonging to a particular community. Although there are a few disparate examples of attempts to bring ethnic Buddhists together in the Canadian setting (e.g., the efforts of Suwanda Sugunasiri in Toronto to form a Buddhist Council of Canada, or the cross-cultural annual assembly of Buddhists in Nova Scotia for *Vesak*[5]), in general ethnic Buddhism in Canada remains culturally exclusivist.

An important reason for this attitude is Canada's official policy of multiculturalism, introduced in the 1970s by then Prime Minister Pierre Trudeau as a means of promoting immigrant integration, but not assimilation, into Canadian society. Other objectives include the reduction of discrimination, and the enhancement of cultural awareness and understanding among the Canadian public. A new federal government so-called Ministry of Canadian Heritage, established in 1993, has assisted the financing of ethnic cultural (but not specifically religious) projects, with the result that in some places, Buddhist 'temples' are in fact found in 'cultural centres' rather than religious edifices *per se*. The essential point is that ethnic Buddhist organizations now have full legal parity with the earlier established Christian churches and Jewish synagogues. Nonetheless, some immigrant spokespersons object to multiculturalism, claiming that it encourages a psychology of separation, 'that people, coming here from elsewhere, wish to remain what they have been; that personalities and ways of doing things, ways of looking at the world, can be frozen in time, that Canadian cultural influences pale before the exoticism of the foreign' (Bissoondath 1994: 43). Despite the pressures of adjusting to a majority society whose world-view is based on Western values, as well as to the effects of modernization and globalization, however defined, ethnic Buddhism nonetheless continues to successfully adapt within a nation that itself has only recently become a truly pluralist society.

A second category of Buddhist affiliation reflected in these chapters is linked with what might be called the Euro-Canadian experience. The search for spiritual comfort and wisdom perceived to be lacking in the dominant Judeo-Christian tradition is a well-known phenomenon in Canadian society. Buddhism has long appealed to non-Asian Canadians. There were pockets of academic interest in a few of Canada's major universities as far back as the 1920s. Later, the social phenomenon of a bohemian lifestyle associated with America's West Coast and the subsequent 'beat generation' had some identification with Buddhism of a type. The impact on Canada was modest; however, as Richard Robinson and Willard Johnson indicate, the impact of D. T. Suzuki (1870–1966) on North American Buddhism at this time was enormous, particularly his separation of Zen from Zen Buddhism.

> From this it followed that Zen's connection with aspects of Buddhist doctrine that were more problematic to the modern, relativistic Western mind – such as the teachings on karma and rebirth, the seeming nihilism of nirvana, and the role of ethics on the Path – were simply cultural baggage that could be dispensed with.
>
> (Robinson and Johnson 1997: 303)

This is not to suggest that the Buddhism transmitted by Suzuki was inauthentic. His teachings on meditation have profoundly affected Western appreciation of this key Buddhist practice.

At the same time, ethnic Buddhism appeared to many Euro-Canadians interested in the faith as being too hierarchical, culturally enclosed, ritualistic and superstitious. The result has been that few ethnic Buddhist centres of worship either appeal to Euro-Canadian Buddhists or reach out to them. Euro-Canadian interest in Buddhism was heightened as well by the Vietnam war, the social and political consequences of which spilled over from America into Canadian society. One result was a significant demand for university courses on Asian religions to better understand and empathize with 'the other side', though Buddhist specialists were relatively rare, with courses taught primarily by Western professors with a historical and philosophical bias rather than from devotional and culturally sensitive perspectives.

In Canada, many Euro-Canadian categories emerged from the mid-to-late twentieth century, among them 'white', 'convert', 'theosophical', 'designer' and 'fusion' Buddhism. 'Celluloid' and 'nightstand' Buddhism further reflect film, media and self-help fascination with such figures as the Dalai Lama and Thich Nhat Hanh. Paradoxically, however, Euro-Canadian Buddhist practice has remained for the most part in some way connected with one of the three great Asian Buddhist *yānas*, however indirectly. Still, there is no real ecumenical movement amongst Buddhists, whether ethnic or Euro-Canadian. It appears that a uniquely 'Canadian' form of the faith is not likely to emerge in the near future, suggesting that particularist schools and sects of the faith will endure. Further, for ethnic Buddhists, adaptation necessitated by generational change, with resulting different expectations, must be anticipated. Yet for the most part it is fair to conclude that Buddhism is a religion free of dogmatic fundamentalism, esoteric restrictions or unusual demands for parochial schooling. The faith in all of its variety and diversity has found a comfortable home in a nation that protects and encourages multiculturalism, tolerance and acceptance.

Notes

1 Paul Bramadat and David Seljak, *Religion and Ethnicity in Canada*. Toronto, ON: Pearson, Longman, 2005.
2 Since at least as far back as 1970, records indicate that the topic of Buddhism in Canada has been directly and indirectly discussed at various meetings of the Canadian Asian Studies Association and the Canadian Society of Studies in Religion by such powerful contributors as Harold Coward, Willard Oxtoby and Judith Nagata.
3 Jan Nattier, 'Who is a Buddhist? Charting the Landscape of Buddhist America,' in Charles Prebish and Kerreth Tanaka, *The Mary Faces of Buddhism in America*, Berkeley, CA: University of California Press, 1998.
4 Statistics Canada, *2001 Census*, Selected Regions for Canada, Provinces and Territories. A further breakdown of these statistics indicate that the median age of Buddhists is 38 (compared to 31 for Hindus and 41 for Jews); and that 217,780 are foreign born and 74,000 Canadian born.
5 There are occasionally multiple spellings of certain names and terms. In this book, some of these spellings have been systematized (e.g. Wesak appears as *Vesak*). Elsewhere, culturally sensitive names referring to the same deity or individual have retained specific spellings (e.g. Kuan Yin sometimes appears as Quan Yin, Guan Yin, Guanyin, Kannon).

Bibliography

Amore, Roy (1979) *Developments in Buddhist Thought: Canadian Contributions to Buddhist Studies*. Waterloo: Wilfred Laurier University Press.
Bissoondath, Neil (1994) *Selling Illusions: The Cult of Multiculturalism in Canada*. Toronto, ON: Penguin.
Coward, Harold and Kawamura, Leslie (eds) (1978) *Religion and Ethnicity*. Waterloo, ON: Wilfred Laurier University Press.
Dorais, Louis-Jacques (1993) "Vie religieuse et adaptation: les Vietnamiens de Montréal," *Culture*, 13(1).

Dorais, Louis-Jacques, Pilon-Lê, Lise and Nguyên Huy (1987) *Exile in a Cold Land: A Vietnamese Community in Canada.* New Haven, CT: Yale Center for International Area Studies.

Fields, Rick (1981) *How the Swans Came to the Lake: A Narrative History of Buddhism in America.* Boulder, CO: Shambala.

Hori, Victor Sōgen, Hayes, Richard P. and Shields, James Mark (eds) (2002) *Teaching Buddhism in the West: From the Wheel to the Web.* London: RoutledgeCurzon.

McLellan, Janet (1999) *Many Petals of the Lotus: Five Asian Buddhist Communities in Toronto.* Toronto, ON: University of Toronto Press.

Numrich, Paul D. (1996) *Old Wisdom in the New World: Americanization in Two Immigrant Theravada Buddhist Temples.* Knoxville, TN: University of Tennessee Press.

Prebish, Charles S. (1979) *American Buddhism.* North Scituate, MA: Duxbury.

Prebish, Charles S. (1999) *Lurninous Passage: The Practice and Study of Buddhism in America.* Berkeley, CA: University of California Press.

Prebish, Charles S. and Tanaka, Kenneth K. (eds) (1998) *The Faces of Buddhism in America.* Berkeley, CA: University of California Press.

Robinson, Richard H. and Johnson, Willard L. (1997) *The Buddhist Religion: A Historical Introduction.* New York: Wadham.

Statistics Canada (2001) *2001 Census* (www.statcan.ca).

Tanaka, Kenneth J. (1999) "Issues of Ethnicity in the Buddhist Churches of America," in Duncan Ryūken Williams and Christopher S. Queen (eds) *American Buddhism: Methods and Findings in Recent Scholarship.* Richmond: Curzon Press.

Tepper, Elliot (ed.) (1980) *Southeast Asian Exodus: From Tradition to Resettlement: Understanding Refugees from Laos, Kampuchea and Vietnam in Canada.* Ottawa: Canadian Asian Studies Association.

Van Esterik, Penny (1992) *Taking Refuge: Lao Buddhists in North America.* Arizona State University Press, co-published with Centre for Refugee Studies, York University, Toronto: York Lanes Press.

1

BUDDHISM IN BRITISH COLUMBIA

James Placzek and Larry DeVries

Buddhism in British Columbia is a complicated and intriguing subject. This is due to its gathering presence in the province over at least one hundred years, and to the wide range of Buddhist sects and organizations that continue to profoundly contribute to the province's multicultural society. Research for this chapter involved extensive travel and interviews with many Buddhist leaders and devotees. It also included a questionnaire, and a roundtable discussion among local Buddhist leaders in July 2004, aimed at determining the strength of the faith in the province, issues of infrastructure, and both national and international connections with other Buddhists.[1] Jim Placzek undertook the study and write-up of the Theravāda and Vipassanā groups and Larry DeVries researched and reported on the Mahāyāna and Vajrayāna groups. The chapter has been adjusted by the editor of this volume, and he acknowledges that it differs from the original submissions. It contains as well an appendix by Victor Chan on the impact of the visit of the Dalai Lama to Canada, specifically to the city of Vancouver, in the spring of 2004. The chapter opens with a brief geographical perspective of British Columbia in order to set the scene. Next, it gives a short historical sketch of the faith in British Columbia. We then proceed to a detailed review of the Theravāda and Mahāyāna presence, particularly its 'ethnic' and 'convert' dimensions. It concludes by indicating that the ongoing robust proliferation of the faith continues unabated, largely because the province has become a much sought-after location for Asian immigration.

Turning to the first point, British Columbia can be conveniently divided into three regions. One is the Lower Mainland (Greater Vancouver and areas that can be reached within two hours, either inland along the Fraser River Valley or up the coast). This region contains most of the population, and provides by far the largest concentration of Asian Buddhists, especially those whose families have immigrated to Canada in the past two decades. A second region is the Islands, including Vancouver Island (with the province's capital, Victoria), and the Gulf Islands. A third region is the interior, including the Coastal and Rocky mountains. In general Vancouver and the Lower Mainland act as the center of Buddhism in the province. Some lower mainland groups have a strong web of connections with other groups either in the form of separate congregations or retreat centers. Other strong connections exist between Buddhist groups in British Columbia and those elsewhere in Canada (especially Montréal) but also with established headquarters in the USA (especially the West Coast), Europe, and 'home temples' in Hong Kong, Taiwan, and Japan.

A major relevant feature is the peninsular nature of Vancouver and the land prices that tend to separate it (and several suburbs) from the rest of the administrative entity known as the Greater Vancouver Regional District (GVRD). There is, moreover, a well-recognized but little-mentioned distinction between East side and West side in Vancouver, again clearly reflected in real estate prices (and ethnicity – most older Asian communities, including nearly all of the Buddhist groups, cluster on the East side). From downtown Vancouver, prosperous suburbs are visible on the mountain slopes of the north (where there are no Buddhist groups) and northeast (only a few Buddhist groups), to the alluvial basin to the south, where suburban Buddhist groups predominate and flourish. Moreover, Buddhist groups have spread quite purposefully inland to the east, following Highway 1 through the Fraser Valley in precisely the direction of urban growth dictated by land values proportional to distance from the urban core, yet qualified by commuting distances to urban congregations or supporters. The vast interior of the province is characterized by mountain ranges which are numerous in all directions but the south. Perhaps significantly, the only swift and simple exit from Vancouver by ground is to the south, about one half hour to the American border. This reflects the fact that many of the British Columbia Buddhist groups also have roots within organizations in the United States.

To summarize a 'Buddhist geography' of the province in 2004: roughly sixty groups are located in the city of Vancouver, thirty in the outskirts, twenty-five on Vancouver Island and about a dozen in the interior. Buddhism in British Columbia is a largely urban or urban-determined phenomenon. Demographically, Buddhists numbered 2.2 per cent of British Columbia's roughly four million people in the 2001 Canada Census, the ninth largest religious group in the province. Buddhists are no longer considered an oddity or a curiosity to the majority in provincial society. Since the 1991 census, the increase in the number of Buddhists has been 134.8 per cent. Excluding some very small groups under 1 per cent of the population, Buddhism is by far the fastest-growing religion in British Columbia. Vancouver has roughly half of the province's four million people, and Buddhists represent 3.8 per cent of the population in this principal city.

For Vancouver, the 2001 Canada Census indicates that almost five times more Buddhists are foreign-born (59,153) as opposed to Canadian-born (13,220). Of these foreign-born Buddhists, 27,015 had immigrated during the years before 1991, and even more (32,110) came in the decade between 1991 and 2001. This is attributable to the rapid influx over the last decade of Koreans, Vietnamese, and Chinese from Taiwan and China, but especially Chinese from Hong Kong – due in part to Canada's liberal immigration laws which for a time welcomed entrepreneurs and professionals who could prove they were bringing skills and prosperity to the country. Buddhism continues to grow due to this immigration, with the influx overwhelmingly urban-based. At only 2.2 per cent of the British Columbia population, Buddhists are still a very small minority. They are, however, a remarkably visible community. This is due in part to the fact that many local Buddhist centers are extensions of extremely wealthy 'home organizations' in Asia. In recent years some very impressive architecture has been constructed by Chinese, Japanese and Korean groups, giving them a higher public profile than their actual numbers may warrant. Arguably, these sites may in future even support what could be termed 'tourist Buddhism,' where Buddhists travel to such famous locations both as pilgrims and as tourists.

Despite the developing presence of identifiable Buddhist communities, in general British Columbia Buddhists are only slowly communicating across sectarian boundaries. There are only occasional efforts to do so, mostly by 'convert' Buddhists and interfaith organizations. The visit of the Dalai Lama in 2004 was a catalyst for such meetings. There is also a community web source called *Dharmalog*, offered as a Buddhist bulletin board for upcoming events, especially retreats. The webmaster hopes to expand this medium into a discussion forum and virtual community center for all Buddhists in the province. But at present, British Columbia is nowhere near developing an umbrella organization representing all local groups, similar to the Northwest Dharma Association in Washington State. Our own roundtable discussion was a modest beginning for a regular forum. But the collapse of a similar organization in Toronto, though quite successful for some years (McLellan 1999: 31–4), is a sobering lesson.

A second focus of this chapter concerns the history of Buddhism in the province. The Buddhist groups of longest standing in British Columbia are connected with the earliest Asian immigrant populations, specifically the Chinese and Japanese. Although contact is recorded to have begun in 1788 and 1833 respectively, the first continuous settlers arrived in the form of Chinese participants in the Fraser River Gold Rush of 1858 (Wickberg 1982: 13) and Japanese 'second sons of poor farmers, fishermen, and labourers' in the late 1870s (Watada 1996: 23–5). Early Chinese settlers formed British Columbia's first Chinatown in Victoria, developing in the latter part of the nineteenth century organizations to meet the physical and social needs of the mostly male community with the formation of the 'Chinese Freemasons' (*Zhigongtang*), the Chinese Consolidated Benevolent Association in 1884, various associations based on kinship, place of origin, or dialect, a school, several Christian churches, and three or four temples or shrine rooms. The earliest of these was a one-storey brick temple erected to the Hakka local deity Tam Gung in 1876, later moved to the top floor of the Yen Wo Society (Lai 1991: 60–8) built on the same site. This temple is no doubt related to a roughly contemporary temple dedicated to Tam Gung in Wong Nei Chung village in Hong Kong (Hayes 1971: 195). Another shrine, 'the Palace of Sages,' served to pay respects to Confucius, Hua Tuo, Zhao Yuan Tan (*Zhao Gongming*), Tian Hou, and Guan Yu on the third floor of the Chinese Consolidated Benevolent Association (Lai 1991: 67–8). Thus, while it would be unusual if there were not some interpenetration of Buddhist and popular practices, there is little evidence of the former among the largely male and labouring-class early Chinese settlers in British Columbia. Interestingly, these two temples are prototypical of some contemporary types of Buddhist sites, either in a private home or on an upper floor in a building devoted to business activities.

By contrast, Buddhism was established quite early in the Japanese community in the lay-oriented form of long standing and wide diffusion in Japan, namely Jodo Shinshu. This was due to a combination of Meiji government encouragement of emigration to North America and active proselytization by the Nishi Honganji (Amstutz 1997: 31–3, 62–3). Several years of devotion and discussion led to the founding of the first temple in Vancouver in 1905 (Watada 1996: 39). The first place of meeting, a dining room in the Ishikawa Ryokan, was replaced in 1906 by a refurbished home, and in 1911 by the first new building, the Franklin Street Buddhist Church (Watada 1996: 47). A number of groups grew among the substantial Japanese population of Vancouver Island, the Gulf Islands, and the Lower Mainland. In 1921 the Canada Bukkyokai was formed, leading to the establishment of the Buddhist Churches of Canada in 1933 (Watada 1996: 59, 78). But virtually the entire Island community was lost in the internment of Japanese Canadians by the government of Canada 1942, resulting in scattered communities which still persist in the provincial interior between Hope and New Denver.

The vicissitudes of these communities under the racism of the first half of the twentieth century have been well studied and continue to provide reflection. In the second half of the same century, Buddhism underwent a transformation in North America due to both immigration and what might be called the American Cultural Revolution. A mere thirteen years after extending suffrage to the Japanese and Chinese, Canada began a steady liberalizing of immigration policy which, combined with the counter-cultural search for religious meaning, led to the accelerating growth of Buddhist communities in British Columbia. The early part of this period is marked by the beginnings of the present concentration of Buddhist groups in the Vancouver area with the founding of the Universal Buddhist Temple in Vancouver's Chinatown in 1968, the Zen Centre of Vancouver begun in the late 1960s in private homes and chartered in 1970, and the Khalu Rimpoche group Kagyu Kunkhyab Chuling Tibetan Buddhist Centre in

1972, all still very active. An early precursor on the Theravāda side was Anagarika Dhamma-Dinna, a nurse, a sculptor, and athlete originally from Austria who was ordained in Sri Lanka and returned to British Columbia to begin teaching in the late 1960s.

Parallel to these developments were the beginnings of Buddhist studies at the University of British Columbia (UBC) with the first courses in Buddhism in 1964 (Overmyer 1990: 8). By the early 1970s Buddhist studies appear in full swing, as described in a graduate student's description of seminars in textual study: 'essentially a continuous phenomenon with three professors, [Leon] Hurwitz, [Arthur] Link, and [Shotaro] Iida' (Arntzen 1990: 37). Buddhist studies at UBC were furthered by the anthropologist Michael M. Ames and the scholar of Chinese religions Daniel L. Overmyer whose careers began in the 1960s and 1970s and continue into the present century. Under the regime of multicultural policy, these strong roots burgeoned in the final decades of the twentieth century with the number of known Buddhist groups in the province expanding to about 135 in virtually all traditions of both Asian and Western origin. Ironically, despite such strong roots and manifest growth in public interest and practice, the province's four academic Asian Studies programmes (University of British Columbia, Simon Fraser University, University of Victoria, and Langara College) remain without a regularly funded basic course in Buddhism.

A third focus of this chapter is the contemporary phenomenon of Buddhism in British Columbia. Although Buddhism in British Columbia is for the most part marked by specific ethnic Buddhist communities and denominations, there are also 'convert' Buddhists (their numbers are not large in comparison to the former). For the most part, this chapter uses the nomenclatures 'ethnic' and 'convert' to distinguish two important constituencies, recognizing fully the inadequacies of these terms and searching for something that would cut across the 'ethnic–convert' distinction. 'Convert' Buddhists tend to be white, middle-class and usually fairly well-educated Canadians. 'Ethnic' Buddhists are those who were born into specific communities, usually overseas, but sometimes into strongly maintained ethnic communities in the province comprising second- and third-generation Canadians. It could be argued that in certain circumstances, 'ethnic' and 'convert' are blending into each other, as some individuals or meditation groups gravitate toward an ethnic teacher and tradition, some converts even taking formal ordination. At the same time, 'ethnic' communities are finding it increasingly difficult to maintain a strong identity in succeeding generations due to cultural assimilation, secularization and other social forces. Accordingly, it is not uncommon to find 'convert' and 'ethnic' Buddhists sharing the same tradition. But in general, there is very little actual physical contact between them, even when they become 'parallel' congregations. Not a few 'convert' groups have a Theravāda connection, a subject to which we now turn, focusing first on the Thai experience.

In 1978 Ajahn Chah of the Thai Forest Tradition visited Vancouver, inspiring a group of local Thais to attempt to establish a monastery (*wat*) in the province. Buying land and putting up buildings could be labelled the 'build it and they will come' approach, but 'build the community first' was the advice given to the group by the monks of Ajahn Chah's teaching lineage. Up to the late 1990s, Wat Washington Buddhavanaram in the Seattle-Tacoma area attracted many British Columbia Thais as a place to make merit. Then Luang Phor Viriyan Sirintharo, a prominent monk from Bangkok's Wat Dhammamongkol, arranged for the purchase of a former Christian church in East Vancouver, consecrated in 1992 as Wat Yanviriya (Wat Yan for short). Luang Phor (a popular honorific for senior monks) tells of a dream that he would find a large block of jade in British Columbia to fashion the world's largest jade Buddha image. On a trip to the province in 1991, he learned that just such a block had been found. With the backing of some wealthy people in Bangkok, the gigantic 35-ton block was purchased and shipped to Bangkok, where the desired image was carved. Large fragments were fashioned into other images, one in Luang Phor's Niagara Falls branch. In the tradition of entrepreneurial Thai monks, Luang Phor Viriyan has to date founded seven Thai *wats* in Canada, including three in Ontario, and three in Alberta. Though Luang Phor now has a string of Canadian *wats* to supervise, Wat Yan in Vancouver was his first, and, as it turned out, his most troublesome. Although Wat Yan had an executive committee from the beginning, Luang Phor developed a strategy of finding a community leader in each site and entrusting the management of the *wat* to that leader. The managers that Luang Phor preferred for Wat Yan were not able to project themselves as overall community leaders, and conflict developed with others in the Thai community. Because of these power struggles over the *wat*, some groups of Thais invited other monks on their own initiative, with the intention of establishing an alternative to Wat Yan. The essential broad-based unity and leadership of the Thai community, however, was still lacking, as was the important funding from Bangkok, and these efforts ended with the monks returning to Thailand. It is also worth noting that the leaders of the various factions were all women.

Conflicts also arose over secular use of the *wat*, for example Thai language classes for children, or community meetings. Eventually all such activities were forbidden, and all such requests had to be forwarded to Luang Phor in Bangkok. This restricted use of the *wat* made it difficult for other Theravāda monks to stop over at Wat Yan while travelling through Vancouver. Although attendance was reduced, the *wat* continued to function as a central gathering place, especially for newly arrived Thais. As well, throughout the troubled history of Wat Yan there has always been a core of Buddhist faithful who participated and made merit, ignoring the power struggles that surrounded them. In principle, 'build the community first' is a more effective strategy than 'build it and they will come.' However, in the case of Wat Yanviriya, the latter strategy appeared to succeed when the *wat* began to function as a kind of community center, as is traditional in Thailand. Currently in 2005 Wat Yan is operating with two monks from Thailand, new management, and increased attendance, but the essential problem of community input into the functioning of the *wat* has not been solved.

Wat Yanviriya was established as a Thai community wat, but Luang Phor is well aware of the potential for 'convert' Buddhists in the West. He has established what he calls the Willpower Institute (*sathaaban jittanuphaap*) at his home *wat* in Bangkok, and is establishing branches of this institute in his Canadian *wats*. Luang Phor's goal is to promote world peace through meditation. The direct way to encourage meditation is to train meditation teachers. Luang Phor opens the annual training sessions himself, and graduates take a four-day forest retreat in northern Thailand. Recruits have been both Thai and non-Thai.

Despite this potential, further support from Thailand for new Thai Buddhist enterprises in British Columbia is unlikely, as the community of ethnic Thais remains relatively small and divided. More likely the Thai Forest Tradition, represented in British Columbia mostly by Western monks, will be able to satisfy the needs of the more contemplative Thai practitioners, while Wat Yanviriya will continue to act as a venue to make merit in the traditional sense, and as a central place for the Thai community, especially more recent immigrants.

In contrast to the factionalism present among the Thai community in British Columbia, the expatriate Lao community has been characterized by unity. While most of the Thais came as individuals with an entrepreneurial spirit, or as the wives of Caucasian Canadians, the Laotians mainly came as refugees – often in entire families – and some of their elders had been members of the old Lao elite. Over the past twenty-five years, most Lower Mainland Lao families have gravitated to Surrey, a suburb of Vancouver well known for its multicultural environment. There, they maintain their community around several leading elders.

A short history of Lao Buddhism in British Columbia centers on Ajahn Santi (Bhikkhu Kittisaddho), who bears the physical scars of the 'Secret War' fought in Laos during the 1960s and early 1970s. He ordained as a monk in Laos, and after three years in a refugee camp, arrived in Montréal in 1984. From 1987 to 1990 he resided in Vancouver with local support, mostly from northeastern Thais. In 1990 Ajahn Santi decided that it was too much of an effort for a few local families to support him, and he disrobed for seven years. Eventually, with the help of local Lao leadership, he reordained, and this has led to welcome stability among the two hundred supporting families in the Surrey area. In 1999 the Lao Buddhist Association bought their present residence in Surrey, which is now the Lao-Canadian Buddhist Temple ('Wat Lao' for short).

The Lao-Canadian Buddhist Society further plans to invite some young, well-educated monks from Laos who speak both Thai and English. As well, some local Western Buddhists have recently stayed at Wat Lao, which will certainly change the tenor of the *wat*. At present, Wat Lao has the usual problems of being a religious center in a residential neighbourhood (such as complaints about too many cars on religious festival days). The Society is looking for a site further from Vancouver where they could construct both a *wat* building and a community center for their many religio-cultural events. Wat Lao could also develop a closer relationship with the Theravāda 'Forest *wats*' in British Columbia and neighbouring Washington state. For the immediate future, Wat Lao will probably maintain reasonable stability within the firm Lao community structure. Buddhism is reviving in Laos, but as the nation is extremely weak economically, there is unlikely to be much support from the 'old country'. Within Canada, the much larger and more settled Lao community in distant Montréal remains the major source of inspiration and legitimacy.

British Columbia has also attracted many Sri Lankan immigrants with a Sinhalese cultural identity, many of whom have retained a close relationship with Buddhism. This community is centered primarily in Surrey. Here, the Sri Lankan Buddhist Vihara Society, supported by over two hundred devotees, is able to maintain a monastery with one or two resident monks from Sri Lanka. The Society is not associated with any particular monastery in Sri Lanka. A prominent lay patron, Kirthi Senaratne, has made efforts to move the Buddhist Vihara Society toward interfaith dialogue and a broader pan-Buddhist view, but the current membership feels a strong need for a more classic 'ethnic' approach. Thus a *dhamma* school for children, including instruction in the Sinhala language, is an additional feature of this society. However, in 2005 they were offering day-retreats in English.

A third British Columbia ethnic Theravāda community is associated with the Burmese, particularly the Manawmaya Theravāda Buddhist Society and monastery (*kyaung*), established in 1991 and now situated in a former Baptist church in Surrey. Manawmaya has the support of about one hundred and fifty regular patrons, but some of its events attract hundreds of visitors and worshippers. Their weekly sitting sessions and *dhamma* teaching for non-Burmese are popular. There are two Burmese monks in residence, and when they give *dhamma* teachings to non-Burmese, translation is provided by the very knowledgeable layman Myat Htoon. An interesting example of the ongoing importance of Burmese traditional customs is the maintenance of the *shin byu* (male adolescent ordination and initiation ceremony) by the temple community. In May 2004, the Manawmaya monastery was able to establish *sima* (consecrated space) in which to ordain eight local Burmese–Canadians as novices (*thamanay* or *samanera*), following the advice of a visiting Sayadaw, U Janakabhivamsa, a 75-year-old Burmese monk of fifty-five 'rains retreats.' All other Theravāda Buddhist monasteries within the community (the Laotian and Sri Lankan monasteries in Surrey) were invited or gave consent. A minimum of five monks was required, and in this case they had nine: three Burmese, one Canadian, one Lao, and four Sri Lankan monks. The space was consecrated by first chanting scriptures on all sides, then placing eight natural stones around the periphery and connecting them with a string. After the consecration the new monks were ordained as novices for the first time in British Columbia.

As indicated by the example of the Manawmaya monastery, although Theravāda Buddhism in British Columbia may be most closely identified with specific ethnic groups, it also has an interesting and important outreach to 'convert' Buddhists. Of the several Theravāda-based organizations with this focus, arguably the most visible is Dhamma Surabhi Vipassanā associated with S. N. Goenka, an Indian national who studied in Burma with Sayagyi U Ba Khin. This famous organization has attracted strong financial backing in British Columbia and is able to offer free ten-day retreats for about thirty people each time in its new retreat center near Merritt, in the interior of the province. A second organization is the Theravāda Buddhist Community of Vancouver, a network of local sitting groups and sponsored classes in Buddhism and *vipassanā* ('inward vision', 'insight meditation'), brought together by the efforts of Brian Ruhe, a Theravāda enthusiast. In an earlier period, a number of local British Columbians were inspired to become teachers of *vipassanā* by the Theravadā Anagarika Dhamma Dinna (1913–90). Originally from Austria, the Anagarika was trained in Sri Lanka, but taught the Theravāda tradition in the province for over thirty years. Other Theravāda groups take as their spiritual source what is generally called the Vipassanā Movement in the United States, associated with the International Meditation Society (IMS) in Barre, Massachusetts, and its western affiliate, Spirit Rock Meditation Center in Marin County, California.

Alan Wallace (2002: 37–8) considers the *vipassanā* movement to be the most recontextualized form of Western Buddhism. Its origins lie squarely within the tradition of the Burmese monk Mahasi Sayadaw (1904–82), who focused on meditation and 'basic awareness,' while reducing emphasis on such things as ritual, temple devotions, merit-making, doctrine, and reliance on the *sangha*. Thus this important Theravāda movement had already undergone a 'stripping down' of traditional elements before it was offered to Western students. The Western Vipassanā Movement is 'loosely bound, if at all' to its Theravāda roots (Fronsdal, in Prebish and Tanaka 1998: 176). Further, while some practitioners strictly adhere to the teachings and the teachers of IMS-Spirit Rock (the source of their own legitimacy), IMS-Spirit Rock itself is somewhat eclectic in its own sources of legitimacy, which include Tibetan and Hindu teachers, independent thinkers, and certain trends in Western psychology. The operative factor seems to be whether a teaching is effective in dealing with the personal issues that so often block a meditator's progress, illustrating the essential theme of human psychology at the core of the movement.

In British Columbia, the IMS-Spirit Rock groups have in turn inspired the Karuna Meditation Society (KMS), the first *vipassanā*-focused organization to bring together local people with an interest in meditation and in Buddhism, but with no ethnic temple or ethnic community to turn to. Its founders were Michelle Mills and Kristin Penn (Ms Penn was still active in the group in 2004). For many years it produced the journal *Karuna*, which had a wide readership beyond the province. From this initiative, the Westcoast Dharma Society evolved in 1995, and also 'Vipassanā BC,' a network of like-minded sitting groups composed of teachers and practitioners of meditation and mental health. The Westcoast Dharma Society retains an emphasis on retreat management, bringing in IMS-Spirit Rock senior teachers. 'Vipassanā BC,' on the other hand, is guided by local teachers, the hardworking team of Adrianne Ross and Joanne Broatch, two senior teachers trained directly by Jack Kornfield, a founder of Spirit Rock. As elsewhere in North America, in British Columbia most non-ethnic practitioners and virtually the entire local *vipassanā* leadership are women. While there appears to be a large reservoir of common agreement and goodwill among these *vipassanā* groups, they are in a historic process of maintaining legitimacy through contact with spiritual sources, and this always involves a hierarchy, whether acknowledged or not. One *vipassanā* trainer calls it a 'fine dance.' In her case, her mentor at Spirit Rock is a student of Jack Kornfield, and this becomes a factor in her relations with people who were trained by Kornfield himself, or other founding teachers. It is a subtle network of relationships that echoes, rather than embodies, the rigid hierarchies of traditional Theravāda communities.

A final British Columbia Theravāda 'convert' group, Birken Forest Monastery, might have been discussed as an ethnic Theravāda organization because of its strong formal ties to a discipline and to the Ajahn Chah lineage in Thailand, but in fact it strategically focuses on Western converts. The first practitioner was Bhikkhu Sona, a British Columbia convert with a deep interest in what he calls the 'healing power of the forest.' After ordination with the Sri Lankan Bhavana Society in West Virginia, and after some years with the Ajahn Chah lineage at Wat Pah Nanachaht in Thailand, in 1994 Bhikkhu Sona fashioned a hermitage in Birken Forest near Pemberton, British Columbia. This so-called 'shack monastery,' with Bhikkhu Sona and a monk from Germany, Ven. Piyadhammo, was arguably the first Western Theravāda monastic site in Canada. In the beginning there were no laypersons to offer food, so Ven. Piyadhammo volunteered to disrobe until a steward could be found. When he reordained at the Pemberton site in 1995, it was the first Theravāda ordination of a non-ethnic *bhikkhu* in the province. While retaining the name Birken Forest, in 1998 the monastery became more 'formalized' at a new site near Princeton British Columbia. In 2000, they moved yet again to their present location in a forest near Knutsford, outside of Kamloops. Birken Forest monastery now has a spacious new building and is 'very well supported,' according to Bhikkhu Sona, now popularly called Ajahn Sona after a Thai tradition of according the title of *ajahn* (teacher) to monks of over ten 'rains' retreats. Birken has become an anchor point for both 'convert' and ecumenically-minded ethnic Theravāda Buddhists in the province. In adapting to local conditions, Birken has increased the use of English over Pali chanting, and has adapted the monastic robes to the severe British Columbia winter – but only in minor ways. It is important to recall that in the Theravāda tradition it is the robes which are honoured, not necessarily the person wearing them. 'Our ethical rules remain virtually identical from the time of the Buddha,' reports Ajahn Sona. This fits with Numrich's discussion of American convert Theravāda Buddhists, where he remarks on 'a clear strain of conservatism on *vinaya* matters, which may characterize this group' (Numrich 1998: 156). Birken Forest Monastery has also enhanced the importance of women, and Ajahn Sona supports the re-establishment of full women's ordination as *bhikkhuni.* Somewhat like the Burmese Monastery in Surrey, a consecrated ritual space was established at Birken in November 2003, and two Caucasian Canadians became the first Canadian-born *bhikkhus* ordained by Canadians in Canada. They had both lived at Birken as postulates for two years. Their preceptor (*upajjaya*) was Ajahn Pasanno, another senior Canadian monk in the Ajahn Chah tradition (currently the co-abbot of Abhayagiri Forest Monastery in northern California). Twelve Theravāda monks participated in this historic ceremony. (But as of 2005, one of the new monks has already disrobed, underscoring the main challenge to propagation of this tradition – the scarcity of senior monks.)

The Ajahn Chah international headquarters is at Britain's Amaravati Monastery, and in 1997 it established the Abhayagiri Forest Monastery in northern California. Abhayagiri has in turn rapidly become the center of the Thai Forest Tradition in North America. As the ordinations at Birken indicate, many British Columbia Theravāda devotees, including Thais, will turn to Abhayagiri as the highest available local source of Thai Forest legitimacy. In turn, Birken benefits from the proximity of Abhayagiri, participating in this link back through Amaravati in Britain to Wat Pah Phong in Thailand, the 'mother *wat*' of the Ajahn Chah teaching lineage. Birken's legitimacy is neatly illustrated by a series of photographs hung on the wall at the entrance to the main building: the photos are of respected Thai Forest Tradition teachers, ending with Ajahn Sona. In the end, legitimacy lies in the perceived discipline and morality of the monks themselves. In this respect, Birken Forest Monastery seems secure, based on Ajahn Sona's dedication, vision, and his own practice. One criticism occasionally heard of Ajahn Sona is that his standards are so high. All are welcome to share the healing powers of Birken Forest and to cultivate their minds. But only a few can 'make the cut' to ordination.

To sum up, Theravāda Buddhism in British Columbia may be heuristically divided into 'ethnic' and 'convert' categories, but all groups must establish their legitimacy. Thus close attention is paid to the orthodox transmission of ordination and teaching. Also crucial is strict adherence to the *vinaya*, code of conduct for the *sangha*, including ascetic commitment, as the monastic component of Theravāda builds and maintains its own 'field of merit' in the province. Inevitably, the future of Theravāda in British Columbia will depend on a vibrant monastic *sangha*. Paul Numrich comes to the same conclusion, citing the well-known scriptural tale which defines a successfully transplanted Buddhism as one where locally born and raised youth can ordain locally (in Prebish and Tanaka, 1998: 149). This makes the Manawmaya and Birken Forest ordinations especially historic. Because of the monk–laity symbiosis, people in Theravāda cultures do not feel at ease when there are no monks to support: they cannot make merit. This feeling grows stronger if people are experiencing some relative economic success. The result is the demonstrated need to invite monks to a location, and to make it attractive for them to stay. Given this cultural imperative, arguably devotees are willing to support any monks who might be available. If they are deemed to be disciplined, ascetic, and knowledgeable monks, so much the better. When the goal is preserving Buddhist culture for an ethnic Theravāda Buddhist community, each organization comes up against specific challenges, such as factionalism and cliques among its own membership. Unless a Buddhist center has a strong program for children, time will see a gradual fading out of the need to maintain traditions, especially as immigrants assimilate into Canadian culture. Among the ethnic Theravāda groups reviewed here, only the Sri Lankan organization has a well-developed children's program. Such children's programs are also rare in the largely non-ethnic Vipassanā Movement, whose practitioners tend to be younger people without children, or baby boomers whose offspring have 'left the nest.' All of the ethnic groups surveyed here have to deal with non-ethnic or 'convert' interest in their faith. Among the groups surveyed, it appears the Sri Lankan center does not go out of its way to cater to non-Sinhalese seekers. On the other hand, Wat Yanviriya does have an 'international program' for bringing non-Thais closer to Thai approaches to the *dhamma*. On a more modest scale, the Burmese Manawmaya center also provides an outreach to converts, as does Birken Forest Monastery and the Dhamma Surabhi (Goenka) retreat center. Richard Seager has summarized the historic transfer of Buddhism to the West, and his argument applies well to Theravāda Buddhism in British Columbia: such transmissions take generations of a 'winnowing process,' and the most likely survivors will be 'communities that positioned themselves to be viable over the long term' (in Prebish and Baumann 2002: 118).

Turning now to Mahāyāna and Vajrayāna Buddhist centres in British Columbia: in 2004 a list of these groups maintained by DeVries indicates an estimated one hundred and twenty five such associations and sites in the province. In addition, these are found among the Asian groups of longest standing, namely Chinese, dating largely from 1858 (Lai 1988: 15; Wickberg 1982: 5) and Japanese, dating from 1877 but with the first Japanese Buddhists actually recorded in 1901 (Watada 1996: 25, 36). As a result not only of deep historical roots in British Columbia but also social changes in North American society and immigration in the latter half of the twentieth century, Mahāyāna and Vajrayāna groups are found virtually throughout the province. These factors necessitated an approach to their study which was qualitatively different from that employed for the Theravāda groups above. This aspect of the survey was undertaken by DeVries in the summer and fall of 2004 with extensive field work, participant-observation, and interviews supported in part by a grant from the Langara Research Committee. As a practical convenience, the groups are arranged according to the ultimate geographical origin of their respective lineages.

This multifaceted topic can perhaps be initially approached by recognizing an important variable that gives Mahāyāna and Vajrayāna Buddhism in British Columbia much of its shape and texture – the actual site of Buddhist devotion and presence, as a temple, a place of community identity, and in one instance even as a museum. Many early Mahāyāna congregations began simply with meetings in the home of a follower. It is still the case that a number of groups assemble in a dedicated shrine-room in a home, which may also serve as residence of the group leader or visiting teachers. A second less well represented but significant category is the practice of establishing a place for religious observance within a commercial site. Though not a Buddhist temple, an example (noted above) is the historic Tam Kung Miao founded in 1877 in Victoria's Chinatown and now situated above a grocery on Government Street. Other more recent examples are represented in Vancouver's Chinatown, notably the Foo-Kwok Kwanyin Buddhist Association, established in 1990, the Taiwan-associated Zheng De Fo Tang, founded 1992, and Sherab Chamma Ling (Tibetan Bon Buddhist Centre) founded by the resourceful Geshe Yong Dong in a simple office suite above an automotive parts store in Courtenay. A third type is a house remodelled to accommodate religious activity. Good examples are the Tashi Choling Mahāyāna Buddhist Meditation Society incorporated 1980 in Nelson, the Lions Gate Priory in Vancouver (in place since 1986), and Po Lam Buddhist Association (Bao Lin Xue Fo Hui, offshoot of a major monastery of the same name in Hong Kong), established in 1994 in a former home on a spacious parcel of agricultural land in Chilliwack. Fourth, a one-time Christian church is not infrequently found for use as a temple, e.g., the Yi Tung temple in Kelowna, a former Full Gospel church. In another example, the Universal Buddhist Temple began in Vancouver's Chinatown in 1968, moved in 1977 to a former church building, and was renovated with a winged roof in 1989. A fifth distinct type of site is the 'suburban temple,' represented by several striking architectural edifices belonging to three traditions: Japanese

Jodo-shu (in Coquitlam), Korean Chogye (Langley), and Chinese Pure Land (Richmond), forming a remarkable contrast between city and suburban Buddhist communities.

Turning now to identifying specific ethnic Mahāyāna and Vajrayāna communities, one of the oldest and most visible is that associated with the province's long-standing Japanese community. The year 2005 marks the centenary of the establishment of the Buddhist Churches of Canada, a major Japanese (Jōdo Shinshū) Buddhist organization. One of the most important sites for the history of this association is in New Denver, deep in the province's mountainous interior. There the Nikkei Internment Centre sets down the history of what happened to the Japanese citizens of British Columbia during World War II. Under the well-documented harsh conditions of the internment camps (separation of families, shacks built of green lumber that shrank to admit winter cold and summer heat), members of the community had produced out of materials at hand a *butsudan* (altar) as an expression of their spiritual commitment. It is still in place and the focus of occasional ceremonies. Panels of blue and pink carved with lotuses in green and rose flanked the green, white, black and gold wisteria motif doors that opened onto the *honzon*, a blue, white and gold Amida emitting blue and white rays. Incense burners were placed on a hand-made table in front, framed by a purple and white hand-stitched wisteria cloth banner. The Centre remains a testimony to the internment experience, but also to the Japanese Canadians who remained in the interior of the province after 1945, in such communities as Midway and Greenwood where practitioners are mainly a few elderly *nisei* folk and more substantial populations in Kamloops, Kelowna, and Vernon.

Jōdo Shinshū is the oldest of the province's continuing Buddhist groups with a base in Japan. The history of the community is marked by what informants describe as the first and second evacuations (to the interior during the War, and some to Japan itself after the War). Visits to sites of former communities, such as Cumberland on Vancouver Island, a former thriving centre and now only a graveyard, or a gathering for Obon (commemoration of the dead) in 2004 at a graveyard in Victoria, keep the community in touch with its provincial historical roots. Jōdo Shinshū clerics based in the Vancouver area and Kelowna or Kamloops generally circulate as itinerant ministers, presiding over such religious events as Obon at smaller communities on Vancouver Island and in the interior. Jōdo Shinshū clergy may also move between provinces and even between Japan and Canada, the latter usually undertaken for the purposes of education and ordination at Nishi Honganji in Kyoto. Training for initial-level ordination (*tokudo*) is now possible through 'distance learning' and in English through the Institute of Buddhist Studies in Berkeley, California. From a Buddhist ecumenical perspective, it is noteworthy that the 'boundaries' of separate Buddhist traditions are periodically penetrated on occasions such as the November 2004 British Columbia Jōdo

Shinshū Convention in Kamloops, at which the Theravāda Bhikkhu Sona of the nearby Birken Forest Monastery was invited to speak.

Tozenji Seizan Buddhist Studies and Cultural Centre in the Vancouver suburb of Coquitlam is significant, in part because it also reaches out to Westerners. Constructed in 1989, it follows the Seizan Jodo Shinshu (Pure Land) tradition and, according to Keith Snyder (interview 8 August 2004), one of two priests of the temple, seeks full identification with Komyoji temple in Kyoto. Funds for the temple were raised in Japan by the founder and head, Zuichou Hashimoto. The furnishings are beautifully traditional, with the main sanctuary finished in *tatami* mats. The main practice of the temple is *nembutsu* and study of Jodo-shu scriptures. However, since 'everyone has different inclinations,' the temple also has such activities as cultural programs, tea ceremony and flower arrangement (*ikebana*) classes, and martial art instruction in a finely crafted *dojo*. The permanent members of the temple number about twenty, but up to four hundred attend certain key events. Most devotees are 'new first generation' Japanese (*shin-issei*).

Japanese Buddhism is also represented by various schools of the Zen tradition which have been transmitted to British Columbia either directly from Japan or indirectly via the United States. Among the former is the Shinzan Zen community, consisting of a small number of ordained clerics and followers of the Japanese Rinzai master Shinzan Miyamae Roshi, chief priest of the Gyokuryuji in Seki city in Gifu prefecture, Japan. The mission of Roshi Shinzan is to disseminate the Rinzai teachings to lay persons in Japan, Canada and other Western countries (interview 22 September 2004). His teachings are particularly addressed to those who might be blocked from the traditional curriculum, particularly with regard to *koan* study. Shinzan Miyamae Roshi has been coming to British Columbia for twenty years. Since 1999, he has taught at the Shinzanji (Heart Mountain Temple), a sanctuary established for him in Victoria by Eshin Melody, one of several students in British Columbia ordained by the Roshi in the Rinzai tradition. An indirectly related group is the Kelowna Zen Centre founded in 1994 by William Bates, who was ordained by Roshi Miyamae at Gyokuryuji. Thus, a kind of 'trans-Pacific' relationship has developed in which the teacher's lineage is perpetuated by British Columbia residents ordained in Japan, and sustained over time by bi-annual visits of the Roshi. This Zen school in both Japan and Canada is directed toward a lay constituency in a deliberately non-traditional manner. Thus the Rinzai *dharma* circulates not only between both sides of the ocean, but also between layers of the *sangha*, and perhaps most significantly between traditional and innovative levels of the tradition itself.

Another Zen Buddhist community (and site) is associated with the Amazenji temple in Golden, close to Yoho National Park. Amazenji derives from *ama*, meaning 'the feeling of mutual giving and receiving between mother and infant.' It was founded in 1996 as a Zen training temple with

Soto roots for women, although it now permits men in most events. A small permanent sitting group of a few members is complemented by an 'electronic *sangha*,' a group of about twenty-five women Zen practitioners linked to Amazenji worldwide. When the director, Kuya Minogue, was asked how the online time differences were handled, she indicated that they ignored it, and that this made it 'very powerful – you can just feel this wave of practice coming across the world as it swept over each member of the group in turn.' Kuya Minogue has clearly positioned herself in the social vanguard of a Canadian Japanese Buddhist outreach – even having spent one year with a Buddhist group on Baffin Island – and also doctrinally, having written a number of articles combining feminism and Buddhism, and breaking with previous traditions not only as 'too patriarchal,' but also too solidified or authoritarian (interview 18 July 2004). She strongly identified with her teacher Okamura Shohaku who left the Soto temple Sojiji as 'too institutionalized' and started 'meditating and teaching . . . totally divorced from institutions. Wherever I go, I start a sitting group.' Amazenji seeks to represent the *dharma* as centred in both Buddhism and feminism.

Three final Zen groups in Vancouver arrived as part of an early influence from the United States. The earliest of these is the Zen Centre of Vancouver (Rinzai) growing out of sitting groups of the late 1960s, founded in 1970, and now with branches in nearby Bowen Island and Victoria, all connected with Mt Baldy in California and affiliated with Rinzai-ji in Los Angeles. The Zen Centre's resident monk is Eshin John Godfrey who, in addition to teaching, supervises retreats and *tokudo* training as well as volunteering as a clear and engaging speaker to university classes. The Lions Gate Buddhist Priory (Soto) was founded in 1985 with monks ordained in the tradition of Jiyu Kennet Roshi's Temple of the Order of Buddhist Contemplatives, Shasta Abbey, Mount Shasta, California. Lions Gate is led by Rev. Koten Benson with the assistance of the Rev. Aurelian, the first monk to be ordained in the tradition in British Columbia. The Shasta Abbey tradition is well known in North America and perhaps represents the Zen tradition most uniquely assimilated, with its plainsong chanting in English. The Mountain Rain Zen Community is the newest in British Columbia, founded in 2002 and 'based upon the tradition of Shunryu Suzuki Roshi' (website) and formerly part of the Karuna Meditation Society. It includes members also connected with the UBC Zen Society founded by Leonard Angel in the early 1980s as well as those ordained under Zoketsu Norman Fischer and The Everyday Zen Foundation in San Francisco, with associated groups in Washington state, New York City, and Mexico (website). Finally among groups of Japanese origin, Lotus Sutra groups are represented in Vancouver by Sōka Gakkai International whose global network is well known, and a small group of Risshō Kosei-kai practitioners associated with a faction in Seattle. Though small in numbers, the latter is frequently represented in interfaith activities in Vancouver.

Mahāyāna Buddhism in British Columbia is also clearly identified with a substantial Chinese community, one with roots going back over 200 years. Early settlement, however, seems to have reflected popular and Confucian religious practices, rather than Buddhist (see above). Growing in the period following immigration reform in the mid-1960s, the community greatly expanded with an immigration influx from Hong Kong, Taiwan, and the mainland during the 1980s and 1990s, largely through Canadian government business immigrant and investor categories and incentives for entrepreneurs. In general terms, these categories attracted between four and six thousand immigrants apiece every year for two decades. Reflecting again on the outwardly visible impact of this immigration on the province, especially in the Vancouver suburban area, it is not difficult to connect the new 'suburban temples' such as the Ling Yen Mountain temple (as well as Tozenji and Seo Kwang-sa) with these social and economic factors. This trend, coupled with a gradient of greater to lesser land prices radiating from Vancouver outwards, tended to favour new development in the suburbs. With the combination of early roots and later intensity in immigration, the city of Vancouver has many Chinese Buddhist organizations and temples, some of which have already been mentioned. Among the others are the Buddhist Compassion Relief Tzu-chi Foundation of Canada, associated with the Tzu Chi Cultural Center in Taiwan, and the Gold Buddha Monastery, also known as Sagely City of the Dharma and associated with Dharma Realm Buddhist Association and City of Ten Thousand Buddhas in Talmage, California. These groups are oriented toward a combination of religious practice and social outreach, and in addition have strong 'world mission' components or ties with groups in the United States. Thus, they may also be thought of as urban area religious service organizations containing an ethnic component (such as Chinese language classes or religious services), but transcending this role with such activities as social services, outreach to students, and translation projects.

But the newest and most lavish architectural expressions of Chinese Buddhism in British Columbia are found in Richmond, a suburb bordering directly on Vancouver, where the number of Buddhist adherents has more than tripled from 3,000 in 1991 to an estimated 11,000 in 2001. Richmond has long been known for the Quan-yin temple (also known as the International Buddhist Society), a spectacular red-roofed edifice on the arterial route of the Steveston Highway. The temple has been at this location since 1981. In addition to regular instruction in both seated and walking meditation, the temple abbot, Rev. Guan Cheng, conducts regular services in Chinese on Sunday and presides over such lay activities as food bank donations. The temple advertises itself as an 'internationally recognized tourist attraction that aims to introduce Buddhism to the Western world through education, charitable giving and superlative Chinese arts and craftsmanship' (International Buddhist Society website). Richmond is also the site of two other well-known Taiwanese Chinese Buddhist groups. The first of these is the Vancouver International Buddhist Progress Society of Ven. Master Hsing Yun, founded as a branch of the Fo Guang Shan in Kaohsiung, Taiwan. A second is identified with Master Sheng Yen's Dharma Drum Mountain Buddhist Association, which also has 'chapters' in several surrounding communities. Arguably, however, the visual culmination of Chinese Buddhist presence is to be found in the Ling Yen Mountain Temple in Richmond on land donated by a Taiwanese businessman who emigrated to British Columbia in the 1980s. Here the public face of Buddhism in British Columbia has reached its zenith, an immense 1,543-square-metre (16,600-square-foot) edifice constructed in 1996 on former farm land, and perceived as a spiritual as well as cultural centre for anyone who wants to learn more about Pure Land Buddhism and Chinese culture. Work has continued well into 2004, aimed at expanding the temple from the original $3.5 million project to a $45-million edifice, including a ten-story Buddha image in a fourteen-story tower, its height limited only by the Richmond building code's consideration of flight paths to the nearby Vancouver International Airport. From a multicultural perspective, it is interesting to note that the Ling Yen temple is a strategic part of a well-known phenomenon in two Vancouver suburbs – that of the so-called 'highway to heaven' – indicating a series of religious edifices of varying religions built along highways leading to Richmond and in Burnaby. (For example, the former has successively, from north to south, Cornerstone Evangelical Baptist Church, Richmond Chinese Free Evangelical Church, Vedic Cultural Centre, Dharma Drum Mountain Buddhist Association, Al-Zahraa Islamic Centre, Guru Nanak Niwas Gurdwara, the Ling Yen temple and the Richmond Bethel Church.) The Ling Yen temple itself is part of a 'church planting,' an offshoot of two other temples, one founded in 1984 in Taiwan and one in 1992 in Hong Kong. The Richmond Ling Yen temple commemorates the connection to the Taiwan Ling Yen Shan Temple by its size and décor. It seems clear that these visible architectural statements are enthusiastically received by temple members as objective expressions of the Buddha *dharma*.

A third ethnic Mahāyāna Buddhist community is represented by two Korean temples, Seo Kwang-sa in Langley and Dalma-sa in Coquitlam, both considered branches of the 'Three Jewel Temples' (Sambosa) in Gyeongsang, Korea, and both associated with six Korean Buddhist organizations in Ontario. Although it is estimated that only about ten per cent of the Korean community in British Columbia are practicing Buddhists, congregational attendance at the Langley temple is reported as reasonable and as consisting of nearly equal numbers of men and women (rather than a predominance of women as in Korea). The two Korean temples contrast considerably in terms of architectural presence. The Coquitlam temple is in a home, with only the plaque next to the door to distinguish it as a temple. On the other hand the Langley temple, Seo Kwan-sa, is a truly magnificent replication of a Korean temple following traditional methods of construction. It was completed in 2001 on a spacious parcel of land also occupied by the home which had served as the previous temple since 1994. Although the larger Korean population is in Coquitlam, the Langley site was chosen based on its less expensive real estate prices. Korea-founded tradition is also present in British Columbia with Kwan Um School of Zen, a group of Zen centres founded by Seung Sahn, which has practitioners in Vancouver as well as the Interior towns of Balfour and Slocan Park.

A fourth Mahāyāna community is associated with the Vietnamese. In Vancouver, the World Vietnamese Order's Chan Quang ('True Light') Temple is the largest. First located in a converted home, it has moved several times before settling at its present location. The temple is served by Ven. Dai Duc Thich Chan Hoa and one novice, Thich Tue Hien. Chan Quang is very traditional in serving the ceremonial needs of a substantial local community, around one hundred at weekly services and up to ten times that number at special events, such as Lunar New Year. The temple follows a Pure Land practice and the monks are both careful and flexible regarding the Vinaya and performance of ritual tasks for the congregation. The mission of the temple according to the abbot is directed primarily to the Vietnamese community and remains specifically ethnic as there are not yet Western converts, and perhaps also because the Vietnamese community still consists mostly of first- and second-generation immigrants. What seems particularly important about the temple, however, is the activity and engagement of the resident clerics, and the energy and business sense that went into the acquisition of three new Buddha images for the temple. These striking figures reach from red lacquered pedestals almost to the ceiling of a large hall on the second floor used for congregational services. Covered with gold leaf, the images were made in Hong Kong for the temple. Many of the red-lacquered furnishings of the sanctuary and in the congregational dining hall are, not unexpectedly, from Vietnam. Throughout the temple, the ambience is one of splendour and activity. The triad of images of Shakyamuni, Guanyin, and Kṣitigarbha, the gleaming furnishings, the red carpeting, and the many inscriptions along the walls of the rooms serve to convey a message of a certain prosperity in the *dharma* attained by the Vietnamese community in the Vancouver area. There are also Vietnamese temples and communities on Vancouver Island in Victoria and Nanaimo, the fastest-growing city in British Columbia, as well as groups connected with mindfulness practice in the tradition of Thich Nhat Hanh in Victoria, Sooke, North Vancouver, and Vancouver. A group of nuns at the Bao Lam Temple established in a converted home in Vancouver is led by Bhikshuni Thich Tinh Phap. A suburban group, Avatamsaka Buddhist Temple (Hoa Nghiem Temple), founded in 2002 in Burnaby, recently appeared in international news as it announced its intent to donate proceeds of the sale of its retreat centre in Mission to the relief effort for the 2004 Indian Ocean tsunami.

The vigour and dedication of the British Columbia Vietnamese community is also manifest in a newly established temple near the American border, Chan Ngyuen, located in the suburb of Langley. Like Hoa Nghiem, the group also maintains a monastic centre named Thon Doai Pagoda in the quiet outskirts of the Fraser Valley town of Mission and also belongs to the Vietnamese Unified Buddhist Congregation of Canada. The Langley temple is located on virtually the same road as the Seo Kwan-sa, but on the other side of town, distant from the incessant traffic of Highway 1, near the US border and the piquantly designated '0 Avenue.' This is an area of mists and margins of many kinds, comprising river-bottom, tidal mud-flats, handsome hobby farms gradually overtaking land occupied by tiny homes of an older generation, and the neglected land of the border itself. The temple also shares this feeling of transition, driven by the hard work of a first- and second-generation immigrant congregation, with a growing third generation much in evidence. A visit on a typical Sunday worship service revealed a large rectangular two-storey white building, surrounded by the rank weeds of alluvial land. However, huge piles of weeds around the building spoke of prior work parties. Children were everywhere, along with men and women, a nun, several monks in work clothes and three dogs. The abbot, Thich Thay, a middle-aged man in army surplus khaki, spoke in a quiet and deliberate manner with many people about personal, religious, and practical matters such as installing switches in the new toilets. Services are conducted upstairs in a very large hall with brightly polished floors and an altar with a white image of Shakyamuni, table coverings of red cloth, and a symmetrical arrangement of tall flowers, 'wooden fish' and bell, and incense burner. Thay worked in a refugee camp in Malaysia for many years, in particular with children. He was convinced by others that he was needed in Canada. In a long conversation (26 September 2004), he made reference to a metaphor of a swan whose serene gliding is driven by powerful activity below the surface. (Thay is also a practicing poet.) Though this seemed to apply to the quiet energy of Thay and the young monks of Chan Ngyuen, it also applies to a community assuming its place in British Columbia society and ultimately in provincial history, echoing Field's imagery of the arrival of Buddhism in America.[2]

We turn finally to Tibetan Buddhism in British Columbia represented by upwards of thirty groups and a number of distinguished figures. Although this is not the case elsewhere in North America, the Tibetan traditions seem to be the sole representatives of Vajrayāna in the province, if one omits the somewhat ambiguous 'True Land Buddha School' headquartered in Redmond, Washington and with several branches in the Vancouver area. Many of the British Columbia groups, such as Shambala, are quite well known and well established throughout North America and elsewhere. The earliest Tibetan group to appear was that founded by Kalu Rinpoche upon his arrival in British Columbia in 1972 (after his stay at the University of Washington in Seattle). This is the Kagyü Kunkhyab Chuling Tibetan Buddhist Centre in the Vancouver suburb of Burnaby, the first of sixty such centres established in the West and the 'North American Seat' of Kalu Rimpoche's tradition. Significant to this tradition is Kunzang Dechen Osel Ling, at Mt Tuam on Salt Spring Island, well known as having been the site of the first three-year Vajrayāna retreat in North America. British Columbia is also the residence of at least three other distinguished Tibetan Buddhist leaders: Jetsun Kusho Chimey Luding, who is a sister to the present head of the Sakya lineage and founder of Sakya Tsechen Thubten Ling in Richmond; the Gelukpa Ven. Zasep Tulku Rinpoche, founder of Zuru Ling Tibetan Buddhist Mediation Centre in Vancouver, Tashi Choling Mahāyāna Buddhist Meditation Society in Nelson, and the international Gaden for the West; and Lama Tashi Namgyal, founder in 1974 of the Sakya Thubten Kunga Choling (Buddhist Dharma Centre of Victoria). These centres have succeeded over the years in producing a number of eminent and active members, both lay and monastic.

Vancouver Island is home to quite a few Tibetan Buddhist groups. Among these is Thubten Choling, founded in 1984 in Duncan, between Victoria (the provincial capital) and Nanaimo. One of its founders, Maria Karuna, a practicing Buddhist of thirty years, indicates that Thubten Choling presents Buddhist teachings from both a Mahāyāna and a Vajrayāna perspective. A key 'interfaith' focus is also indicated by some of the activities of a young resident teacher, Lama Kalzang Dorje, who has undertaken such activities as spiritual encounters with First Nations peoples. Practices at Thubten Choling take place in a medium-sized room adjacent to Karuna's home. In this way, it is typical of quite a few British Columbia Buddhist sites located in such residential spaces. Outside is an 'enlightenment *stupa*' built in the mid-1990s and a symbol of both cosmic oneness and religious and communal cooperation. The *stupa* is white, about twenty feet high, containing an image of Sakyamuni painted by a local artist, Toti Lewis, and with images of Mañjúrī, Avalokiteśvara and Vajrapani attached to the side walls. Monks and teachers of various Buddhist schools offered ceremonies during the construction, with all four Tibetan Buddhist sects represented at the consecration. Also on Vancouver Island the Bhutanese Nyingma teacher Ven. Lama Chimi Kinley presides at the Yeshe Khorlo Nyingma Centre of Victoria, which he established in 1995. The newest Tibetan group is led by Canada's first Bon cleric, Geshe Yong Dong Losar. After initial experience in Terrace and Kitimat, in 2003 this resourceful teacher established the Sherab Chamma Ling Tibetan Bon Buddhist Centre in Courtenay. Geshe Yong Dong maintains a teaching schedule that includes outreach to followers on Quadra and Gabriola Islands, Port Alberni, Tofino and Vancouver as well.

In the Interior town of Westbank, near Kelowna, the Karma Kagyü Center Okanagan was established in 2002 as a branch of the worldwide Lama Ole

Nydahl Diamond Way (a literal translation of 'Vajrayana'). The oldest Tibetan tradition in Canada has been present in British Columbia since 1979 as the Crystal Mountain Society. The group, a network meeting in the houses of practitioners, sees itself as 'non-denominational, emphasizing the development of a Western expression of Buddhism' and follows Venerable Namgyal Rinpoche (1931–2003), a Westerner trained in both Theravāda and Vajrayāna traditions, recognized by His Holiness the XVIth Gyalwa Karmapa as an incarnation of the Namgyal Tulku (see website). The group maintains a sixty-acre forest retreat centre on Galiano Island and is associated as well with Sunshine Coast Retreat House in the coastal town Roberts Creek.

This account of the Tibetan Buddhist groups in British Columbia is selective rather than exhaustive. A forthcoming study by DeVries, Dan Overmyer, and Don Baker of UBC will supply more detail.

In conclusion, one very important consequence of the field work for this chapter is the way that one thing would lead to another – a new group added as a result of a conversation, unseen or unknown connections uncovered between known groups, or even in some cases information new to the informants themselves relayed through the study. One of the most fascinating aspects of the research, which was necessarily partly historical and partly synchronic, proved to be the glimpsing of a remarkable web or perhaps several webs of associations between current and past Buddhist groups and institutions, what might be called a 'pattern of circulation.' An indication of this came from a discussion with a Taiwanese monk at San Hui (Three Practices) Monastery, a small group in the Fraser Valley town of Chilliwack. Chilliwack is situated about two hours' drive from Vancouver and is best known for its agricultural produce and its share of the 'bible belt' conservative Christian communities. But within the last decade, Chilliwack has become the site of at least four Buddhist monasteries. As we discussed this movement of Buddhists and Buddhist groups between Vancouver and the outlying areas, the San Hui monk ventured the speculation that there were considerably more Buddhist sites in the province than either he or we were aware of. Monks, nuns, and loosely associated Buddhist groups in general may simply purchase a house which may then be occupied by themselves or others over an indeterminate period of time, coming and going between the province and overseas locations as freely as the seemingly ever-changing immigration laws permit. Here indeed is a clear indication of a 'transnational' circulation – not of entrepreneurs and capital resources, but rather a 'circulation of *dharma*.' This 'circulation' involves movement of both individuals and groups, of information and awareness, and it both creates and represents a complex system of associations across boundaries of all sorts – geographical, denominational and ethnic. Such 'circulation' appeared at all levels of the study. Thus, while visiting the Po Lam monastery in Chilliwack, we happened to arrive at the same time as a group of nuns visiting from the

Ling Yen Mountain Temple, hours away in Richmond. A visit to Fu Hui Temple in Vancouver introduced us to a nun acquainted with Do Ming, the abbess of Fa Yu (Dharma Rain) monastery in Chilliwack, who, it turned out, was leading services at the International Buddhist Temple near Langara College, Vancouver. A somewhat different 'pattern of circulation' was observed in the Tibetan-based groups in the province. Members had often become familiar with the group or teacher through their individual travels, often in Asia. Virtually all these groups were associated with international networks (such as the Kagyu Kunkhyab Chuling Tibetan Buddhist Centre). In general, bulletin boards and shelves of pamphlets at both Mahāyāna and Vajrayāna temples and centres typically advertised unique international relationships and awareness of other groups.

In addition to this 'inter-group' and international circulation, there appeared a circulation of a different order often quite deliberately traversing boundaries valorized in academic studies, including the present one. The Po Lam nuns and the San Hui monks actively train in the Chilliwack Vipassanā (Goenka) groups and one, the abbess Ven. Sik Yun Kit, is also in training as a *vipassanā* teacher. Thus, monastics are studying meditation under lay teachers. This is not seen as a crossing of monastic–lay boundaries or even in interdenominational terms but rather as a 'practical benefit.' The categories of 'ethnic' and 'convert' often blurred beyond distinction, not only through familiar social processes such as intermarriage, but through conscious crossing of these lines. An example is a Hong-Kong based temple which had embraced a Canadian monk in order to establish an outreach in English utilized by both 'ethnic' and 'convert' Buddhists. When asked where he ordained, the monk politely dismissed the question as not important since the main point was 'to help people in the world.' While some groups studied were oriented toward a specific ethnic group, this may be largely explained by the age of the practitioners or the relative newness of the group to British Columbia. As to the so-called 'convert' groups, many of those of Mahāyāna and Vajrayāna origin were comprised of a distinctly multicultural clientele and are well understood to be international in their scope. Finally, the categories of Theravāda, Mahāyāna, and Vajrayāna may overlap in practice and in any case may not be seen as primary by their practitioners. This is understandably the case in eclectic groups such as the UK-based Friends of the Western Buddhist Order whose centre was founded in 1996 in Vancouver, or the quite small Dr Ambedkar Memorial Association (affiliated with Ambedkar Mission, Toronto), begun even earlier in 1981 by resident director Mohan Bangai, who practices in the Goenka *vipassanā* group. Even groups with a strong denominational heritage may pursue an ecumenical approach. One example noted above is the cooperation of Bhikkhu Sona of the Birken Forest Monastery in Merritt with the 2004 British Columbia Jodo Shinshu Convention in Kamloops, bringing together geographically adjacent Buddhists of separate *yana*s. Another example is the range of clerics, especially of Chinese and Tibetan traditions, who have held services at the Universal Buddhist Temple. When asked about this, the board members simply replied, 'We are happy when we see people are happy.' Basic Buddhist principles subvert taxonomies.

Residency in British Columbia, especially in Vancouver and its suburbs, exposes one immediately to a vast multiculturalism, where the flow of people is similar to the international flow of business in the province. One result is that a traditional temple built in a Vancouver suburb may be no more surprising than a Toyota or Honda made in Canada. In order to come to grips with this relatively new sociology, the method we have made most use of is that of visiting sites and interviewing practitioners. No doubt this determines to a degree the kind of result obtained. With this approach we aimed to bring an element of 'texture' to the study of British Columbia Buddhism. Taking a longer perspective, it seems that studies like this one, with its melange of history, doctrine, practice, popular culture, pamphlets, people, and what not, virtually require an interdisciplinarity typified by the field of folkloristics. What we gathered from so many 'active tradition bearers,' from bookshelves and bulletin boards, seemed like nothing so much as lore. All of these Buddhists and Buddhist groups we studied were active and optimistic. Perhaps the characterization of Buddhism as pessimistic and passive is a mere stereotype now to be left behind. And while descriptors such as 'ethnic' and 'convert' seemed to apply in some circumstances, the multiple examples of an interconnectedness in spirit and practice associated with British Columbia Buddhists increasingly appears to overcome these distinctions, giving the Buddha Dharma a visible identity as a singular faith in a highly diversified Canadian provincial society.

APPENDIX (VICTOR CHAN)

In April of 2004, the Vancouver Coliseum was filled to capacity twice on the same day with crowds eager to hear the Dalai Lama. His Holiness spoke for just under one hour each time. This was in every way both a great Buddhist occasion and, in a strategic way, a kind of inter-faith event. The visit inspired many ordinary Canadians with its message of service and compassion. One example was a 10-year-old child who quietly donated her entire savings to help cover the cost of an eye operation for a small boy threatened by blindness. Her parents were surprised by her altruism but clearly proud of her generosity. They had no doubt that the seed was planted when she had accompanied them to one of the talks at the Coliseum. The Dalai Lama's presence in Vancouver became a catalyst for a reawakening of interest in the universal themes of peace, non-violence, compassion and the education of the heart. Many British Columbians, not all identified with the Buddhist faith *per se*, nonetheless carried the Dalai Lama's message back to their homes and communities. The momentum the Dalai Lama set in motion was considerable, especially when he met with other Nobel laureates and peace champions (Desmond Tutu, Shirin Ebadi, Zalman Schachter-Shalomi, and Joann Archibald) at the University of British Columbia's Chan Center. Among several projects inspired by the Dalai Lama's visit, five might be identified to show the range of his impact. First, the foundation of the InterSpiritual Centre of Vancouver, largely through the initiative of Rabbi David Mivasair and the Shaughnessy United Church in Vancouver. Mivasair became interested in the idea of an interspiritual centre, a contemplative facility where people of different faiths and religions could come together, pray, meditate and learn from each other. He formed a committee to guide the project and, as of the beginning of 2005, the Vancouver City Council and the Vancouver Olympic Committee have endorsed the idea. The city has now earmarked land in the Southeast False Creek area for the centre.

Second, the Vancouver School of Theology (one of Canada's pre-eminent seminaries) has had a notable involvement. Soon after the Dalai Lama's visit, Ken MacQueen, Principal of the School, met with University of British Columbia's Chinese law professor, Pitman Potter, and Professor Don Grayston of Simon Fraser University's Institute for the Humanities, to consolidate ideas triggered by the unprecedented gathering of luminaries in Vancouver. After several months of meetings and a retreat on Bowen Island, plans are well under way for the School to offer a VST degree progam in Peace and Spirituality. Thirdly, the establishment of the Dalai Lama Center for Peace and Education is a direct outcome of His Holiness's Vancouver visit. As Chair of the Organizing Committee for the Dalai Lama's visit, I traveled to Dharamsala in October 2004 to consult with the Dalai Lama. We agreed to collaborate on a Center in his name, an institute of advanced studies where world-renowned thinkers from around the world could come together and explore the Dalai Lama's ideals of peace, universal ethics, and moral education. Plans are underway to locate the Center within an academic institution in Vancouver. Archbishop Desmond Tutu, Tendzin Choegyal (15th Ngari Rinpoche and brother of the Dalai Lama) and former Czech president Vaclav Havel have agreed to be advisors.

Fourth, there is a continuation of an 'Educate the Heart' dialogue in Vancouver. This stems from a roundtable event attended by the Dalai Lama and his celebrated colleagues entitled 'How to balance educating the mind with educating the heart' (one of the most eagerly anticipated events of the Dalai Lama's visit). At the Dharamsala meeting in October 2004, the Dalai Lama agreed to my request that, if possible, he come back to Vancouver for the second 'Educate the Heart' dialogue, to be sponsored by the Faculty of Education, University of British Columbia.

The Dalai Lama's 2004 visit has heightened the prospect that British Columbia will become a global leader in helping to build a new humanity. These objectives include linking people together as a culturally diverse and tolerant society, inspired by the universal ethos that the Dalai Lama spoke so eloquently about. Thus it seems likely that the Dalai Lama will have a meaningful, ongoing relation with British Columbians in the foreseeable future, particularly through the Dalai Lama Center for Peace and Education. Further, it is hoped that his center – and other interfaith initiatives – will provide a powerful incentive for the Dalai Lama to return to a province and city that so enthusiastically welcomed him. And there is no doubt, as demonstrated by the past events of April 2004, that should this be so, he will bring with him some of the most thoughtful and fertile minds of our age.

Notes

1 Associated with this study was a questionnaire, divided into two sections. One was for a group or organization, the other for a specific individual. Sample questions for the group questionnaire were: How long has your group been established in British Columbia? Is it affiliated with a Buddhist centre abroad on in the USA? What are the fundamental principles or beliefs of your group? How is it organized? Does your group have contact with other Buddhist groups in the province? Sample questions for the individual form were: Is there a particular Buddhist teacher you admire or use as a model? Is there a common thread shared by various Buddhist teachers? How does Buddhism fit into mainstream British Columbia society? In the next five years, how do you see Buddhism adapting to Canadian society? About fifty responses were obtained, and the results in part incorporated in the context of this chapter. On the other hand, the Roundtable Discussion, held in July 2004 at Langara College, Vancouver, featured several presenters: Bishop Orai Fujikawa (Buddhist Churches of Canada), Kirthi Senaratne (Theravāda Buddhist Community of Vancouver), Ajahn Sona (Birken Forest Monastery), Joanne Broatch (Vipassana Vancouver), Robyn Traill (Vancouver Shambala Center), Graham Good (Karuna Meditation Society) and John DeJardin (Crystal Mountain Society). They were asked to select topics from a comprehensive list of themes pertinent to the evolution of Buddhism in the West, most of which are found initially in Prebish and Baumann 2002: 35, 160. The presentations were thoughtful and cordial, and CD copies of the discussion are archived at Langara College's Pacific Rim Studies Department.
2 Rick Fields, *How the Swans Came to the Lake: A Narrative History of Buddhism in North America*. Boulder: Shambala, 1981.

Bibliography

Amstutz, Galen Dean (1997) *Interpreting Amida: History and Orientalism in the Study of Pure Land Buddhism* [SUNY series in Buddhist studies]. Albany, NY: State University of New York Press.
Anderson, Charles P., Bose, Tirthankar, and Richardson, Joseph I. (eds) (1983) *Circle of Voices: A History of the Religious Communities in British Columbia*. Lantzville, BC: Oolichan Books.

Arntzen, Sonja (1990) "Leon Hurvitz," *BC Asian Review*, University of British Columbia (UBC) 75th Anniversary Issue.

BC STATS. Ministry of Management Services. www.bcstats.gov.bc.ca/

Hawkins, Freda (1988) *Canada and Immigration: Public Policy and Public Concern*, 2nd ed. Kingston, ON: McGill-Queen's University Press.

Hayes, James (1971) "Visit to the Tung Lin Kok Yuen, Tam Kung Temple, Happy Valley, and Tin Hau Temple, Causeway Bay, Saturday, 7th November, 1970," *Journal of the Hong Kong Branch of the Royal Asiatic Society*, 11.

Johnston, Hugh J. M., Gen. (ed.) (1996) *Pacific Province: A History of British Columbia*. Vancouver: Douglas & McIntyre.

Lai, David Chuenyan (1988) *Chinatowns: Towns within Cities in Canada*. Vancouver, BC: University of British Columbia Press.

Lai, David Chuenyan (1991) *The Forbidden City within Victoria: Myth, Symbol and Streetscape of Canada's Earliest Chinatown*. Victoria, BC: Orca Book Publishers.

McLellan, Janet (1999) *Many Petals of the Lotus: Five Asian Buddhist Communities in Toronto*. Toronto, ON: University of Toronto Press.

Morreale, Don (1998) *The Complete Guide to Buddhist America*. Boston, MA: Shambhala. *The Multifaith Directory: A Resource for Students of Religious Studies 100* [a world religions course at University of British Columbia], unpublished list originally compiled by Donna Schmid in 1987 under the direction of Charles P. Anderson of the Department of Religious Studies.

Numrich, Paul David (1998) "Theravāda Buddhism in America: prospects for the *sangha*," in Charles S. Prebish and Kenneth E. Tanaka (eds) *The Faces of Buddhism in America*. Berkeley, CA: University of California Press, 147–62.

Overmyer, Daniel L. (1990) "Glowing coals: the first twenty-five years of the Department of Asian Studies at the University of British Columbia, 1960–1985," *BC Asian Review*, UBC 75th Anniversary Issue.

Prebish, Charles S. (1999) *Luminous Passage: The Practice and Study of Buddhism in America*. Berkeley, CA: University of California Press.

Prebish, Charles S. and Baumann, Martin (eds) (2002) *Westward Dharma: Buddhism Beyond Asia*. Berkeley, CA: University of California Press.

Prebish, Charles S. and Tanaka, Kenneth K. (1998) *The Faces of Buddhism in America*. Berkeley, CA: University of California Press.

Roy, Patricia (1989) *A History of British Columbia: Selected Readings* [New Canadian readings]. Toronto, ON: Copp Clark Pitman.

—— (1989) *A White Man's Province: British Columbia Politicians and Chinese and Japanese Immigrants, 1858–1914*. Vancouver, BC: University of British Columbia Press.

——, Granatstein, J. L., Iino, Masaka and Takamura, Hiroko (1990) *Mutual Hostages: Canadians and Japanese during the Second World War*. Toronto, ON; Buffalo, CO: University of Toronto Press.

—— (2003) *Oriental Question: Consolidating a White Man's Province, 1914–41*. Vancouver, BC: UBC Press.

Statistics Canada (2001) *Census Canada*. www12.statcan.ca/english/census01/home/Index.cfm

Wallace, Alan (2002) "The spectrum of Buddhist practice in the west," in Charles S. Prebish and Martin Baumann (eds) *Westward Dharma: Buddhism Beyond Asia*. Berkeley, CA: University of California Press, 34–50.

Watada, Terry (1996) *Bukkyo Tozen: A History of Jodo Shinshu Buddhism in Canada, 1905–1995.* Toronto, ON: HpF Press: Toronto Buddhist Church.

Wickberg, Edgar (ed.) (1982) *From China to Canada: A History of the Chinese Communities in Canada.* Toronto, ON: Published by McClelland and Stewart Ltd. in association with the Multiculturalism Directorate, Department of the Secretary of State, and the Canadian Government Publishing Centre, Supply and Services Canada.

Williams, Duncan Ryuken and Queen, Christopher S. (1999) *American Buddhism: Methods and Findings in Recent Scholarship.* Richmond, Surrey: Curzon.

Media

Globeandmail.com (2004) "Building a bodacious Buddha," by Robert Matas. Monday, 2 August. www.theglobeandmail.com/servlet/ArticleNews/TPStory/LAC/20040802/BUDDHA02/TPNational/

Pluralism Project (2004) *International News*, 18 July–17 August. www.pluralism.org/news/intl/index.php?feature=1

Robert Gallagher of the Department of Religious Studies at Capilano College, North Vancouver, BC in 1976 produced a number of educational "kits" under an LIP provincial grant featuring slides and descriptions of religious organizations in the Greater Vancouver area.

The Review (1999) "Richmond, BC's Favourite Since 1932." Internet edition, 5(34), 25 August. www.yourlibrary.ca/community/richmondreview/archive/RR19990825/morenews.html

YahooNews (2004) "Vancouverites learn Big Buddha will be watching them," 9 August. news.yahoo.com/news?tmpl=story&cid=1527&u=/afp/20040809/wl_canada_afp/canada_religion_taiwan&printer=1

Internet

Amazenji website. www.amazenji.org/

Archive for Asian Religions in British Columbia; developed under a BC provincial LIC grant in 1998. www.langara.bc.ca/pacrim/archive (password required).

Baumann, Martin (1999) *A Bibliography on Buddhist Traditions and Schools in the USA and Canada*, June. www.globalbuddhism.org/bib-ambu.htm

BC STATS. Ministry of Management Services. www.bcstats.gov.bc.ca/

British Columbia Folklore Society (2000) *Folklore Heritage in the Pacific Northwest*, Chinatown. collections.ic.gc.ca/folklore/chtown/index.htm

BuddhaNet – Buddha Dharma Education Association, *Buddhist America Directory: British Columbia, Canada.* www.buddhanet.net/americas/can_bc.htm

Buddhapia Internet Buddhist Information Centre. www.buddhapia.com/templeaddr/canada.htm

Buddhism in America: Urban Dharma. www.urbandharma.org/index.html

Buddhist Meditation Society of Northern British Columbia (BMSNBC) website. www.geocities.com/pgjudithus/

DharmaNet International. *Dharma centers in Canada.* www.dharmanet.org/Dir/World/ctr_ca.html

International Buddhist Society. www.buddhisttemple.org

Kagyu Kunkhyab Chuling. *The North American Seat of Khyabje Kalu Rinpoche.* www.kkc.bc.ca/

Mountain Rain Zen Community. www.mountainrainzen.ca/

Northwest Dharma Association. *Dharma Groups for British Columbia.* www.nwdharma.org/buddhistgroups.php?action=list_groups&select=BC

Padmakumara – The Buddhist Teachings of Living Buddha Lian-Sheng website. www.padmakumara.org/index.shtml

Sherab Chamma Ling Tibetan Bon Buddhist Centre website. www.sherabchammaling.com/

Taiwan Ling Yen Shan Temple. www.twlingyenshan.org.hk/index.html

Thomas Kirchner. *Zen Centers of the World.* iriz.hanazono.ac.jp/zen_centers/country_list_e.html

Thubten Choling. *Buddhist Consulting Site.* www.buddhistconsulting.com/Mainweb/thubten.html

Ti-sarana Buddhist Association. *World Buddhist Directory.* British Columbia. www.tisarana.org.sg/Deta per cent20Base per cent20html/North per cent20America/Canada/british per cent20columbia.htm

Tricycle. *Dharma Centers Directory Search.* www.tricycle.com/new.php?p=home

Vancouver International Buddhist Progress Society. www.vanibps.org

2

BUDDHISM IN ALBERTA

Leslie Kawamura

Alberta became a province in the Dominion of Canada in 1905. Its land mass is 661,190 sq. km that today makes up 6.6 per cent of the national total (by comparison, roughly twice the area of Japan).[1] It is 1,232 km from the north to south and 660 km from east to west. According to the census of 2002, the population is over three million.[2] The central focus of this chapter will be on the Buddhist developments in the lower half of the province, particularly in Calgary and Edmonton, the two principal metropolitan areas. A detailed discussion of Buddhism elsewhere will be acknowledged, but not discussed as thoroughly.[3] In discussing the various groups, associations and temples, there are several approaches that one can take. For example, one could discuss them in terms of the ethnic grouping or they could be considered in view of the different Buddhist schools or denominations.[4]

Within the Canadian context, the Chinese and Japanese immigrants[5] into the province of British Columbia marked the first introduction of East Asian Buddhism into Canada. The fact that Vancouver was the city into which the ships sailed from East Asia naturally made it the place where various Buddhist movements took root. As Bruce Matthews notes:

> When Buddhism first appeared on Canada's West Coast, it just 'came along,' so to speak, to minister to specific Chinese and Japanese immigrant communities. . . . For those who did not convert to Christianity, the religion of choice was generally syncretistic, a blend of Buddhist, Confucian, Taoist, and Little Tradition devotion. Less eclectic was the Buddhism of the Japanese, largely the Jodō Shin Shū or Pure Land tradition.
>
> (Matthews 2002)

It can be shown that the first major school of Buddhism in Canada was associated with the Nishi Hongan-ji temple[6] in Kyoto, the form of Buddhism known as the Jodō Shin Shū or True Pure Land Buddhism. Apart from British Columbia, Alberta can certainly be considered one of the earliest provinces where Buddhism thrived as an integral part of the immigrant community. The Buddhist mosaic is quite different today, because compared to the earlier days when Chinese and Japanese forms of Buddhism prevailed, Alberta now has many different immigrant communities with just as many different Buddhist denominations coming from this variegated cultural background.

Nonetheless, the story of Buddhism in Alberta quite rightly begins with the Jōdō Shin Shū, a form of the faith initially planted in the relatively small community of Raymond in the early 1930s. Although it was the Mormons who had the religious stronghold here, it was also the Mormons who gave the Jōdō Shin Shū adherents the greatest challenge to maintain their native Japanese tradition. In spite of the fact that it was Jōdō Shin Shū Buddhism that had the earliest influence and greatest potential for growth in Southern Alberta, it has not flourished, and it is one of the Buddhist movements that has a dwindling congregation today. However, one must wonder whether the declining congregation in Raymond would have been so noticeable had it not been for the mass evacuation of the Japanese from the coastal areas owing to the Canadian government's decision to move them in World War II. The small Japanese population in Raymond prior to that time was suddenly greatly expanded by uprooted Japanese Canadians from British Columbia.[7] After the war, most moved away from Raymond, some out of Alberta altogether. Although there is no doubt that the decision to move the Japanese inland during the war (particularly to the sugar beet fields of Southern Alberta) was an unjust action, with the scattering of the evacuees throughout Southern Alberta, new Buddhist temples were established to accommodate the needs of the local followers. These were in many locations, such as Picture Butte (a temple was established on 28 October 1942); Coaldale (first service held on 31 January 1943, first temple dedicated on 20 March 1943); Taber (in 1947 a group was organized and in 1950 a temple building was completed); Rosemary (beginning in 1947, Japanese Canadian families met in private homes to conduct Sunday School, and in 1958 purchased a former Mormon Church for their temple); Lethbridge Buddhist Church (first Obon service was held on 31 July 1949, with a new temple available on 30 January 1955), and Lethbridge Honpa Buddhist Church (organization formed in January 1966, with sod-turning for the new temple held on August 1970, and a building officially dedicated on 1 August 1970). Among these places of worship, the temples at Picture Butte and Rosemary are now closed owing to the decline in membership. Those in Picture Butte who remained joined the Lethbridge Buddhist Church and those in Rosemary remain as members of the Jōdō Shin Shū Buddhist Federation of Alberta.[8] There is as well the Calgary Buddhist Church, affiliated with the Buddhist Churches of Canada and belonging to the Nishi Honganji Temple tradition.

Calgary is arguably the most important location for Buddhism in Alberta. With a population of over 900,000 in 2003, it is situated some 100 kilometers east of the Canadian Rockies at an elevation of 1,139 metres (3,740 feet) above sea level. Its population is nearly a third larger than that of Edmonton, the provincial capital. The earliest Buddhist organization in Calgary was known as the Hoyukai (Dharma Friendship Organization). This group met periodically when the Jōdō Shin Shū minister from Southern Alberta visited the city. The group gradually organized itself into the Calgary Buddhist Temple, and most importantly established a system of 'Sunday School' Buddhist education for younger members (later renamed the Dharma School). The members obtained a former Croatian Catholic Church[9] and thus established a permanent home for the organization. Nonetheless, Jōdō Shin Shū is becoming superseded[10] by other forms of Buddhism that are growing slowly but steadily in size, influence, and membership outreach to non-Asians. Since the introduction of Buddhism into Calgary by the Jōdō Shin Shū ministers, the city has seen enormous growth in the varieties of Buddhist traditions. Thus, Buddhism in Calgary has been graced with Buddhist followers of the Sri Lankan, Burmese, and Cambodian Theravāda tradition, of the Taiwanese, Chinese, Vietnamese, and Japanese Mahāyāna schools, and of the various Tibetan Buddhist schools. These Buddhist organizations have gradually established themselves within the last twenty years to become some of the largest and most progressive Buddhist groups in Calgary. I want now to outline their activities according to the branch of the faith they represent.[11]

Those belonging to the Theravāda tradition

In the city of Calgary, eight groups ranging from a smaller meditation group to formally constituted temples have the Theravāda tradition as their basis. Some of these have a specific outreach to local Canadians. One of the earliest was formed by Mrs Mechele Calvert in Redwood Meadows. Known as the Dynamic Insight Meditation and Study Group, it still meets in private homes under Calvert's direction, following the Theravāda *vipasannā* tradition taught to her by her spiritual teacher, the well-known Sri Lankan monk, Venerable Piyadassi Thera. Similarly active is the Calgary Theravāda Meditation Society, which began under the leadership of Shirley Johannesen (who trained in the Theravāda 'forest tradition' and is associated with the Abhayagiri Buddhist Monastery in Redwood Valley, California), and Anne Mahoney (who began her Buddhist studies under Anagarika Dhamma Dinna and then continued with Ayya Khema, a celebrated Buddhist nun ordained in Sri Lanka in 1979 at the Parappuduwa Nuns Island). Another Theravāda site is the Yoga and Meditation Center of Calgary, which also doubles as the Center for Vipassanā Meditation, providing introduction to mindfulness meditation classes as well as general courses on Buddhism. The center follows the Theravāda tradition under the guidance of Venerable Bhante Gunaratana, the abbot of Bhavana Monastery, in West Virginia. It offers a variety of retreats conducted by leading monastic and lay meditation teachers from around the world. The Yoga Center is also the home of the Calgary Vipassanā

Meditation and Study Group Sangha, meeting twice a month for chanting, sitting meditation, a *dhamma* talk and study period.[12]

A further Theravāda Buddhist meditation group, the 'Commmunity of Mindful Living – Bow Valley Sangha', was established in 1994 in Canmore, near the entrance to the world-famous Banff National Park. Led by Mary Dumka and also initially following the tradition of the Venerable Piyadassi Thera, Ms Dumka later completed two retreats with Venerable Thich Nhat Hanh and has 'taken refuge' with him. The Canmore group of about twenty continues to meet once a week in a private home. The evening begins with chanting followed by forty minutes of silent meditation, after which the participants listen to tapes on the Buddha-*dharma* or read from Buddhist books. There is a respectable library of Buddhist books, audio and video tapes that students may borrow.

From an ethnic Buddhist viewpoint, and reflecting a specifically Thai Theravāda perspective, is the Dhammayutti Nikaya, or the 'Ratchatham-mviniyaram Buddhist Temple 4' (it received the name because it was the fourth of such temples established after 'Temple 1' in Kanata, Ontario, 'Temple 2' in Niagara Falls, Ontario and 'Temple 3' in Edmonton, Alberta). Ratchathamviniyaram was established in 1998 under the patronage and instruction of the Grand Master, Thai Lao, who was eighty-four years old in 2003. The temple also supports the Will Power Institute, which provides free six-month meditation instructor courses in Edmonton, Calgary, and Fort McMurray, Alberta (and other locations in Canada). The master teacher of these meditation courses is Luang Phor Viriyang Sirintharo, who practiced meditation for many years as a forest monk in Thailand.

Another ethnic Theravāda group, the Khmer-Canadian Buddhist Cultural Centre, has converted a bank building into its temple (it has the unusual feature of a shrine situated in front of the vault!). A large room adjoining the shrine area is used for public lectures, meditation retreats, 'Saturday' *dharma* school (with emphasis on Khmer language and culture), and other activities. From its early beginnings in a house that served as the temple, the move to the new site has made it possible for this group to extend its activities and its outreach to a greater community beyond the Khmer people. It has therefore become a center where the Buddha-*dharma* is occasionally taught to non-Khmer-speaking people. In addition, a meditation program for the Rain Retreat (*Vassa*) takes place every Sunday of the week over a four-month period. Special days such as the Bon Choul Chhnam Khmer (Cambodian New Year), the Maghapuja or the Day of *Dhamma* Ceremony, or the Bon Pachum Ben (Cambodian Feast Festival for Ancestors Ceremony) are always celebrated.

The Sri Lankan Buddhist community in Calgary, the Ehipassiko Buddhist Centre, has recently purchased a house as its 'temple' (*vihara*). Under the guidance of Venerable Werapityiye Sonananda Thero, the centre offers a wide range of spiritual activities, notably meditation, 'Sunday School' and *dhamma* classes for both young people and parents. The purchase of property and the residency of Bhikkhu Sonananda has brought stability to this group that, until recently, met in various centers and halls. The establishment of the temple building has made it possible for the Sri Lankan Buddhists to re-establish their identity as Buddhists within the community. Notably, however, even before they obtained their own temple premises, the largely Sinhala members that constituted this organization were among the most supportive and cooperative of Buddhist activities in Calgary. Their commitment to the Buddha *dhamma* and their trust in it kept them together and produced a harmonious unified group.

The Burmese tradition is focused primarily on the Alberta Vipassanā Foundation, an affiliate organization of the Vipassanā Meditation Centers in the tradition of Sayagyi U Ba Khin, as taught by S. B. Goenka. Born and raised in Myanmar, but settled in India, Goenka began teaching *vipassanā* in 1969.[13] The Alberta Vipassanā Foundation functions out of rented space and is active in organizing a range of activities, from a one-day children's retreat to fairly lengthy ten-day residential retreat courses.

Those belonging to the Tibetan Buddhist tradition

Tibetan Buddhism has had an extensive outreach in the province, largely to Western converts and interested local practitioners. The first Tibetan monk to visit Alberta was Geshe Ngawang Kaldan. Born in Kham province of southeastern Tibet, he studied in Drepung Monastery near Lhasa and was bestowed the rank of Geshe Lharmpa Degree from His Holiness the fourteenth Dalai Lama. In 1974, after many years without a resident teacher, and through the efforts of Mrs Joan Van Loon and others, Geshe Kaldan was invited to Edmonton. In the 1980s he moved to Toronto, but came back to Edmonton in 1992, when he became the resident spiritual director of Edmonton's Gaden Samten Ling center and a spiritual leader of Chokhor Ling in Calgary until his untimely death in 1998. The Edmonton Gaden Samten Ling continues to be a very active group under its present resident teacher, Kushok Lobsang Damchoe. Arguably because of his devotion and magnetic personality, Lama Geshe Kaldan is credited with initiating considerable interest in Tibetan Buddhism in Edmonton and in Calgary, though the Calgary center has since closed.

Secondly, the Akshobya Buddhist Meditation Centre (also known as the Akshobya Kadampa Buddhist Centre) is one of nearly 800 Kadampa Centres worldwide founded by the Venerable Geshe Kelsang Gyatso in 2001. The Calgary resident teacher, Phuntsog, originates from Camrose, Alberta, and after studying at the Chandrakirti Buddhist Centre in Toronto for more than five years, he was ordained as a Kadampa Buddhist monk. In the early stages of the organization's development, Phuntsog (who teaches the Buddhist tradition that began with the great Tibetan Buddhist masters such as Tsong kha-pa, 1357–1419 CE) put up posters and began his propagation of

Buddhism from a basement of an old downtown church. Now located in its new premises, the practitioners of the Calgary Kadampa Sangha are referred to as those 'before from the basement' and those 'after the basement.' During the 'basement days', the organization was something of a family affair, with Phuntsog's mother even baking cookies for the students. The opening of the new centre has dramatically increased its ability to offer a full range of study initiatives consisting of a General Program, a Foundation Program, and a Teacher Training program. As one of the many Kadampa Buddhist Centres established by the Venerable Geshe Kelsang Gyatso, its stated purpose is to promote inner peace and well-being in the hearts and minds of Albertans (in the case of Alberta) and to promote world peace by helping others throughout the world develop an authentic and stable inner peace.[14]

A third Tibetan Buddhist organization is the Marpa Gompa Changchup Ling (or the Marpa Gompa Meditation Society of Calgary), dedicated to the promotion, practice, and study of Tibetan Buddhist meditation and operating under the spiritual guidance of the well-known Vajra Acharya Lama Karma Thingley Rinpoche (residing in Toronto) and the resident *dharma* teacher, Jetsun Rigdzin Khandro, a long-time student of Karma Thinley. Jetsun Rigdzin speaks of her center in the following words:

> We live in an amazing, fast moving and fast changing world. Great progress in science, medicine and technology is raising our living standard to ever new heights. But alongside this positive develop-ment, attachment to materialism also has grown very strong. When we give in to this attachment we become rigid, competitive and irritable. Even though we wish only to be happy and loving, we can see in our own experience how quickly our mind, when challenged, reacts with anger, jealousy and other negative emotions. To heal this situation, Lama Karma Thinley Rinpoche teaches Lojong practice through which many problems and much mental suffering disperse. When self-interest is changed into concern for others, our main trouble-maker, clinging to the self as a real thing (which is the root of all delusion, conflict and suffering), dissolves, and the gate of the heart of our buddha nature opens: *bodhichitta* encompasses all of space like a great sun, and our wish-prayers, like the sun's rays, touch all sentient beings effortlessly, limitlessly. The Mahāyāna teaching says when complete realization of the union of compassion and shunyata is achieved, then ordinary consciousness is gone, and duality and emotional states, too, are gone; there is limitless freedom, peace and wisdom, like the sun rising free from darkness and clouds. At that time universal space and the palm of the hand are not different in size: there is only Buddha Mind. And so, making Lojong practice the basis of our conduct and practice, we can embrace the whole world in compassion and love.[15]

Like many of the other Buddhist groups, the Marpa Gompa followers wish to see happiness pervade throughout the world. In order to give an example of the Lojong teaching, Jetsun Rigdzin Khandro sent me the following Lojong verse:

> When I am happy, may my merit flow to others,
> May its blessing fill the sky
> When I am unhappy, may the sorrows of all beings be mine,
> May the ocean of suffering run dry.[16]

Fourthly, the Diamond Way Centre in Alberta is led by Lama Ole Nydahl, and follows the Karmapa lineage with emphasis on the Guru Yoga meditation on the 16th Karmapa, Ranjung Rigpe Dorje, who introduced it to the West when he visited in 1974. Centers were established in Edmonton in 1993 and in Calgary in 1995. Members share the responsibility of guiding meditation, giving teachings, and answering questions. Frequent guest speakers (such as Erle Eilers, who together with her husband operates the meditation centre in Saarbrucken, Germany) give special public lectures.[17]

Fifthly, since 2000, the Red Deer Meditation Society has been led by Kushok Lobsang Dhamchoe (also a teacher at the Edmonton Gaden Samten Ling, mentioned above), who trained in the Gelug tradition of Tibetan Buddhism. Interestingly, the society is located on the second level of a major shopping centre. Members meet twice weekly to meditate and to learn about Buddhist Philosophy based on Tsong kha-pa's writings. The Society puts out a Newsletter that is published three times a year in January, May, and September. It contains color pictures of events, teachings by Kushok Lobsang Dhamchoe, reports, and schedules of events and meetings.

Those belonging to the East Asian Buddhist tradition

I begin with the considerable Vietnamese presence in Calgary and Edmonton, and the Buddhism associated with their tradition. A Vietnamese Buddhist Cultural Centre[18] began as early as 1982 when Vietnamese devotees rented a building near to their present temple in Calgary. In 1987, the Reverend Venerable Quan came to Calgary as the leader of the congregation, and in 1991 the present-day building was established. This building serves the Vietnamese Buddhist community in various ways and is administered by an Executive Board of ten members. According to Venerable Quan, the precise number of people associated with the temple is difficult to determine, but he estimates that some 1,500 Vietnamese Buddhists attend on a regular basis and that there are some 3,000 Vietnamese Buddhists in the vicinity. The building houses the largest Buddha image in Calgary, so large that the back wall of the temple had to be removed to seat it within the Temple. The Sitting Buddha is twenty feet high and fifteen feet at the base. From a ritual perspective, even more significant than Vesak, the Vietnamese New Year (generally near the end of January) and the Ullambana (held on the full moon in August) attract the biggest crowd of Vietnamese Buddhists to the temple. On Sundays, there are usually two activities, one directed towards the youth (over one hundred generally attend), and the other for the people at large. The youth-oriented activities are aimed to teach them both Vietnamese language and culture, with an emphasis on the Buddha *dharma* (given by the monks or nuns in the Vietnamese language). On Saturdays a 'common service' is conducted, during which participants chant sutras and listen to *dharma* teachings. English services can also be obtained by arrangement on any week day. Recently, a new Sangha Building was constructed. According to Venerable Quan, this is the one and only Sangha Building among the Vietnamese Buddhist organizations in Canada. Because Vietnamese Buddhism is consistent and uniform throughout Canada, the Venerables within this tradition can come together and meet in retreat. Such an event was held in Calgary in June 2003, in the newly built Sangha Building, with sixty monks from across Canada, the USA and Australia in residence. Although in Vietnam it is customary to spend ninety days in such a formal retreat, in Canada this period has been reduced to fifteen days, during which time the visiting monks provide *dharma* talks for the local members of the congregation. This idea of the retreat became part of the Vietnamese Buddhist tradition because at its inception, Vietnamese Buddhism belonged to the Theravāda tradition. Gradually over time, through the influence of Pure Land Buddhism and Zen Buddhism, Amita pietism and Zen meditative practices became the central form of worship in this temple. It is important to note that the temple has a respectable collection of the Buddhist texts, including the Pali Canon and the Chinese Tripitaka.

I turn now to Chinese forms of Mahāyāna in the province. Center Street in Calgary is one of the major thoroughfares that divides the city into the West and East quadrants. Near the northern end of this street is a small temple, actually a home converted into a temple, that houses the Guan Yin Tsu, established in 2001. The shrine room is adorned with the statue of the Thousand-Armed Guan Yin behind an image of Shakyamuni. The Master of the temple, Venerable Xie Hai, comes from Saskatoon, Saskatchewan. The members are mostly immigrants from Taiwan, and thus the language of communication is Mandarin. A rich variety of services are offered. Worship takes place every Sunday, and each Friday, apart from meditation, the *Nenfo* (the calling of the name of Amitābha Buddha[19]) is invoked, *dharma* talk is given, and the *Smaller Sukhāvati-vyūha Sūtra* is chanted. Twice a month, on the first and fifteenth day, a special *sutra* is read and offerings given to the Buddha. It is of interest as well to document the daily practice of the resident monk, who begins his day at 4:30 am, does his morning practice from 5:00 am to 6:00 am, has breakfast, cleans house, meditates, chants *sutras*, and studies between 6:00 am and 11:00 am, makes offerings to the Buddha at 11:00 am, meets people between 2:30 and 5:00 pm, does evening preaching from 5:00 pm to 6:00 pm, after which he meets with no one and goes to bed at 10:30 pm.

Further south along Center Street is an area that can be understood as the new Chinatown of Calgary. There, just north of the Trans-Canada highway, is a cluster of three temples representing the Chinese Buddhist traditions. The first temple, the Indo-Chinese Buddhist Association, was established in 1986 when it built a Chinese-styled temple. Its membership is mostly Taiwan and Hong Kong Chinese, with a few Vietnamese, and they participate as lay-clergy on a daily basis. It is not unusual to see a team of these lay-clergy doing worship services in which, garbed in clerical robes, they chant the *sutras* in Cantonese. Their sanctuary is open every day. The temple also importantly serves the Taiwan and Hong Kong immigrant families as a columbarium where the names (but not ashes) of the deceased are recorded and kept. This custom of preserving the names of the dead is a common practice in all of the Chinese Buddhist temples in Alberta.

The second temple, Pai Yuin or the True Buddha Pai Yuin Temple, was established in 1986, moving from place to place within the city until it settled in its present location at 1809 Centre Street in 1993. This temple is said to be one of 300 'chapters' worldwide, founded by the Living Buddha Lian-Shen (also known as the Grand Master Lu Sheng-Yen). It is a temple having both significant similarities and differences from the usual Chinese Buddhist temples. In the central position of the Shrine is a statue of the Living Buddha Lian-Shen himself, flanked on both sides by other Buddhist images. Somewhat strangely, off to one side there is an image of the Hindu deity Ganesh, and on three of its walls is a variety of Tibetan Tankas. Just as one finds in the other Chinese temples, there are many tablets with the names of the deceased surrounding the Shrine area.

The variety of artifacts found in this temple is not unusual when one understands that the Grand Master, the Living Buddha Lian Shen, a Taiwanese, was once a Christian until the age of twenty-six, when he had a profound mystical experience that led him to study Daoism and Tantric Buddhism.[20] It is said that he has received initiation empowerment in various religious traditions of East Asia. Consequently, Rev. Lian-yan and Rev. Lian-tang, the resident ministers, oversee Group Cultivation and Practice on Sundays (8:00 pm in Chinese and 10:00 am in English), the Bardo Ceremony (on the first Saturdays of the month), ritual offerings to Medicine Buddha, the Planet God, and Pagodas of Bright Light, as well as setting up ancestral shrines in the chapter's Hall of Merit. In order to take refuge with the Grand Master, one should either make an appointment with the 'True Buddha Tantric Quarter' in Redmond (Washington DC) or write a letter to Redmond stating that one has undergone the necessary rituals on the designated days with the intent of seeking refuge, the necessary personal information, and enclosing an appropriate donation. There is also the possibility of taking refuge through the local chapter. The monthly calendar is filled with various eclectic rituals held at the temple. These acknowledge the various deities associated with Buddhism, Daoism and Hinduism, as well as birthdays of certain Tibetan Buddhist teachers, the various heavenly beings, and the Grand Master, the 'Living Buddha' himself.

The third temple is Lian Yin Ching Sus, also known as Lian Yin Buddha Charitable Foundation. The resident monk, Rev. Sik So Huai, arrived in Toronto from Taiwan in 1998 and then traveled to Edmonton in 1999 to set up a temple there (registered with the interesting name of the Lotus Seed Buddhist Community Society). When Rev. Sik So Huai left in 2002 he gave the temple to a Malaysian monk and moved south to establish a temple in Calgary. In 2004, he moved again to his new temple building, which is already too small for his growing congregation. Rev. Sik So Huai seems to attract followers wherever he goes, despite the fact that he is reputed to be a very strict monk (e.g., he refuses to see any woman if she should come to the temple alone; likewise, he once expressed an interest in learning how to roller skate, but decided not to owing to the fact that he felt that the Chinese people would criticize him!). Sik So Huai does not wish to have disciples and claims not to be interested in creating a lineage of any sort, but his reputation is widespread among the Alberta Chinese Buddhist community as one who goes out of his way to help those in need and does so with great compassion and loving kindness. He is interested in nothing but having people hear and enjoy the Buddha-*dharma* (classes consist of chanting, walking meditation, sitting meditation, and prostrations). Because his English is not strong, Sik So Huai invites those trained in Buddhism and who do speak English to assist him in his outreach to non-Chinese-speaking seekers. (The temple has many books in English that are available free of charge to those who are interested, and it is anticipated that Buddhism classes in English will be offered by professors and graduate students of the University of Calgary.) Of those who have joined Lian Yin Ching Sus, only half are originally Buddhists. The remainder have joined his temple most often because they faced a death in the family or some other personal crisis, and Sik So Huai was there to comfort them.

Elsewhere, the Avatamsaka Monastery,[21] a member of the Dharma Realm Buddhist Association, was founded by the Venerable Master Hsuan Hua and established in 1987. The organization purchased a centrally located former Mountain Equipment Co-op building after spending many years in a smaller center. They follow the so-called 'Five Schools' of Mahāyāna that include the precepts or moral rules of the Vinaya; the meditative practices of the Chan School; the study of *dharma*-teaching associated with of the Scholastic School; recitation of the Mantras of the Esoteric or 'Secret School'; and chanting Amitābha Buddha's name, a hallmark feature of the Pure Land School. The head monk, Master Hsuan Hua, is a Caucasian who has complete command of the Chinese language. He has very progressive ideas and has created a strong Buddhist *sangha*. Being committed to education, the Avatamsaka Monastery is in the process of establishing a Buddhist Religious School system, beginning with kindergarten and grammar school. The temple has an exemplary collection of Buddhist materials in its library, including the complete Chinese Buddhist Canon.

In conclusion and by way of summary, because Alberta is such a vast area to cover, there have been attempts to establish umbrella organizations to coordinate Buddhist activities. The earliest attempt was the so-called Alubata-kyoku (Alberta Division) of the Buddhist Churches of Canada. However, within Calgary and Edmonton, unlike the Alubata-kyoku that focused only on the True Pure Land tradition of Japan, there are two other organizations. In the words of Bruce Matthews:

> Others have brought Buddhist groups together in specific locations, such as Leslie Kawamura's International Buddhist Foundation of Canada and Steven Aung's International Friendship Association. Despite their bold names, these efforts are almost entirely confined to the cities of Calgary and Edmonton, respectively, where they continue to do excellent work in bringing Buddhists closer to each other, sponsoring visits by famous monks, helping with temple building and making outreach efforts to non-Asian Buddhists.
>
> (Matthews 2002: 129)

From the above discussion, it is fair to say that from the early introduction of the True Pure Land Buddhism into Alberta in the early 1930s to the later developments during the 1980s and 1990s, the mosaic of Buddhism in Alberta has undergone great changes. Although traditions such as the Pure Land tradition as introduced by the Japanese immigrants may be dying embers, the Pure Land traditions of the Chinese Buddhist traditions are growing in leaps and bounds as Chinese immigration rates surge. Augmenting this growth are new developments taking place in both the Theravāda and Tibetan Buddhist traditions. It is difficult to know how these traditions are faring in other parts of Canada (hopefully this book will inform us of that), but what can be said of Buddhism in Alberta at the present time is that it is a growing concern, albeit within well defined ethnic communities.

Notes

1 There may be centers, institutes, temples, churches or organizations other than the ones discussed in this article in the areas covered here. My apologies if such omissions have occurred. Also, I would like to thank Ms Sarah Haynes and Ms Chrissy Lakusta, both doctoral students in Buddhist Studies at the University of Calgary, for their proofreading of the text.

2 The Alberta Government Website www.gov.ab.ca/home/ and map can be found at www.servicealberta.ca/pages/category.asp?EK=13193&PK=13189
3 For example, even to travel by air from Calgary to Peace River would take a day.
4 It should be noted that some of the organizations that appear in the 'lists' of Buddhist organizations found in the various websites are no longer in existence.
5 In 1877, a Japanese sailor, Manzo Nagano, decided to remain ashore at New West Minster, British Columbia, becoming the first Japanese immigrant to arrive in Canada (Adachi 1991: 9, as quoted in 'Japanese–Canadian Internment,' found at teapot.usask.ca/cdn-firearms/Research/Panic/4-0.html. See also www.lethsd.ab.ca/sheran/new_page_3.htm for additional information on early Japanese immigration. In order to appreciate what happened to Japanese–Canadians following 7 December 1941, see the above websites.
6 Also known as the Honpa Honganji Temple.
7 According to *Kanada Dōbō Hatten Daikan (Encyclopedia of Japanese Immigrants to Canada)*, Tokyo: Nakayama Jinshiro, 1921, Appendix p. 28, there were seven families in Raymond around 1921 and earlier.
8 The Jodō Shin Shū Buddhist Federation of Alberta is an organization affiliated with the Buddhist Churches of Canada since 1980. It is an umbrella organization that takes all of the Jodō Shin Shū temples in Alberta under its wing.
9 Calgary Buddhist Temple website at www.buddhismcanada.com/alta.html provides further information.
10 For a documentary on this issue of decline, see *Vision TV's* series '360 Vision' aired on Wednesday 28 April 2004.
11 No commentary on Buddhism in Alberta would be complete without mention of the Sōka Gakkai International (Canada Calgary Community Center), a member of the Sōka Gakkai International (SGI) with members in more than 180 countries. The SGI is a global organization founded in 1975 with Daisaku Ikeda, the recipient of the UN Peace Award, as the first and current President. SGI Canada, Calgary Community Center, adheres to the basic Buddhist philosophy of Nichiren Daishonin (1222–1282 CE) that emphasizes the sanctity of human life from which peace develops.
12 The information on the Yoga Meditation Center of Calgary was supplied to me by Barbara Ross in an e-mail correspondence of 18 September 2004.
13 For further information, visit the website www.dhamma.org/vipasan.htm
14 I am indebted to Sarah Nesbitt, Education Program Coordinator, who provided me with information regarding the Akshobya Kadampa Buddhist Centre in Calgary.
15 This selection by Rigdzin Khandro can be found on the Marpa Gompa.homepage, www.marpa-gompa.org. Consent to use the materials was obtained from Rigdzin Khandro.
16 ibid.
17 Information derived from website, www.diamondway.org/
18 Information on the Vietnamese Buddhist Cultural Centre is based on an interview I had with the Venerable Quan on 12 October 2004.
19 Here the term *Amitābha* ('infinite light') is used to represent the 'Immeasurable Buddha', whose characteristics are both Infinite light and Infinite life (*Amitayus*).
20 The information given here and in the following sections is based on a handout that introduces the True Buddha School. From the Calgary True Buddha Pai Yuin Temple.
21 Information regarding the Avatamsaka Monastery is based on its website www.avatamsaka.ca and the author's encounter with the monastery on various occasions throughout the years.

Bibliography

Bruce Matthews (2002), "Buddhism in Canada," In Charles S. Prebish and Martin Baumann (eds) *Westward Dharma: Buddhism Beyond Asia.* Berkeley, CA: University of California Press, p. 121.

"Japanese–Canadian Internment", found at teapot.usask.ca/cdn-firearms/Research/Panic/4-0.html and www.lethsd.ab.ca/sheran/new_page_3.htm

Kanada Dōbō Hatten Daikan (Encyclopedia of Japanese Immigrants to Canada) (1921). Tokyo: Nakayama Jinshiro.

Prebish, Charles S. and Baumann, Martin (eds) (2002) *Westward Dharma: Buddhism beyond Asia.* Berkeley, CA: University of California Press.

3

BUDDHISM IN SASKATCHEWAN AND MANITOBA

James G. Mullens

The history and development of Buddhism in Saskatchewan and Manitoba replicates general patterns found in the rest of Canada, though on a scale that reflects the smaller populations of these provinces and their later dates of settlement. This chapter offers an overview of the history and present state of Buddhist community membership and practice in Saskatchewan and Manitoba.[1] The chapter takes two principal sociological dimensions into account: Asian-ethnic Buddhist groups that primarily follow traditional Buddhist practices as part of their cultural and community lives; and Euro-Canadian Buddhist groups whose membership is comprised primarily of individuals who have taken up the study and practice of Buddhism out of personal religious enquiry.[2]

Asian-ethnic Buddhist groups in the Prairies

Saskatchewan (SK) and Manitoba (MB) are Canada's central Prairie Provinces with populations of 980,000 and 1.2 million respectively.[3] They are both largely agricultural areas with a predominantly European immigrant population base. Inherent economic and social conservatism, combined with a cold climate, have made the provinces less attractive to Asian immigrants than other parts of Canada where diverse employment opportunities and larger Asian populations make settlement and adaptation easier. Nonetheless, sufficient numbers of Asian immigrants have become established in the region to foster and support the development of Buddhist community groups. Buddhists in Saskatchewan and Manitoba are estimated to number about 10,000. The majority – about 9,500 – are of Asian descent and live in the urban centers of Saskatoon, SK (pop. 225,000) Regina, SK (pop. 190,000) and Winnipeg, MB (pop. 670,000).

Buddhism came to the Prairies in the late 1800s with Chinese immigrants who moved from Alberta, British Columbia, and Ontario, and some who also arrived from the United States. Chinese communities observing Buddhist rites and practices formed in Saskatoon, Regina and Winnipeg by the early 1900s (Li 1990). A small number of Japanese also migrated to the Prairies during this period, but there was little growth or expansion of Buddhist communities until after World War II. Increased Asian immigration from the early 1970s onward saw the arrival of new Canadians from many Buddhist lands, including Burma, Cambodia, Korea, Laos, Sri Lanka, Tibet, and Vietnam.

These various Asian groups are at different stages of adaptation to the Canadian social context, though all are concerned with cultural retention in which religion plays an important role. The smaller groups, such as the Burmese, Cambodians, Koreans, Laos, and Tibetans do not as yet have sufficient numbers to establish independent temples. Consequently their main vehicle for cultural preservation is the home and occasional use of rental premises or the facilities of the larger Buddhist groups for community religious gatherings. Today there are Asian community groups of sufficient size among Chinese and Vietnamese Canadians in Saskatchewan to support their own Buddhist temples. This is also the case in Manitoba, which in addition has a Japanese community large enough to maintain a Buddhist 'church.' The Vietnamese, though recent arrivals, have sufficient numbers to support community temples that also serve as centers for second generation cultural preservation. The older and more established Chinese and Japanese communities that also have Buddhist associations and religious institutions are, on the other hand, presently experiencing the inevitable long-term effects of acculturation and assimilation. The Japanese in particular are concerned about reversing a dwindling temple membership.

Ethnic Buddhism in Saskatchewan

According to recent statistics, Saskatchewan has approximately 2,000 Buddhists, though this figure does not reflect the full extent of Euro-Canadian involvement. The majority of Buddhists in the province are members of the Chinese and Vietnamese ethnic communities in Saskatoon and Regina, which number about 8,000 in total. Asian-ethnic settlement in Saskatchewan began in the late 1800s with the arrival of Chinese contract labourers. Chinese communities that emerged in Saskatoon and Regina in the early 1900s have maintained an enduring presence since. Saskatchewan Chinese mainly emigrated from the region around Canton and are now involved primarily in business and education. There are active community associations and languages schools in both Saskatoon and Regina. A small number of Japanese, Koreans and Sri Lankans came as regular immigrants in the post World War II period. During the 1970s and 1980s over 2,000 Vietnamese refugees together with a small number of Burmese and Kampucheans were settled in Saskatchewan. Several Tibetan families also settled briefly in the 1970s but have since departed to other parts of Canada.

A visible Asian-ethnic Buddhist presence has been late in emerging in Saskatchewan and still remains comparatively small. The appearance of Buddhist institutions was prompted primarily by the arrival of the Vietnamese and the initial establishment of small centers in Saskatoon and Regina in the late 1980s as places for weekly prayer gatherings. With population growth and financial stability, the Vietnamese community in Saskatoon founded the Chanh Tam temple in the mid-1990s for regular religious gatherings and to provide a venue to host short- and long-term visits by monks and nuns from outside the province to teach and officiate at ceremonial occasions. Chanh Tam temple is located in a large single-storey bungalow on the west side of the city of Saskatoon. It is owned by the community and has been remodeled to provide upstairs space for a shrine and prayer room with a dining area, kitchen and bedroom suite downstairs. The shrine area includes a wall mural depicting the Bodhi Tree, an altar with seated statues of Sakyamuni and Amitābha, and a life-size figure of Kuan-Yin. An ancestor shrine and book-cases of scriptures are also located on the main floor. In the spacious yard surrounding the temple are a garden with a second large Kuan-Yin statue and a garage that has been redesigned as a workshop and clinic space for acupuncture and other health treatments that are provided on an occasional basis by local practitioners. There is a membership of about 150 with a regular weekly attendance of twenty to thirty.

Chanh Tam Temple practices in the Pure Land tradition and is a member of the Union of Vietnamese Buddhist Churches of Canada, an independent organization established by the Venerable Thich Thien Nghi of Montréal. The Saskatoon community pooled resources in 2002 to bring a resident nun from Vietnam who presides over weekly devotional practices and attends to the general needs of the community. In addition to its weekly meetings, the community gathers to celebrate the major Buddhist festivals. The temple also hosts the visits of monks from other Buddhist traditions, e.g., Tibetan, Sri Lankan, and Burmese when they come to the city to teach or meet their respective ethnic community members. Developments in Regina have paralleled those in Saskatoon, with gradual increase in financial strength leading to the establishment of the Hai Duc Pagoda – also a Pure Land temple. Hai Duc Pagoda is located in a renovated church building with sufficient space to also serve as a community center for the Vietnamese population of that city.

The Chinese Buddhist presence in Saskatchewan is most clearly evident in the Avalokiteśvara Buddhist Temple of Saskatoon, founded in the late 1990s. The temple's relatively recent appearance represents the second Asian-ethnic Buddhist group in the province with a visible institutional profile. Established by members of the local Chinese community, including some of its Vietnamese Chinese, Avalokiteśvara Temple practices in the Pure Land tradition of the City of the Ten Thousand Buddhas. This temple is also located on the west side of the city, three blocks away from the

Chanh Tam Temple in an older three-storey building that was originally an Eastern Orthodox Church. The temple has a dining area and kitchen facilities downstairs, a spacious shrine room with altar and statues, and assembly area on the main floor, and a mezzanine area above this with a resource library with books and tapes in Chinese and English. These resources are available to temple members and the general public interested in Buddhism. There are residence quarters at the rear of the premises.

Avalokiteśvara Temple holds regular weekly gatherings led by a resident monk brought from California and also organizes celebrations for major Buddhist festivals and religious observances. There are also monthly vegetarian suppers open to the public that are held to raise funds for community needs. Temple membership is between 100 and 150 individuals, of whom twenty to twenty-five attend services on a weekly basis.

Ethnic Buddhism in Manitoba

The Buddhist presence in Manitoba is concentrated in Winnipeg, which is by far the largest city in the province with a population nearing 700,000. Winnipeg is multi-ethnic with citizens of predominantly European origin, though it also has a representatively large and diverse aboriginal population, as well as an influential Jewish community. Asian immigration to Winnipeg began with the arrival of Chinese entrepreneurs in the late 1870s, leading to the foundation of the first Chinese community association in the 1880s (Li 1990). There is an enduring Chinese presence in Winnipeg to the present day, currently numbering just over 10,000. The Chinese community has a number of cultural and business institutions, as well as a Buddhist temple.

The other Asian-ethnic groups who have settled in Winnipeg and established a visible Buddhist profile are, chronologically, the Japanese, who came in the 1940s and currently number about 1,400; several Tibetan families who arrived in the 1970s and still remain few in number; Vietnamese refugees and their subsequent family reunification arrivals during the 1970s and 1980s who now number close to 4,000; and Sinhala Buddhist Sri Lankans who settled in Winnipeg from the 1980s through 1990s, with a community of about 150 today. There are also small communities of Korean and Laotian Buddhists in Winnipeg that hold religious gatherings in family homes, but do not have sufficient numbers to establish centers that would give them a public presence.

The Chinese community of Winnipeg is the oldest Asian-ethnic group in the city and due to its relatively large numbers and dynamic business sector has a high public profile. The major institution that fosters its presence in the city is the Winnipeg Chinese Cultural and Community Centre which is located in the downtown core and active in civic affairs. This large center hosts a number of events and festivities open to the public throughout the year and houses attractions of various kinds that make it a prominent Winnipeg landmark. It has a library and cultural displays, and also sponsors language classes and courses in traditional arts for the city's Chinese community.[4] The Chinese Buddhist Association and its small Pure Land community temple, in contrast, have a low profile, do not garner public attention, and are not advertised or promoted outside the Chinese community. The temple is located in a remodeled house in an older residential area and is geared primarily to the needs of older Chinese citizens. The Buddhist Association provides memorial services for individuals and members of extended families and observes major Buddhist festival occasions with formal rites.

The next oldest community of Asian settlers in Winnipeg is Japanese–Canadian. Their Manitoba Buddhist Church was established in 1946 as the cultural and religious center for over 1,000 Japanese–Canadians who were resettled in Manitoba during World War II and welcomed to remain in Winnipeg at war's end. The Manitoba Buddhist Church is one of sixteen members of the Buddhist Churches of Canada, a federation of Jodo Shinshu institutions founded in 1905.[5]

The spacious Manitoba Buddhist Church building was constructed in the early 1950s and still stands today, having been renovated and extended twice. Rev. August Hideo Nishimura was its first minister, instituting a language school, Sunday school and regular Sunday services for 600 active members in the early years of the church.[6] There are presently about 1,400 Japanese in Winnipeg, mostly descendants of the original founding community. However, church membership has been declining due to out-migration, intermarriage, and assimilation. The Church presently has 200 members, fifty of whom are Caucasian. Twenty-two of the original founding elders of the community are still alive, while 97 per cent of the congregation is intermarried.

The Buddhist Churches of Canada adopted the Protestant 'church' model in interior design and the manner of services. The building has a spacious prayer hall with bench seating and a beautiful, priceless carved rosewood altar that was originally in the Vancouver Church and brought to Winnipeg after World War II. There is office space and classroom space, as well as a large kitchen and dining area in the basement. Weekly religious services are attended by a small but devoted group of members, while the entire membership participates in a number of major celebrations held throughout the year. During services, liturgical chanting is done in the Japanese language, but the remainder of the worship is conducted in English. Declining membership since the 1980s has presented a number of challenges to the membership, including finding new ways to keep youth interested and involved, developing resources in English to foster the faith, and maintaining financial viability.

The Manitoba Buddhist Church is fortunate to have a minister who is able to address these. Sensei Fredrich Ulrich is the fifth minister since the church's founding. Sensei Ulrich is an American-born naturalized Canadian of German and First Nations family heritage. He became minister of the Manitoba Buddhist Church in February 1999 and is one of a few non-Japanese clergy in the Buddhist Churches of Canada (BCC). Sensei is married to a Japanese–Canadian and they have two daughters. Prior to his appointment with the Manitoba Buddhist Church, Sensei Ulrich was a school teacher in Edmonton and pastor to the small Shin community there for a number of years.[7] Sensei Ulrich has a rich and varied background that has served him well in his ministry. In addition to his ordination in the Jodo Shinshu priesthood through the Institute of Buddhist Studies,[8] Sensei has completed Christian seminary studies and is a First Nations elder trained in traditional Native American spiritual disciplines. He holds graduate and postgraduate academic degrees and has a Second Degree Black Belt in Kempo Karate. Sensei is also an author and essayist who writes on a variety of topics ranging from Buddhist philosophy to responsible citizenship in a multi-ethnic society.

In addition to keeping contact with the larger BCC organization for its support in maintaining and fostering its traditions, Sensei Ulrich also looks to ways that the local church community can use its social resources and experience with interfaith marriages, inter-racial families and bilingual families to contribute to the wider Winnipeg society. He has brought the church community into the Manitoba Interfaith Council and offers 'meditation training in loving kindness' for anyone interested. As part of a wider outreach, Sensei travels widely in Canada and the United States offering workshops based on Buddhism, Christianity and Black Elk's Vision, conducts children's spiritual education seminars, gives talks and lectures, and engages in traditional pastoral work.

Another important Buddhist group is associated with the Vietnamese community, the third most recently established Asian group in Winnipeg. Though the Vietnamese are the second largest Asian immigrant population, with over 4,000 in total numbers, only a quarter are practicing Buddhists. Three hundred belong to the Chanh Dao Buddhist Association Temple, which is located in a large refurbished church in an older area of the city. The church was purchased by the Vietnamese Buddhist community in the 1990s through internal fundraising, public outreach and the help of other Winnipeg Buddhist community groups. Their Chanh Dao Temple is a three-storey building with a finished basement area, with adjoining shrine rooms on the main floor. The larger of these contains statues of Sakyamuni Buddha, Kuan Yin, and Jiso Bodhisattva; the smaller room houses an ancestor shrine with votive tablet racks and large urns for incense offering. The second and third floors have meeting areas, classrooms, a library, offices and rooms to accommodate visiting teachers and guests. The basement has a well-equipped kitchen and large dining area.

Buddhist services at Chanh Dao are held on Sundays, and language classes and other community events also occur there on a regular basis. *Dharma* instruction is offered by a lay teacher as the temple does not have a resident monastic. However, monks and nuns are regularly invited from outside to give teachings, officiate at ceremonies and festivals, and guide the community in its religious formation. Chanh Dao Temple, like Chanh Tam Temple in Saskatoon, is a member of the Union of Vietnamese Buddhist Churches in Canada founded by the Venerable Thich Thien Nghi. The venerable abbot visits the community regularly and also sends his monks and nuns to Winnipeg at the request of the community and when opportunity arises. Chanh Dao Temple also makes its facilities available to other community groups. In this way it serves as the institutional home for the Winnipeg Sri Lankan Buddhist community's Manitoba Buddhist Vihara, which uses the Temple facilities for its own purposes.

The Manitoba Buddhist Vihara was founded by Mrs Radhika Abeysekera, a lay Buddhist who came to Canada with her husband and children in the 1980s. Finding no local Sri Lankan Buddhist *sangha* to provide religious instruction for her own family and other Sri Lankan Buddhists in Winnipeg, Mrs Abeysekera proceeded to create the Manitoba Buddhist Society in 1989. Beginning with only ten members, the group quickly grew to a registered membership of sixty-seven youth and sixty adults, representing virtually the entire Sri Lankan Theravāda community in Winnipeg. The Vihara membership is predominantly Sri Lankan with a handful of Euro-Canadian members. The group meets weekly on Sunday at the Chanh Dao Vietnamese Buddhist Association Temple, which allows them its use for a couple of hours. Ceremonies are conducted in English with some chanting in Pali. The Vihara's classes include preschool, junior, intermediate and advanced *dharma*. There is also youth and adult meditation instruction. The youth help maintain the website for the Vihara community, including its regular newsletters, schedules and photos. This Theravāda congregation meets regularly through the year starting after the first long weekend in September until the end of June, with a break in July and August. The Vihara community began conducting Vesak *puja* in the late 1990s and its members observe the eight lay precepts in conjunction with Vesak, Founding Day (when Buddhism came to Sri Lanka), and the traditional date of the founding of the Bhikkhuni Order. On May full moon *poya* day there is a two-day Vesak celebration involving the whole community. On Mother's Day community members go to St Norbert's nursing home in south Winnipeg to perform dances and share refreshments with the seniors' community there. There is also a day of ceremony, chanting and meditation at the Peace Pagoda at the St Norbert's Arts Centre held as part of Vesak. Members of the community are also actively encouraged in the day-to-day practice of generosity, virtue and meditation.

One of the important features of the Vihara is the extent to which Mrs Abeysekera has involved herself in *dhamma* transmission to her community and beyond. From shortly after the time of her arrival in Winnipeg, Mrs Abeysekera and her husband began hosting regular visits of Buddhist monks, nuns and spiritual leaders to the city. Staying in her home, these learned visitors offered instruction in all aspects of the *dhamma* to the community. Radhika Abeyesekara's earnest study of Buddhist tradition has equipped her with a deep knowledge of the *dhamma*, and through her teaching, inspiration and association with the visiting professional Sinhalese *sangha*, three men and one woman have followed through for ordination. She is also the author of many books on the *dhamma*, and her works are used in a number of overseas Buddhist communities as the syllabus for their classes.[9] The Vihara keeps in contact with other Vihara centers in Vancouver, Mississauga, Toronto, and Ottawa, as well as in the United States and Great Britain.

By way of summary, ethnic Buddhists of Winnipeg have been supportive of one another's community needs over the years. One notable expression of Buddhist community solidarity is the city's World Peace Pagoda, the fifth of its kind in North America. The Pagoda was built in 2000 at St Norbert's Art Centre south of Winnipeg with the combined efforts of the Buddhist groups of the city, under the guidance of Sayadaw U Thila Wanta, a respected Burmese monk who has played an active role in establishing Buddhism in Canada.[10]

Euro-Canadian Buddhism in the Prairies

As in Canada generally, Euro-Canadians in Saskatchewan and Manitoba were initially introduced to Buddhism through popular literature in the early twentieth century. Those with greater interest could become more knowledgeable about Buddhism through the aegis of the Theosophical Society which had active lodges in both prairie provinces from the 1920s to the 1980s.

After World War II, travel to Asian countries brought contact with Buddhist traditions in their lands of origin, and the arrival from those countries of teachers capable of, and interested in transmitting Buddhism to Euro-Canadians. Over time, an increasing number of non-Asians have taken on the role of teachers and facilitators in the study and practice of Buddhism. Today there are at least 500 Euro-Canadians in Saskatchewan and Manitoba involved in the practice of Theravāda, Zen, Tibetan Vajrayāna, and Pure Land traditions, with many others taking an informal interest through university classes, visiting speakers, retreats and personal reading.[11]

Euro-Canadians generally do not belong to Asian-ethnic Buddhist community groups unless they have married a member. This applies equally to groups where English is the language in which services and teachings are conducted, notably among the Sri Lankan Theravāda and the Japanese Pure Land groups in Winnipeg. Even in these cases, the number of non-Asians involved is small. Euro-Canadians primarily belong to groups connected with Asian teachers and traditions nevertheless, though these connections are gradually becoming mediated by other Euro-Canadians who have themselves become teachers. Dakshong Rinpoche in Winnipeg is the only master of Asian origin permanently residing in the Prairies who ministers to a predominantly Euro-Canadian following. In contrast, there are over a dozen Euro-Canadian *dharma* teachers in Saskatchewan and Manitoba who have studied with Asian masters in Asia and the West. These teachers, in addition to guiding Euro-Canadian groups in their areas, also sponsor visits of monks, nuns and lay masters in the various traditions which they represent. This helps to support their groups' practice as well as their own, and maintains a regular connection with their respective lineages and study centers beyond the local region.

Euro-Canadian Buddhism in Saskatchewan

The emergence of a Euro-Canadian Buddhist presence in Saskatchewan has occurred gradually and informally over the past two decades. The first such group was established in Saskatoon in the 1980s by Gelongma Wangchuk (Sister Anne McDonough), student and disciple of the late Namgyal Rinpoche. Gelongma Wangchuk continues to lead the original Saskatoon Dharma Group which has ten regular members who meet weekly. In the early 1990s, the Saskatoon Buddhist Studies Group was organized by individuals with varying backgrounds and degrees of experience to provide a venue for non-sectarian study, meditation and discussion of Buddhist thought and practice. Open to anyone with an interest in Buddhism, the group maintains a steady presence in the city with approximately fifteen members. The SBSG meets on a weekly basis for meditation and fellowship and remains unaffiliated. The Tibetan tradition in Saskatchewan has been introduced through the visits of a number of Buddhist monastic groups and individual teachers who have conducted presentations and retreats through the 1990s and early 2000s. Hosted primarily by the Canada Tibet Committee and other interested individuals, the Saskatoon and Regina areas have seen the visits of a number of Buddhist teachers, including Amchok Rinpoche, Karma Lekshe Tsomo, Lobsang Samten, Geshe Khenrab, Geshe Kalden, Glenn Mullin, and the monks of Drepung Loseling, Ganden Jangtse, and Sera Je monasteries. But despite the wide public interest in these visits, no Tibetan teacher has yet become established in Saskatchewan.

Euro-Canadian Buddhism in Manitoba

Other recent additions to the Buddhist profile of Saskatchewan involve meditation and study groups organized by local individuals who have connections with traditions elsewhere. The most active of these is the Insight Meditation Society Group in Regina, led by Dana White, which practices in the IMS tradition. There are regular Insight Meditation retreats in the province with invited teachers such as Joanne Broatch and Sharda Rodgell from Spirit Rock, California who help foster the small practice groups that meet regularly in Regina and Saskatoon. Further relatively new groups centered in Saskatoon are the Saskatoon Ch'an Meditation Group (which practices in the Dharma Drum Mountain tradition of Linji and Caodong Zen as taught by Master Sheng-yen); the Saskatoon Zen Centre (which practices in the Soto/Rinzai Zen tradition of Shunyru Suzuki Roshi and Roshi Philip Kapleau); and the Saskatoon Community of Mindful Living that engages in 'Mindfulness meditation practice' in the tradition of Thich Nhat Hanh. These groups each have memberships ranging from ten to twenty members and meet on a regular basis to engage in their respective practices. Finally, Sōka Gakkai International has a presence in Saskatoon, and though not a full-fledged branch, it maintains a regular practice schedule with occasional participation in public lectures and presentations. Importantly, the Saskatoon Buddhist groups have recently founded an informal 'Buddhist communities association' to support one another and raise Buddhism's profile in the city.

On the other hand, in Winnipeg there are several other individuals and smaller groups who have brought Buddhist traditions to Euro-Canadians. Notable amongst these are Ven. Dakshong Rinpoche, an independent Tibetan lama with a dedicated following practicing in the Nyingma tradition; Gyurme Dorje (Gerry Kopelow), a student and disciple of the late Namgyal Rinpoche, who offers regular teachings and opportunities for practice; and Soka Gakkai International, with its active branch in the city. Winnipeg also offers opportunities to practice in the *vipassanā* traditions of G. N. Goenka, and the Insight Meditation Society. Another unique phenomenon is the Canadian Tibetan Buddhist Society of Manitoba, the longest established group with a predominately Euro-Canadian membership. It was founded in 1985 by Ven. Dakshong Tulku, a married Tibetan lama who immigrated to Canada in the 1970s. Dakshong Tulku is the resident teacher of the Dorje Drak Dharma Centre in Winnipeg and its associated retreat facility Dakshong Gonpa, a rural center outside the city. Though a recognized incarnate lama and scholar in the Nyingma tradition of Tibet and trained as a teacher in India, during his first ten years in Canada Dakshong Tulku was not a *dharma* teacher and worked at a number of laboring jobs to support his family. In the mid-1980s he was asked by a small group of Euro-Canadians to teach on a regular basis and established Dorje Drak Centre as a member-supported charitable organization. Beginning with practice in family homes and rental premises, steady growth in the group led to the purchase of premises for the first permanent center in 1993. The present location of Dorje Drak Centre is a two-storey home in a residential area purchased in 2000. Dakshong Rinpoche and his wife live on the upper floor, there is a shrine room and meditation area on the main level and one of the group members stays in the basement. Rinpoche is now a full-time *dharma* master supported by his students and available to them at all times. The Centre has fifty members, thirty of whom live in Winnipeg and participate in practice on a regular basis. The group meets four mornings and three evenings a week, with extended times on special dates and occasions. There are monthly retreats every third Sunday; a *tsok* offering on the tenth day of each lunar month; evening *dharma* classes twice a month focusing on the Bodhicharyavatara; and *pujas* on Tuesday, Wednesday and Friday evenings centering on Amityus, Tara and Guru Rinpoche – all in all a very active organization. There is also at least one group retreat each summer at Dakshong Gonpa, which is located on a large section of land beside a river in the countryside, though the Gonpa is in use year-round.

Dorje Drak Centre is structured like a traditional Tibetan training school. When a student decides to take formal refuge, he/she pledges a comfortable amount of financial support and is expected to follow through with that promise. The group believes in having only what it needs for its maintenance and no more. Internal politics have never become an issue, as the group's focus is entirely on practice. When Dakshong Rinpoche is away, tapes are use to continue the practice. The group is evolving and has recently begun training senior members as 'chant masters.' For the most part the group remains within its own circle of community and when there is public involvement outside it, the level is measured and well-focused. Dakshong Tulku occasionally gives talks at schools and multifaith gatherings and helps translate ceremonies and lectures when visiting monks come to the city. On occasions when the Chinese government has sent performing arts groups who present ostensibly Tibetan cultural and religious practices, the members of Dorje Drak Centre have engaged in silent protest and reached out to the public through pamphlets and discussion sessions. On 10 March, 'Tibetan Uprising Day' commemorations are also held in locations where the public can become involved. Though there is no organized relief program to assist Tibetans in Tibet, members take personal initiative in sending clothing and funds to help people there. Dorje Drak Centre has also been active in support of the local Buddhist communities in Winnipeg, participating in building the Peace Pagoda and fundraising for a new roof and heater for the Vietnamese temple. Several members are involved with care for the sick and dying, practicing compassion and loving kindness on an individual basis. They also have contact with people in prison and provide assistance to them in various ways.

On the other hand, the Dharma Centre of Winnipeg is another group that actively fosters Buddhist practice among Euro-Canadians in Manitoba. Founded in 1991, the Dharma Centre is guided by Gyurme Dorje (Gerry Kopelow), a senior student and disciple of the late Namgyal Rinpoche. The impact of Namgyal Rinpoche (Leslie Dawson) on Canadian Buddhism has yet to be fully assessed. The Dharma Centre of Winnipeg is one of a dozen centers in Canada and abroad that are affiliated with the Dharma Centre of Ontario founded by Namgyal Rinpoche in 1966. Namgyal Rinpoche in turn was first ordained as Ananda Bodhi in the Burmese Theravāda tradition by

U Thila Wanta in the late 1950s, and subsequently took his Tibetan title, with ordination, from the 10th Gyalwa Karmapa in the 1970s. Namgyal Rinpoche traveled widely and trained a number of students who are now active *dharma* teachers. His approach to *dharma* instruction was to synthesize and enhance the Buddhist teachings with the inclusion of spiritual wisdom from other religions, as well as actively integrating art, psychology, science, and appreciation of nature.

Gyurme Dorje was a student of Namgyal Rinpoche for over twenty-five years, receiving lay ordination and teaching empowerment from him. A man of diverse interests and capacities himself, Gyurme is a professional photographer and an accomplished writer, lecturer and teacher in his field. He is also a community activist involved in fundraising and other charitable work for a variety of service agencies. His role as a religious teacher has also led him to active involvement in the Winnipeg Interfaith Council. His Dharma Centre of Winnipeg is involved in a variety of spiritual activities. There are regular Sunday meetings for teachings and meditation, as well as evening talks on a variety of Buddhist-related topics. These are held at the Centre's city location, a single-storey building that has been remodeled to create an open, airy studio that serves well as a practice space for students and venue for public gatherings. The Centre also organizes retreats at St Benedict's Retreat and Conference Centre outside Winnipeg and hosts visits from fellow students of Namgyal Rinpoche who lead practice, confer empowerments and give lectures on a wide range of subjects. One of the significant contributions that the Dharma Centre has made to Buddhism in Manitoba is initiating and coordinating the construction of the Peace Pagoda in south Winnipeg. It was Gyurme Dorje's respect for his teacher Namgyal Rinpoche (and by association for his teacher's teacher U Thila Wanta) that led to the pagoda's creation. With funding assistance and community support from Buddhist groups in the city, and a site provided at St Norbert's Art Centre to erect it in, the pagoda has become a well-known and respected symbol of Buddhism in the province.

With regard to *vipassanā*-based meditation, the Manitoba Vipassanā Foundation in Winnipeg, though small, maintains regular practice according to the Burmese Theravāda tradition. There are three *vipassanā* centers in Canada that follow in the meditation tradition of Sayagyi U Bakhin, as taught by S. N. Goenka. The Winnipeg group has several experienced members who have actually practiced with S. N Goenke and they organized the first and so far only ten-day *vipassanā* meditation course in Manitoba in 2003. The *vipassanā* group meets twice monthly and plans to begin conducting ten-day meditation courses annually starting in 2005.

Finally, Winnipeg is also home to one of the eight branches of Sōka Gakkai International in Canada. SGI Winnipeg was founded in 1964 by Mrs Toshiko Friday and a local Euro-Canadian friend. There are now eighty active members in four groups around the city, twenty per cent of whom are of Japanese descent. Members meet in homes on a regular basis and as a full group weekly. Membership in SGI Winnipeg is increasing and the branch now has is its own premises which were inaugurated in November, 2004. SGI Winnipeg also has an active student club at the University of Manitoba to which visiting Japanese exchange students are invited and welcome to become involved.

Conclusion

The Buddhist presence in Saskatchewan and Manitoba is relatively small when compared to more populated and cosmopolitan regions of Canada. Nevertheless, the history and present state of Buddhist community development in the Prairies offer useful insights into the way Buddhism is being woven into the fabric of our national life. As in the rest of Canada, Buddhist groups can be broadly distinguished as either Asian-ethnic or Euro-Canadian. The number of Asian–Canadians living in Saskatchewan and Manitoba is no more than 30,000, of which Buddhists comprise approximately one-third. Asian immigrants began to settle in the region more than a century ago, with the last thirty years being the most active period. There is sufficient data from this to outline factors and features that characterize the processes of Asian-ethnic Buddhist community development.

It is important to realize that Asian-ethnic Buddhism is fundamentally culture-bound and practiced primarily to satisfy the needs and purposes of self-contained ethnic groups. Another salient characteristic of Asian–Canadian immigrant communities is the large number of languages and diversity of cultures involved in them. Buddhism, as a religious form, is only one feature of larger cultural matrixes that are challenged by the forces of acculturation. This is coupled with the fact that collectively these communities practice Theravāda, several forms of Mahāyāna, and Vajrayāna Buddhism. There is little time or capacity for them to reach out to each other or to the larger Canadian society. Their efforts seem largely to preserve their particular cultural traditions or Buddhism as they understand it. The many strands of Asian or ethnic Buddhist tradition only become entwined when some exceptional effort is made to join them, such as building the Peace Pagoda in Winnipeg, which creates public awareness of Buddhism generally but serves no group in particular.

Another factor that must be taken into account is the fact that Buddhist traditions, like ethnic languages, start to lose their social relevance as descendants of the original immigrants become mainstream Canadians. The data from Saskatchewan and Manitoba indicate that Asian-ethnic Buddhism is no more immune to the pressures of acculturation and assimilation than the many forms of Euro-ethnic Christianity in the Prairies. These also thrived during the first generations of settlement but have greatly altered their configurations with the passage of time. The data on Saskatchewan and Manitoba show that Asian-ethnic Buddhism is faced with the same issues that inevitably arise when immigrant communities age and adapt.

One final factor worth noting with respect to the development of Asian-ethnic Buddhist communities is the potential for problems to arise when a community decides to establish and thereafter maintain a community temple. This issue is only slowly becoming apparent in the Prairies because of the small number of institutions involved and their recent establishment, but is evident nevertheless. The Buddhist religious heritage of any of the Asian-ethnic 'source' nations is diverse in itself, with many schools and lineages that vie for recognition. There is potential for divisive internal politics when choosing which of these will be asked to visit a temple or send a resident teacher to serve it. This process can undermine community integrity if not well managed and adds to the complications already present in establishing a community and maintaining its stability in a new land.

Buddhist community development among Euro-Canadians faces a different yet equally challenging set of social variables. Buddhism is relatively new to Canada and as there are no established constituencies to draw from, emerging groups must gather and increase their numbers by attracting membership from a relatively small percentage of the public that is sufficiently attracted to Buddhism to consider practicing some form of it. This situation is complicated by the tendency for newly interested persons to initially engage in short-term involvement with more than one group as they learn more about Buddhism and what they wish to gain from practicing it. While it is true that all Buddhists rely on the capacities of their teachers to guide them in practice, Euro-Canadian Buddhists especially need teachers who can also shape interested individuals into viable communities and practice groups. The relative success of the small but dedicated groups of Euro-Canadian Buddhist practitioners is attributable to the organizational abilities and long-term dedication of the teachers, both Asian and Western, who have fostered stable and dependable relationships with their students and followers. The gradual transition that is occurring from the exclusive reliance on Asian Buddhist masters to a growing number of well-trained Euro-American Buddhist teachers is an important element in the development of Buddhism in the region.

Due to the relatively small number of Euro-Canadian Buddhists in Saskatchewan and Manitoba, one must be cautious when trying to estimate which of the Buddhist traditions is currently having the greatest success in attracting a following and for what reasons. This region of Canada has a history of tolerance for religious sectarian diversity, but this tolerance is founded on an inherent Christian conservatism. There is an understandable reluctance to challenge or upset this locally established norm with overt displays of difference. Though further research would be required to verify the full range of factors involved, this conservatism is likely one reason why the practices that currently command the most interest among Euro-Canadians new to Buddhism in Saskatchewan and Manitoba are the relatively low-key Zen and Vipassanā/Insight traditions. The teachings and practices involved here have fewer elements of ritual, worship and liturgy that require language proficiency and other culturally specific knowledge or paraphernalia to be competent in their performance. It is also the case that the most basic forms of sitting, walking and breathing meditation, when coupled with the observance of Buddhism's fundamental moral principles taught by these groups, constitute a viable practice that does not conflict with other beliefs, practices, or views of religion that enquiring individuals might still wish to hold while exploring Buddhist traditions.

At the same time, one cannot contest the fact that Dakshong Rinpoche has created a stable group of Vajrayāna practitioners that continues to grow in numbers, albeit slowly, or that there is considerable public interest in Tibetan tradition when its representatives come to visit. This suggests that more Euro-Canadians would enter into this tradition if there were more teachers available to guide them in it. This is particularly true for Saskatchewan where there is no resident master to cultivate those who do have an interest in Vajrayāna.

The tradition that appears to hold the least overt appeal for Euro-Canadians in Saskatchewan and Manitoba is Pure Land Buddhism in its various forms. This may be because Pure Land practice in this region is still closely tied to Asian cultural traditions that in most cases require language skills to enter into without difficulty. It is also possible that Pure Land tradition appears similar to devotional Christianity and Euro-Canadians interested in Buddhism wish to experience types of religious practice that are demonstrably different from those with which they already feel familiar.

As indicated above, the history of Buddhist community development in the Prairies spans little more than a century, with much of it concentrated in the past three decades. It is remarkable that in this short period of time all the major forms of the Buddha *dharma* have been transmitted to this region of Canada and are being authentically practiced by Asian-ethnic and Euro-Canadian Buddhist groups. It is too early to predict which of these will survive over the long term, or whether distinctive modes of institutional organization or practice founded on uniquely Canadian views and values will emerge as adaptation proceeds.

There is clearly an existing potential and arguably a growing need for Buddhist groups to begin to work together for the protection and preservation of Buddhist tradition in its various forms. Fostering a sense of Buddhist ecumenism and forming organizations through which it can be exercised will develop ideas and skills that Buddhist groups can use to shape a collective future as each continues to maintain and develop its particular aspect of Buddhist heritage that has successfully taken root in Saskatchewan, Manitoba, and in Canada as a whole.

Notes

1 The materials in this chapter are based on site visits and interviews in Saskatchewan and Manitoba and supporting research conducted from the summer of 2003 through to the fall of 2004. I wish to extend my heartfelt appreciation to the teachers, group leaders and institutions described in this chapter for welcoming my enquiries and for their unstinting cooperation and hospitality during my research visits. I also wish to thank Ms Rachel Lemke for her fieldwork assistance in the Winnipeg area and St Norbert's Art Centre for providing a base of operations there. All credit for this work goes to them – any errors in it are the responsibility of the author.

2 The terms 'Asian-ethnic' and 'Euro-Canadian' are used for convenience here to broadly delineate the geographic and ethno-cultural backgrounds that distinguish the major Buddhist constituencies in Canada. Ethno-cultural factors among the Asian–Canadian groups play a central role in the way their respective Buddhist traditions are practiced. This is not the case for Euro-Canadians whose ethno-cultural backgrounds have no particular bearing on the form of Buddhism they take up.

3 General population figures and related statistics cited in this chapter are based on the 2001 Census (Statistics Canada 2001) and its associated provincial reports, with updates where available. See www.statcan.ca

4 Winnipeg Chinese Cultural and Community Centre details available at: www.wcccc.ca/

5 Buddhist Churches of Canada website: www.bcc.ca/

6 Manitoba Buddhist Church website: www.manitobabuddhistchurch.org/

7 For a short biography see www.manitobabuddhistchurch.org/about/personnel.htm

8 IBS site: www.shin-ibs.edu/intro1.htm

9 Radhika Abeysekera's publications: www.bodhileaves.com/

10 For a description of the building of the peace pagoda: www.dharmawpg.com/essaypa.htm

11 Approximately 500 Euro-Canadians indicated Buddhism as their religion on the 2001 census; 300 are accounted for in the present research, an additional 200 regularly engage in some form of Buddhist practice not connected with a particular group. Euro-Canadians with informal connections to local groups who have occasional involvement in activities such as retreats, lectures, celebrations amount to perhaps another 500.

Bibliography

Li, Peter (1990) *The Chinese in Canada*. Toronto: Oxford University Press.

Statistics Canada (2001) *2001 Census*, provincial reports (www.statcan.ca).

4

BUDDHIST DIVERSITY
IN ONTARIO

Kay Koppedrayer and Mavis L. Fenn

Of any province in Canada, Ontario has the largest numbers of Buddhists. According to the census figures of 2001 (Statistics Canada 2001a), Ontario's 128,320 Buddhists made up over 42 per cent of Canada's total. Only British Columbia, with 85,540 Buddhists, comes anywhere close to this figure. Forty-two per cent seems substantial, but in reality, the number is small. Like the rest of Canada, Ontario is by and large inhabited by people who identify themselves as Christian; a little over 74.5 per cent of the population of over 11 million in 2001 cited one form or another of Christianity as their religion.[1] Other religious identities (Muslim, Jewish, Buddhist, Hindu, Sikh, and other religions) were found among just over 9 per cent of the population, while 16.3 per cent claimed no religious affiliation. The number of Buddhists thus is quite modest, with only 1.1 per cent of Ontario's population in Ontario identifying Buddhism as their religion.

The raw census figures, however, do not tell the whole story about the history and presence of Buddhism in Ontario. They reveal who in a particular year was willing to tick off the box on a form to let their religious affiliation stand on public record. These figures do not tell us who the Buddhists are, what kinds of traditions and practices they follow, what kinds of commitments, dreams, or purposes they have, nor of ways their presence contributes to Canadian life. The figures likewise reveal little about other ways that Buddhism shows up in Ontario. The numbers point to people who identify as Buddhists, but is there a presence of Buddhism apart from, or in addition to those who call themselves Buddhists? What about others who might in one way or another have been influenced by Buddhist thought? Or changed because of an encounter with a family of Buddhist immigrants? Or who have become more politically astute after reading about the Dalai Lama's visit to Toronto in 2004?

As Thomas Tweed reminds us (2002: 21), the encounters with Buddhism in places like Ontario can happen in a range of different situations, including not only living within a tradition, but all sorts of other ways such as reading, seeing material objects (either in a religious context or not), and in the doing of things. Tracking the adherents of a religious tradition is one way of documenting its presence, and even that can miss many people who have various interests in the tradition, everyone from those whose life is infused with Buddhist elements, to those who are drawn to any range of non-Western traditions, to people who use Buddhist meditation practices for purposes such as alleviating stress, to those with a casual interest or curiosity, to those who may in one way or another come into contact with Buddhist material without having any idea of its relationship with Buddhism.[2] Counting the numbers of Buddhists in any region in Canada is important, but the larger story is much richer than any bare numbers can show.

In this chapter, we attempt to provide some glimpse of that larger story. Buddhists and Buddhist centres are part of Ontario's social reality, and in the pages that follow we flesh out some of the rich contours of these centres and communities of practitioners. In addition, we recognize that there are other ways that elements of Buddhism, traces of Buddhism, influences, understandings, awarenesses, aspects, and so on, show up in the religious, cultural, social and even physical landscape of Ontario. These histories commingle what is happening in Ontario with larger global processes, larger histories in an increasing arena of transnationalism.

Where the Buddhists are and who they are

By far, most of Ontario's Buddhists live in greater Toronto, over 75 per cent in fact (Statistics Canada 2001b). Of the Buddhist population in other cities and regional centres, none comes anywhere close to Toronto's numbers; Ottawa has just under ten thousand, Hamilton 4,725, London 2,610, in comparison with Toronto's 97,165. Smaller centres and cities more removed from the large density of population of Toronto and its surrounding areas, or what is known as the Golden Horseshoe, reported smatterings of a population self-identifying as Buddhists. Most of the Buddhists in Ontario, especially in the Golden Horseshoe, are from immigrant communities. A reading of figures from the 2001 census across categories (Statistics Canada 2001a, 2001b, 2001c, 2001d, 2001f, 2001g), such as languages spoken at home, place of birth, and ethnic affiliation, suggests that over 84 per cent of Buddhists in Ontario are new or 'newer' Canadians, with East and Southeast Asia the predominant places of origin. Likewise, the demographic bulges which indicate when people immigrated reflect Canada's changes in immigration laws, when educational and employment qualifications replaced country of origin criteria allowing settlement by people from Asia and other parts of the globe (Matthews 2002: 122); the decades from 1971 through 2001 show the largest numbers. From the 1960s to the 1970s, the numbers jumped nearly eight-fold, and a decade later again doubled. Among these immigrants were some whose resettlement in Canada was the result of conflict in their homeland. Included are Vietnamese, ethnic Chinese from Vietnam, Khmer and Lao refugees who settled in the 1960s through the 1980s. The 1990s and the years since the turn of the century have seen new waves of Chinese immigrants resulting in part from China's repatriation of Hong Kong in 1997 and from political changes in China since 1989. Matthews (2002: 122–6) outlines the successive waves of immigration that have contributed to the Buddhist population in Ontario.

With its employment opportunities, community and social services, and clusters of immigrant communities, greater Toronto has remained the area of immigrant settlement, and it is where most Buddhist temples, centres and community gathering places are found. Janet McLellan's chapter in this volume reviews their make-up and activities (see also McLellan 1999). However, the rest of Ontario is not without Buddhist centres. A recent examination of George Klima's web listings of Buddhist centres (Klima and Ouellet 2004a, 2004b, 2004c) and BuddhaNet's *Buddhist Directory, Americas*, Ontario (2004) finds more than sixty, with groups and centres located in every region of the province except for the more sparsely populated northerly areas and the extreme western part of the province near the Manitoba border. Even there, however, census figures (Statistics Canada 2001b) report small numbers of Buddhists in cities and towns, such as Kenora (80), Timmins (60), and Kirkland Lake (10).

By no means exhaustive (as they generally do not include informal meditation groups and may omit Buddhist community organizations still coalescing that have not yet established a public presence), these listings are nonetheless revealing of the different 'Buddhisms' present in the province and the institutional formation they show. Some of these listings are study groups and meditation groups with no permanent site as the gatherings rotate by meeting in different members' homes; others purposely avoid the creation of any infrastructure (or as one group, the Kadam Chanchub Ling of Ottawa, puts it, 'no money, no politics, no agenda' [Klima and Ouellet 2004c; cf. Morreale 1998: 317–18], an impressive statement of cohesion considering the group has been meeting since the late 1970s). In comparison, some of the centres are modelled after retreats and hermitages, while others recreate Buddhist temples similar, but not without adaptations and changes, to those found in different parts of Buddhist Asia. Yet others are much more syncretic, blending different models, different purposes and various traditions. These different types of centres, the various needs and clientele they serve and the Buddhist traditions and practices they include, map out how Buddhism is becoming rooted in Ontario.

The different Buddhist traditions represented by these centres

A complete range of Buddhist traditions –Theravāda, Mahāyāna, Vajrayāna and eclectic forms – are represented in the Ontario beyond Toronto.[3] Centres that emphasize the Theravāda tradition are of several different sorts. The first consists of temples that have been founded through the efforts of a defined ethnic group or affiliated ethnic groups whose origins are from a specific region in South and Southeast Asia. Laotian and Cambodian temples are the main examples, with Thai and Sinhalese temples and centres also gaining presence. The orientation of such temples is expressed by Wat Lao Veluwanh of Caledon, which explains on its website that 'most of the members of the Wat Lao are Laotian Canadians who immigrated to Canada over the past 20 years, bringing with them their Buddhist culture and Laotian heritage. The community's desire to construct a temple reflects not only the ties to their cultural past, but also adoption of Canada as their new homeland' (Wat Lao Veluwanaram 2004).

A similar statement is found on the Khmer Buddhist Temple's website: that its mission includes preservation of Cambodian culture, Khmer traditions, the moral values of the Buddhist religion; that the temple should serve as a place of spiritual worshipping for Cambodian people, and that in cooperation with other organizations and communities, the temple and its activities should work to increase the awareness of and understanding of the Buddhist religion and Khmer society within Canada (Theng and Ek 2004). The celebration of traditional holidays, the inclusion of local practices carried on from a homeland, an emphasis on inter-generation activities, a concern for the education of children, language classes, and the offering of a range of services – legal, financial and other counselling, translation – make these temples community centres as well as religious centres. Serving immigrant families who have settled in sufficient numbers in a given part of the province, their associations are with a local ethnic group or cluster of ethnic groups, but they also attract people from outside of these particular ethnic communities. Regular meditation sessions often draw a mixed clientele. Continuity, matched by adaptations and adjustments, are characteristic features, as are some of the challenges these organizations face. These can be financial, but they are also religious concerns related to maintaining a monastic presence. The ethnic communities that support these temples are still setting roots and growing and have not yet developed a monastic community here; by and large monks necessary for so many activities must still be imported.

A second type of Theravāda centre are those which are Asian in origin and orientation, but have broadened their clientele to serve Theravāda Buddhists of all nationalities. Wat Ratchadham 2 of Niagara Falls, affiliated with a network of Thai temples located elsewhere in Ontario and the rest of Canada as well as back in Thailand, is an example. The 2 in Wat Ratchadham 2's name signals that it is a branch temple of another Wat Ratchadham, this one in Kanata, near the nation's capital, Ottawa. The Niagara Falls location of the second Wat Ratchadham is significant as it is a popular tourist site, one of the few sites in Ontario that has immediate recognition almost anywhere in the world. The large jade Buddha image it houses draws visitors, while the temple gives them the opportunity to pay homage to the Buddha. Further activities include the daily offering of food to the resident monks, chanting, group meditation and *dharma* talks (Wat Ratchadham 2 2004).

Centres that have affiliations with a Theravāda tradition in Asia, either through resident and/or visiting teachers of Asian ancestry or through a Canadian of non-Asian ancestry associated with an Asian Theravāda lineage, monastic organization or teaching tradition, make up a third type. In general, these centres emphasize meditation through regular instruction in *vipassanā* techniques and in some cases more formal retreats. Ranging from quite small-scale groups, such as the Hamilton Meditation assembly, which offers both weekly meditation at members' homes to much larger residential retreat centres modelled after the forest hermitage-style of the Theravāda tradition, they attract individuals and families, many of whom come from non-Buddhist backgrounds, and whose interest is in experiencing Buddhist teachings through praxis. Meditation as taught by Thai and Myanmar lineages are predominant.

Northern and central Ontario have several well-established Theravāda retreat centres of this sort. The oldest, situated on a large property near Thunder Bay, is the Arrow River Forest Hermitage (previously the Arrow River Community Centre), begun in 1975 on land donated by a student of Kema Ananda (née Eric James Bell). The Hermitage is modeled on a forest monastery. It offers a range of activities including long-term and short-term retreats under the direction of Canadian-born Ajahn Punnadhammo. Ajhan Punnadhammo became a student of Kema Ananda in 1979 and was initially trained in the meditation method of the Burmese master, Mahasi Sayadaw. He ordained in Thailand in the Forest tradition of Ajahn Chah in 1990 (Arrow River Forest Hermitage 2004) and, when Kema Ananda died of cancer in 1996, he returned to operate the Centre – which then took on a more monastic direction. After Kema Ananda's death his son and disciple, Michael Bell, relocated to the Kitchener-Waterloo area where he and his wife Melanie teach both *jhāna* and Insight meditation. (There are eight *jhānas* leading to progressively higher levels of concentration. Of the relationship between *jhāna* and *vipassanā*, Bell notes, '*Jhāna* development tames the mind and Insight practice penetrates the nature of the mind.')[4] Currently, Michael and Melanie Bell are preparing for a three-month retreat. Another older centre is the Ontario Vipassanā Centre, or Dhamma Torana, near Barrie. Dating to the 1980s, it is affiliated with a larger network of centres in North America and abroad that follow the teachings of S. N. Goenka, known among other things for the prisoner-treatment programs using *vipassanā* meditation introduced in India and the USA. The Buddha Sasana Yeiktha (International Meditation Centre) of Severn Bridge follows in the lineage of the late Ven. Mahasi Sayadaw. Dating to 1994, it offers formal organized retreats with senior meditation masters from Myanmar in addition to the regular retreats and meditation sessions run by its resident nun, Sister

Khemanandi (Buddha Sasana Yeiktha 2004). The site of the retreat is in Muskoka, about 150 km from Toronto. Due to severe weather conditions it is open only from May to October. Formerly, Sister Khemanandi conducted a weekly meditation session at Fenbrook Correctional Institute in Gravenhurst but ill health has forced her to suspend these sessions. Another, the Ottawa Buddhist Society, is more eclectic. With affiliations with several centres and teachers located outside of Canada, it draws on teachings from Sri Lanka, Thailand and Myanmar (Ottawa Buddhist Society 2004).

A fourth type offers a specifically North American adaptation of *vipassanā* meditation, such as the meditational style of mindfulness-based stress reduction developed by Jon Kabat-Zinn, or what might be called recombinant techniques, derived from *vipassanā*, but reworked and adapted for a North American context. These groups offer weekly meditation and discussion and periodic retreats (Klima and Ouellet 2004a, 2004b).

Mahāyāna and Vajrayāna centres

A similar pattern of temples and centres with different make-up, orientation, and ethnic configurations obtains among the Mahāyāna and Vajrayāna centres, though there are differences pertaining to the histories of the communities involved, and the traditions they follow, within Canada. The oldest of the centres of the first sort – temples whose members share an Asian ethnicity – are the Hamilton Buddhist Temple and the Thunder Bay Buddhist Fellowship, each dating to 1949. Affiliated with the Buddhist Churches of Canada, their orientation is Jodo Shinshu, and membership largely Japanese. As Layman has discussed elsewhere (1976: 57), the relatively early date this organization took shape has contributed to an organizational style consciously modelled after Christian churches. The date is significant in another way: it is after the World War II period of internment of Japanese Canadians and points to the reestablishment of Japanese communities after 1945 (Watada 1996). Participation in the temple's activities in the early years contributed to a sense of Japanese Canadian identity and a sectarian understanding of Jodo Shinshu beliefs and practices. Recently, however, with the growing interest in Buddhism and through its ties with other Buddhist groups, more and more non-Japanese have begun joining (Watada 1996).

Also of the first sort are the numerous Vietnamese temples and associations, Pure Land and Vietnamese Zen, located in major centres such as Hamilton, Windsor, London, Kitchener, Ottawa, that serve the local communities. Some are affiliated with the larger organizations; the London chapter of the International Sangha Bhiksu Buddhist Association (centred in California under the direction of Thich Giac Nhien), a Vietnamese Zen temple, is one such example. Located in a residential district in a renovated school, the temple declares its presence by the figure of Quan Yin flanked by two lions at the entrance. Its resident director and primary teacher is Bhikshuni Suko

Lien, a disciple of Thich Giac Nhien sent to serve the community here. She and two resident monks who frequently travel to other Vietnamese communities make up the temple's staff. Practice, including a program for non-Vietnamese practitioners, includes meditation, chanting, and what is known among Zen practitioners as *oriyoki*, a practice using the alms' bowl in which participants practice mindfulness by learning to hold the bowl properly, accepting the food properly, and eating with mindfulness. The Vietnamese-speaking and English-speaking practitioners meet on different days. Bhikshuni Lien gives numerous talks each year to students and teachers from the public school system who visit the temple to learn something about Buddhism. Another umbrella organization is the Vietnamese Unified Buddhist Congregation of Canada, which has a centre in Ottawa.

Thich Nhat Hanh's teachings also have followers among the Vietnamese community. The Deiu Khong (Marvellous Emptiness) Temple in Ottawa draws both Vietnamese and non-Vietnamese to its activities, with separate meditation practices scheduled for English-speaking and Vietnamese-speaking people. This is not the only group that follows the Engaged Buddhist teachings of Thich Nhat Hanh. A meditation group in Gloucester draws together Vietnamese, English and French-speaking practitioners. The Pine Gate Sangha of Ottawa (the nucleus of Friends for Peace), led by Ian Prattis, a professor of anthropology and religion at Carleton University and an ordained member of the Tiep Hien Order, draws people who have a broad-based interest in spirituality and social issues, including environmental concerns (Prattis 2004). The Sangha's engaged activism is the focus of their activities.

The different Chinese communities in Ontario likewise have their own temples and organizations. McLellan's chapter in this volume and previous work (McLellan 1999) discusses the Fo Guang Shan temple and the Buddha's Light International Association, and also the Cham Shan temple. Both have presence in other parts of the province and indeed the world, and both engage in outreach activities to help disseminate their Buddhist teachings to a wider, but largely ethnic Chinese audience. Buddha's Light International Association, with an active agenda of propagating Buddhism worldwide including programs of 'localizing Buddhism' (Fo Guang Shan Temple 2003), has a chapter in Ottawa, and an affiliated organization, the International Buddhist Progress Society of Ottawa. Recently, Fo Guang Shan opened a non-profit tea house in the Waterloo area. In part, the mandate was to provide a place where students from the two area universities could come, meet and eat well-prepared vegetarian food. The tea house also provides a permanent site where people can learn about humanistic Buddhism. Currently, there are *dharma* teachings and meditation training in Chinese and English on alternating Mondays. Every few months there is chanting. All the teachings and meditation training are provided by monks and nuns from the Mississauga (Toronto) Fo Guang Shan temple. They lead the chanting as well. The practitioners, however, are not as separated as those studied by Numrich (Numrich 1996). The Chinese chants are translated into English, and translation is provided when necessary at teaching and meditation sessions. The Lotus Tea House and the Buddha's Light International Association of Toronto, of which the Waterloo group is a sub-chapter, are fairly involved in the broader community, participating in multicultural events and the United Way. In the case of the Cham Shan temple, it has affiliate temples in Hamilton and Niagara Falls. Its Ten Thousand Buddhas World Peace Saria Stupa, a traditional temple complex built in 1995, with its meditation halls, *stupa* (relic container), meeting rooms, library and art gallery, also serves as a religious centre for Chinese Buddhist and other tourists with its highly visible seven-tiered copper roof (e.g., Canadian Copper and Brass Association 2001). In this way, the World Peace Saria Stupa is an example of a centre with ethnic associations that opens outward to others. Indeed, one of the reasons for choosing Niagara Falls was to make Buddhism visible and available to a broader community. There are tours of the temple complex, a daily service in Mandarin with English translation, and a three-day retreat once a year that focuses on the Surangama Mantra that draws between fifty and a hundred people. In addition, on Saturday and Sunday in the summer the temple provides lunch for tourists.

Of all the Buddhisms in North America, Zen was what initially had the most appeal to non-Buddhists (Prebish 1979: 127). In Ontario, there are a few Zen centres that draw a largely non-Asian clientele, but these are indeed few, and not in any way disproportionate in relation to other Buddhist centres, perhaps because of the relative degree of access Ontarians have had to other Buddhist traditions, given the history of the introduction of different Buddhisms to the province. Vietnamese Zen temples, already mentioned, draw followers not only of Vietnamese but also of other ethnicities, leading on occasion to 'parallel congregations,' to borrow Numrich's phrase (Numrich 1996: 63–74). Other Zen centres attract Western followers. The White Wind Zen Community of Ottawa, dating to 1985, is a well-established group of students, mainly Caucasian, of the Western-born Ven. Anzan Hoshin. Following an interpretation of Dogen's teachings and made up of both monastic and lay members, the community has a number of innovative features including a long-distance training program, implemented in 1995, that allows students who otherwise might be solo practitioners due to their geographic distance from any Zen community to sustain student–teacher contact through regular email exchanges. In effect, this enables a virtual community, but one grounded in practice, as participants in the long-distance program are expected to maintain 'committed sitting,' thirty minutes of meditation at a regular time at least once a week (White Wind Zen Community 2004). Another Zen group which draws practitioners from a broad-based population is the Kingston Zendo, which meets at Kingston, Ontario, Queen's University, and is an affiliate of the Montréal Zen Centre (Montréal Zen Centre 2004).

Another Buddhism that has become a focus of attention due to global politics is Tibetan Buddhism, perhaps the most popular Buddhism in the West at present. When Canada agreed to accept a small number of Tibetan refugees in the early 1960s, Lindsay, Ontario, was one of the places they were settled. In spite of the challenges of relocation, members of the community have managed to maintain ties to their religious traditions and have some access to religious teachers in their own community and to teachers who continually come through Ontario. Tibetan Buddhism has also attracted much interest in the past few decades as an alternative to the religious traditions North Americans were born into or to the absence of religion in their lives. As a result, Ontario, like much of the rest of North America, has seen a small proliferation of Tibetan Buddhist centres, catering to non-Tibetan North Americans.

The Karma Kagyu and Nyingmapa traditions are especially well represented with groups in Ontario, such as Niagara Falls' Karma Kagyu Buddhist meditation centre, that are linked to larger communities of worldwide centres. Two Nyingmapa organizations, the Palyul Foundation, which maintains Orgyan Osal Cho Dzong, a 200-acre retreat facility in southeastern Ontario (near Madoc), and the Palyul Namdrölling Foundation, which maintains the Chamundi House, an hour outside of Ottawa, complement the range of teachings offered.

Other Mahayana Buddhist-based traditions that are international in scope are established in Ontario. The Kulata Buddhist centre of Kingston, founded in 1998, is one of a network of over 900 New Kadampa Tradition centres and groups located in 35 countries associated with Ven. Geshe Kelsang Gyatso. Also popular are the teachings of Chögyam Trungpa Rinpoche, whom James Coleman in his study of North American Buddhism describes as the teacher who more than any other shaped the face of Tibetan Buddhism in the West (2001: 73). That Shambhala International has a presence is not surprising, considering its headquarters are located in Canada, as Matthews' chapter in this volume discusses. Shambhala International, formerly Vajradhatu, an example of Buddhist-based religious movement adapted to conditions in the West, was part of the larger phenomenon of new religious movements in the late 1960s and 1970s. (Though not Tibetan Buddhist in orientation, the Sōka Gakkai, which has had a formal presence in Ontario since 1975 in Ottawa, is another of the earlier Buddhist movements that has attracted followers.)

Shambhala's place in Ontario is marked by centres in Toronto and Ottawa, and a group centred on Shambhala teachings which meets in Alliston, near Lake Simcoe. In addition to the Shambhala centres, the presence of Chögyam Trungpa's community in Canada has had other impacts on Buddhism in Ontario. One has been the way Gampo Abbey, the monastic retreat founded by Chögyam Trungpa in Cape Breton, Nova Scotia, has proved to be an important resource centre and training ground for Buddhist practitioners and teachers from Ontario. A Karma Kagyü centre in the Kitchener Waterloo region, Palpung Yeshe Chokhor, owes its origins to a fortuitous encounter at Gampo Abbey. A Canadian-born nun, Ani Sonam Lhamo, whose training was in a Nyingma lineage, had gone on retreat to Gampo Abbey, Cape Breton, where she met the Tibetan-born Lama Karma Phuntsok. Her invitation brought him to the heavily populated southern Ontario Kitchener-Waterloo area where he now teaches. Palpung Yeshe Chokhor, which exists in a space donated by a member, provides evening meditation sessions and regular teachings. Importantly, Tibetan language classes are also offered. An interest in ensuring transmission of the teachings is evinced in a children's program called the 'Little Buddha's Club,' held bi-weekly. The Centre has recently achieved charity status, which they hope will assist with additional financial aid. To date, they have had a very successful art showing of Lama Phuntsok's art work (2002) and a Tibetan dinner/dance fundraiser (2003). Both events brought Palpung Yeshe Chokor to the attention of the broader community in the Kitchener-Waterloo area.

The Karma Kagyü Buddhist Meditation Centre of Niagara was founded by Chöje Lama Namse Rinpoche in 1983. This centre was made possible by Professor John Mayer and Lama Namse's invitation to his Holiness the 16th Karmapa to perform the Vajra crown ceremony in St Catharines in 1980. In what must be a unique gesture, the Unitarian church donated their manse to use as a *dharma* centre. In 1985 Lama Namse returned to Toronto to develop his temple there, but he has always stayed in close contact with the group. To reinvigorate the centre he performed Chenrezig empowerment in 2002. The group currently meets at the centrally located Folk Arts/Multiculturalism Centre in St Catharines. It provides meditation instruction and classes on Buddhist philosophy, and hosts empowerments and teachings by visiting lamas. Chenrezig *puja* is practiced weekly and Tara *puja* twice a month.

Another Buddhist teacher, Yeshe Wangpo of London, Ontario, is a student of Thrangu Rinpoche of the Karma Kagyü tradition. A North American by birth and a monastic since the early 1980s, his formation includes twelve years' residency at the Gampo Abbey, noted above as the centre for Vajradhatu/Shambala. Yeshe Wangpo founded the Nyingje Companions (Centre for the Development of Meditative Arts and Contemplative Understanding) whose website combines Western literary arts and Buddhist teaching, echoing the way Shambala, under the influence of its founder Chögyam Trungpa, integrated various arts 'to erode the boundary between aesthetic and ordinary perception, and to free up . . . creative expression' (Butterfield 1994: 216). The purpose of the Companions is to provide teaching and support for those who do not have a local *sangha*, for example individuals who are in prison or homebound. Since moving to London, Yeshe's prison work has been limited to mail, telephone and e-mail. Unlike the Christian tradition, prison outreach is not funded by a central Buddhist organisation in Canada. Internationally, there is Angulimala, a British-based prison chaplaincy established in 1977 which received recognition by the British penal system in 1985 and has chapters in Scotland, and contacts in America, Russia and Nepal (Angulimala 2004; Angulimala's founder, the Venerable Ajahn Khemadhammo, recently received the OBE for his prison work). Yeshe Wangpo also teaches Sunday mornings at the London (Ontario) Meditation Group by request (formerly the London Vipassanā Group). He initially tried teaching within the context of Tibetan culture but that proved ineffective. He was charged by his teacher to teach Buddhism in a way that would relate to Westerners. Teaching in London for four years, he came through the request of students who were receiving teachings via the internet and felt that there was a teaching vacuum in their region. Most sessions are held in Yeshe Wangpo's apartment where he teaches Vajrayāna practice and meditation. The group is composed mostly of Caucasians who range in age from 14 to 72, with the majority being in the younger age range. While he believes that Vajrayāna practices have a lot to offer, Yeshe Wangpo chooses a practice according to student need. This factor came up numerous times in interviews with teachers from various traditions. In line with his belief in non-attachment to religious beliefs, his students also take the precept: 'Do not harm another's faith.' Yeshe Wangpo also has a very interactive style. He believes that teaching is also learning. While he may be able to guide students because of his experience, he learns much from them as well. For him, he avers, there is mutual transformation.

Yeshe Wangpo's work with both Karma Kagya and Vipassanā leads to a final category of Buddhist practice centres consisting of those whose history and teachings draw upon more than one tradition. Like Yeshe Wangpo, some have affiliations with Asian lineages, but are more eclectic in their combinations of teachings and in their histories. Another example is to be found at the Blue Heron Dharma Centre of Hamilton, founded by Sa Di Ni Tjnh Quang who is also the resident *dharma* teacher. Sister Tjnh Quang is a Western Buddhist nun ordained three years ago in Vietnam in a Vietnamese Zen lineage. Her personal history, drawing upon several different forms of teachings, is not uncommon for Western Buddhist teachers. For Sister Tinh Quang, it includes work as a psychotherapist and training in gestalt therapy. She attended the Toronto temple of Samu Sunim for almost a decade and studied with him for about a year and a half. She left to study with Thich Tam Dang and Thich Tri Thanh at the Chua Huong Dam Temple in Hamilton. While the Centre has moved occasionally in its eight-year history, it began and now continues in Sister Tinh Quang's former home, which has been transformed into a Dharma Centre. Sister Tinh Quang's living quarters are upstairs. Most of the members are Caucasians in their middle years. Teachings and practices at this centre draw upon Vietnamese Zen (Thien) and Theravāda traditions and are an interesting blend of the traditional and modern. There is chanting in English, Pali and Sanskrit, meditation instruction, yoga and special ceremonies: Vesak (Buddha's birthday), Precept and a Rose ceremony constructed for Mother's Day. There are frequent seminars: Chinese medicine, dreams, *dharma* in daily life, a Reading Group as well as a vegetarian cooking class, and a once a month *dharma* class for children. Sister Tinh Quang sits on the Hamilton-Wentworth School Board Interfaith Advisory Committee and the centre offers mindfulness-based counselling and therapy for couples. She has studied the works of Thich Nhat Hanh and integrates it in her teaching. The Centre would like to do more socially engaged work with the homeless and for the cause of the environment but faces a problem shared with many groups that are not Asian-based – inadequate financing. While both Asian and non-Asian Buddhist groups practice *dana* (meritorious giving), Asian groups tend to be larger and have a longer tradition of significant giving. Several groups expressed a desire to expand and develop classes especially for children but were hampered by a lack of both human and financial resources. While the Blue Heron Dharma Centre primarily combines Zen and Theravāda traditions, other combinations are also found, sometimes involving a fusion of different practices and traditions resulting from the relationships their leaders have had with various lineages and teaching traditions. Others again foster exchanges by inviting preceptors from different traditions and lineages to teach. In addition, there are centres such as the Waterloo Riverview Dharma Centre, Peterborough's Buddha Place, and the Dharma Centre of Canada that are inclusive of all Buddhist traditions. Operating under the guidance of a spiritual advisory committee of ordained *sangha* from the Theravāda, Mahāyāna and Vajrayāna traditions, the mission of the Buddha Place is to increase the awareness of *dharma* and 'to provide a supportive environment for people to learn, practice and share together' (Buddhist Place 2004).

The Dharma Centre, located in Kinmount (Kawartha Lakes) is one of the oldest meditation centres in North America – it was founded in 1966 – and with its 400 acres certainly the largest Buddhist land-holdings in Ontario. It defines itself as 'universalist,' suggesting that beyond the three *yāna* and their numerous schools and traditions, beyond the cultural differences between the Buddhisms of different regions in Asia and the West, beyond the different orientations, is a universal *dharma*. The centre continues to thrive, inviting teachings of all traditions to hold courses and retreats throughout the year, and offering space for individuals wishing to do personal meditation retreats. Its universalist approach reflects its history and that of its founder, the Ven. Namgyal Rinpoche. Canadian-born and just recently deceased (October 2003), he spent decades outside of North America studying and practising with meditation teachers in Sri Lanka, Burma and Thailand, later serving as abbot of a *sangha* association in Britain in the early 1960s. In the late 1960s he was recognized as a tulku by the 16th Karmapa of the Karma Kagya tradition and reordained, having previously been ordained by the Burmese teacher, the Ven. U Thila Wunta Sayadaw. Namgyal's teachings combined these traditions and other experiential forms, and he created a fairly large network of centres in New Zealand, Australia, Japan, Canada and Europe. He is, in effect, one of the several Buddhist teachers Ontario has exported, and an early one at that. In an interesting historical note, Kema Ananda, the founder of Arrow River (Thunder Bay, northwest Ontario), was a student of Namgyal while he was ordained in the Burmese lineage.

The Riverview Dharma Centre was started by Susan Child in 1999 and she continues as the coordinator of the Centre which now has two locations in the Kitchener-Waterloo area. The Centre provides a non-sectarian approach, in that it is open to the teachings of all Buddhist traditions; however, the basis of meditation instruction is rooted in the Theravāda tradition. Child stresses that one does not need to be a Buddhist to attend, nor even be religious; benefit from practice can be integrated into any lifestyle. From the beginning, the Centre has brought in teachers from a variety of traditions. Initially, all programs took place at the Child home. However, as the Centre's range of activities grew, parking became problematic. In July of 2003, the Riverview Dharma Centre rented space in a downtown location. This proved to be a good move as it made activities more accessible than the previous suburban, almost rural area. A survey of the 2003 report to the Board of Directors indicate that finances are 'in the black' and a group of about sixty committed meditation practitioners are involved in the Centre (Riverview Dharma Centre nd). The Centre offers introductory meditation instruction, as well as ongoing meditation training. Members of the Centre have been involved in organizing and participating in an annual Interfaith Peace Walk, since 2001. In April of 2004 they organized a bus to transport people to Toronto to hear H.H. the Dalai Lama speak. The Centre has also been supporting an outreach project in Zambia. As well as their own retreats and programs, the Riverview Dharma Centre website provides a list and contacts for other Buddhist retreats and special events in the area.

Charitable organizations

Temples, *dharma* centres, retreats, and study groups are not the only Buddhist organizations in the province. Also of note are charitable organizations. The Palyul Sangha, discussed above, has an affiliated charitable organization, the Palyul Namdroling Foundation that supports several hundred children of the refugee Tibetan community settled in the Mysore area of south India. Another charitable foundation active in Ontario is the Buddhist Compassion Relief Tzu Chi Foundation. Founded over forty years ago in Taiwan, the Foundation operates an extensive network of chapters worldwide, including its Canadian headquarters in Vancouver and offices in Calgary, Edmonton, Toronto, Mississauga, Ottawa and Montreal. Its activities in Canada date to 1992 for Vancouver, and 1994 for the first Ontario branch office. Based on the *bodhisattva* principle that there should be 'great mercy even to strangers and great compassion for all' (Buddhist Compassion Relief 2002: 2), it is an outreach organization and in its years of operation in Canada, the Foundation has broadened its focus from providing financial and material assistance to low-income families and fundraising to help other non-profit organizations and health-care facilities, to include active spiritual counselling, community volunteerism and care-giving. It also engages in international relief work, and as such is yet another example of how Buddhist organizations in Ontario are often linked to larger global networks.

Observations

Several observations can be made about this diversity of Buddhist temples and organizations within Ontario. First and foremost is the diversity of teachings, practices, and orientations that address and serve different religious purposes. This would suggest that to converse about Buddhism in Ontario is a misnomer: rather, there are many Buddhisms that can be catalogued in several ways – by tradition, by types of practice, by adaptations, by ethnicity of followers, by style of teachings, and so on. This roster of groups marks out the history of settlement by different immigrant groups in Ontario who have come from areas where Buddhism is a living religion. At the same time, it also documents the history of the interest in Buddhist thought and Buddhist teachings in the West, with the considerable variations that appear in the interpretations in any tradition's teachings. The dates when different centres and temples were founded also indicate several decades of development. The earliest, the Japanese Jodo Shinshu groups, mark a beginning of a rooting of Buddhism; the next group, Kinmount's Dharma Centre, dating to the mid-1960s, corresponds with the time of a burst of interest in 'Eastern' religions on the part of North Americans. Subsequent dates reflect when centres and temples mark immigration and refugee settlement patterns, and also tally with North American's phases of experimentation with alternative religions.

Some of the Buddhist groups mentioned in this chapter are highly local, resulting from the presence of a particular teacher or the efforts of a particular community, ethnic group or cluster of people who have identified among themselves shared purposes. At the same time, more than half are associated with larger networks and organizations, some extending throughout North America, others even more international in scope. These larger networks are not confined to any particular ethnic group, or a certain Buddhist tradition, or a style of practice (whether devotional or meditational). There are larger networks serving ethnic Vietnamese Buddhists, large, international Chinese Buddhist groups, international organizations based on *vipassanā* practice, international organizations based on Tibetan teachings, and so on. These constitute what might be called international lineages or schools of Buddhism, whose development is characterized by the increased abilities in international travel and communication, made even easier by the possibility of rapid electronic communication. Most have been introduced into Ontario, in the sense that the organization originated outside of Ontario, but there are exceptions as in the case of the Dharma Centre, where the impetus comes from a Buddhist teacher whose first community was established in Ontario.

In recognizing the significant number of centres and groups that are chapters, branches, or member centres of larger organizations, two observations can be made. First is that the religious and social identities of the people frequenting these centres are fostered in part by a sense of affiliation or connection with a larger community. These affiliations contribute to a collective identity – Buddhist, but also Buddhist of a certain type, a certain tradition, a certain teaching, defined by the presence of a group within Ontario, but nevertheless an identity or association that indicates a transnational presence. A sense of participation in a larger, often multinational movement is implicated by these linkages. In this way, what is found in Ontario is part of what might well be called a global Buddhism, its various traditions spread throughout the world. Some of these traditions may appear localized, but they are nonetheless part of much larger networks.

The second observation relates to the implications of the first. Given these linkages, or even given the diversity we have catalogued, to what degree is it possible to think about a Canadian Buddhism, even in nascent form? We suggest that the make-up, organization and affiliations implicitly operating within the Buddhist groups in Ontario will work against any assertion of a Canadian Buddhism. We suggest that there is a rich and readily documentable presence of Buddhism(s) in Ontario, but that this Buddhism is not unequivocally Canadian in formation, nor will it be in any forseeable future. These centres and Buddhist groups are, instead, a testimony to cultural and religious pluralities criss-crossing an increasingly global community. And they are not the only way that images and ideas of Buddhism have entered into Ontario. We conclude this chapter by considering other ways that networks of information have brought understandings and presentations of Buddhism here. We start with a descriptive anecdote to illustrate just where else Buddhism is found.

In repositories of intellectual history

One of the least likely places one might expect to find traces of Buddhism is in a small town of about 1,500 people in a largely agricultural area some fifty kilometers west of the Kitchener-Waterloo region. Apart from a family of Sikh immigrants who recently bought the local gas station, the population is entirely of European ancestry.

Religion is clearly present. Churches abound; the six within walking distance of the main crossroads offer a representative sample of the liberal, conservative and evangelical denominations found in this part of Ontario. On alternate Sundays clusters of buggies signal the home church meetings of the horse-and-buggy Amish whose farms ring the edge of the community. The area is politically conservative.

Within the gift shops on the main street are cards and plaques that contain biblical verses; unlike shops in larger centres, one finds no *yin-yang* symbols or other motifs borrowing from the 'Orient.' In all these public places, no appearance of any other religious presence besides Christianity can be seen – that is, until one enters the local library. Built in 1906 thanks to a grant by the American industrialist Andrew Carnegie, the library has nothing out of the ordinary with its shelves of fiction, financial management, local history, self-help, gardening books, kids' books and so on, but in its catalogue is no small collection of Buddhist materials.

More than just world religions' texts and survey materials, the collection includes over a hundred works, organized under 41 headings. A decent range of Buddhist traditions – Thai, Tibetan, Zen, Theravāda, Soka Gakkai, even Socially Engaged Buddhism – are represented, as well as textual translations of materials from the Pali Canon, various renderings of the Buddha's life story, and even a collection of Milarepa's verses. Among the ten items from the Dalai Lama are both print and audio materials documenting his teachings; works by other Buddhist teachers popular in North America, such as Thich Nhat Hanh, Pema Chödrön, Chögyam Trungpa Rinpoche and Surya Das, are also present.

Beyond the categories of traditions, translations, survey materials and works by popular teachers are the thematic ones: sub-headings under Buddhism include love, compassion, anger, interpersonal relations, meditation, aging, and money. The entry for the last category is Kulananda and Dominic Holder's *Mindfulness and Money* (2003). It is checked out, as are a goodly number of the other works. Thich Nhat Hanh's *Anger: Wisdom for Cooling the Flames* (2001), Chögyam Trungpa Rinpoche's *Heart of Buddha* (1991), and Franz Metcalf's *What Would Buddha Do?* (2002) are among the 20 Buddhist works checked out on a summer day in 2004. Given the appearances of the community one might not expect to find consumers of Buddhist material, but in different homes in this community there are people who have been reading (or hoping to read) the popular and inspirational writings of all sorts of Buddhist teachers and others.

The original publication dates of works in this collection are also telling. The works range from late nineteenth-century introductions of Buddhism to the West to the most recent therapeutic indulgences. Paul Carus' *Gospel of Buddhism*, the 1972 reprint of the 1898 work that shaped North American understandings of Buddhist thought, is present, as is Hesse's *Siddhartha* (1992) (also checked out). Some representative scholars of the mid-twentieth century show up (Dumoulin, but not Suzuki), and certainly the most recent reflect what is trendy. Likewise, there are a few works that Canada might claim as her own. Tim Ward's *What the Buddha Didn't Teach* (1991) is on the shelves; Pema Chödrön's connections with the Gampo Abbey in Nova

Scotia give a Canadian setting to her *Wisdom of No Escape* (1991), while David Swick's (1996) account of Chögyam Trungpa Rinpoche's relocation of his Shambhala community to Halifax documents some of the history of Buddhism in Canada.

While few people, if any, in this community would self-identify as Buddhists, and none can claim Buddhism as their family's religion, over a hundred years of publications have brought these different presentations of Buddhism here. Intellectual trends, curiosities, fashions, and an increasingly global circulation of ideas have all contributed to the making of this collection. Eclectic insofar as it reflects the vagaries of library acquisitions along with the idiosyncrasies of a near century of librarians, the holdings are not completely random, as the works document the intellectual history of Buddhism in North America. It also is evidence that people even in a more rural area of Ontario are nonetheless influenced by and participants in larger intellectual and social processes, one of which at present is an interest in Buddhism.

As a subject in the public school curriculum and elsewhere

As a subject of study Buddhism has found its way into the public school curriculum, albeit in a small way, since the early 1970s. That time saw elective world religions courses introduced at the secondary level. Their presence may not seem unusual, but in fact their introduction presaged significant shifts in public policy at provincial and federal levels of government. Up through the 1960s, religious education or 'knowledge,' meaning by and large Christian formation, was part of the Ontario public curriculum, on the understanding that such education contributed to students' moral education and thus to good citizenship. Such offering during two time periods a week was incumbent for school boards. Students of other religious backgrounds could petition for exemption; still the policy came under increasing criticism from the mid-1960s for pedagogic reasons as well as concerns for religious freedom (Wideman *et al.* 1994). The implementation of recommendations of a Committee on Religious Education appointed by the Government of Ontario (1969, cited in Howse 2004: 4) saw its replacement with a religiously neutral approach to moral education in addition to the introduction of optional world religions courses offered to grade 11 and grade 12 students.

Behind these recommendations were several factors, including recognition of a changing cultural landscape in Ontario, particularly changing demographics in light of the new immigration laws; the prevalence of secular humanist values in educational theory; and shifts in public policy to endorse religious and cultural plurality seen in pronouncements on multiculturalism, notably the 1971 statement by Prime Minster Pierre Trudeau that the government was adopting a policy to 'support and encourage the various cultures and ethnic groups that give structure and vitality to [Canadian] society.' While multiculturalism has not been without its critics, under this policy, the definition of good citizenship tacitly included respect and appreciation for cultural and religious diversity. One way students in the public system could gain an understanding of religions other than their own was by taking the world religions course. Using basic textbooks the course offers a standard introductory historical survey of Buddhism which includes basic summaries of central doctrines and beliefs. From its inception, it has been optional and whether it is taught depends upon the teaching resources of any individual school. Nonetheless, it has been one way in which a number of students in Ontario have received a formal introduction to Buddhism. Occasionally it sparks sufficient interest in a student to be followed by self-directed explorations, the seeking out of Buddhist centres or the taking of further courses.

At the post-secondary level, courses on Buddhism or including a section on Buddhism are found at many colleges and at all Ontario universities. Even before 1972, when all accredited post-secondary institutions (including what had previously been religiously affiliated schools) came under public governance, students at some institutions were offered instruction in the histories, tenets, beliefs and practices of other religions. For example, at Waterloo Lutheran University (now Wilfrid Laurier University), a world religions course was a requirement of all undergraduates from the 1950s through the 1970s. Strengths in Buddhism are found in the religious studies and philosophy departments at the University of Toronto, Brock, Wilfrid Laurier, McMaster, and the University of Waterloo. No institution at present offers an MA or PhD specializing in Buddhist studies *per se* (though graduate theses on Buddhist subjects of one kind or another are often defended in at least three of these institutions), but efforts spearheaded by Suwanda H. J. Sugunasiri in Toronto have lead to the opening of Nalanda College of Buddhist Studies, 'the first Canadian seat of learning approved by the Government of Ontario as a non profitable charitable organization to run post-secondary courses for "the systematic study of Buddhism"' (Fernando 2000). Among its objectives are to foster the academic study of Buddhism, to meet the educational needs of Buddhism in Canada and to facilitate personal spiritual growth (Nalanda College 2004).

Other ways that more formalized instruction on Buddhism occurs outside of Buddhist centres is through speakers series or study sessions organized by churches and community groups. Churches from a wide spectrum of Christian denominations – Lutheran, Anglican, United, Unitarian – routinely organize sessions in which representatives of other non-Christian faiths or scholars from nearby departments of religious studies are invited to explain the tenets of their tradition. Occasionally the sessions move into a mode of inter-religious dialogue, but mostly they are information sessions. Even the Christian Evangelical Fellowship active on university campuses have sponsored religious debates and discussion on various topics such as salvation and the afterlife in which they have invited Buddhist and other cross-faith participants. Such engagements have not been restricted to Christian groups. An active Ahmadiyya group in southern Ontario has since 1980 organized topical forums in which they have sought commentary from speakers from other religious traditions, including Buddhism. Religious groups are not the only groups who have sought out information on different religious traditions. Civic groups such as groups of young business leaders have also run series presenting world religions, and there are organizations, such as the Centre for Spirituality at Work, which organize presentations along the lines of Lloyd Field's 'Buddha in the Boardroom' (2005), a consideration of how Buddhist ethics can be integrated into responsible corporate governance. And, for those individuals wishing to cast their nets anywhere in the world for information on Buddhism, cyberspace offers near infinite possibilities. Even a search restricted to Buddhism and Ontario returns some 47,000 'hits' on 'Google.'

These educational efforts are matched by efforts within the Buddhist community. A central concern of Buddhists who have settled in Ontario over the past few decades is the transmission of Buddhist ethics and understanding to the next generations. The recent Vesak celebration at the Phommaviharan temple in Kitchener was markedly oriented towards the children of the community. While the ceremony included ways for the community members to make merit through offerings to the quorum of senior monks in attendance, the central talk given by the teaching monk of the temple, presented in English, advised a large group of children seated right up front of the ethical expectations found in the lay precepts and how those expectations reflected the Buddha's life and teachings. This temple offers regular Sunday school sessions for the children.

Efforts directed towards youth are found at other Buddhist temples, as seen in the activities they list on their websites. For example, the activities of the Ottawa chapter of the Vietnamese Buddhist Youth Association (started in Vietnam some fifty years ago and modelled in part on the YMCA/YWCA), include outdoor activities, leadership training, cultural awareness, and Buddhist study, all efforts to help shape the next generation.

The presence of Buddhism through free-floating objects and symbols

Not all aspects of Buddhism found in Ontario are set within informed contexts. Like elsewhere in North America, Ontario can offer ample examples of the commodification, sales and trafficking in Buddhist icons, images and symbols. A walk through many of the markets still found in Ontario's cities and towns inevitably encounters an importer who offers among other goods knock-offs of Tibetan *thanka* paintings produced in Nepal or resin images of a pantheon of Buddhas and Bodhisattvas. The buyers of these images sometimes know what they are buying and sometimes do not. Often they have some general ideas but are hard pressed for specifics, and despite some awareness of its religious associations, what is purchased may end up as art or as a display piece, its presence alluding to something, an 'Eastern' tradition, a contemplative moment, a possibility of some other state, a repository of yearnings and desires. What the Buddhist icon or symbol represents in these instances is something that points beyond itself to whatever conceptual domains these symbols evoke – but only for those whose attention is caught, and that actually cuts across large segments of the population. Buddha images have appeared in native homes in northern Ontario as well as native homes near the Six Nations reserve outside of Brantford and in homes of all different ethnic backgrounds; they have appeared in affluent homes and in poor homes, in urban areas and in rural areas. Level of education is not necessarily an indicator, nor is travel or job. The Buddhas are present because they can be, because Ontario, like the rest of North America, is a participant in these processes of global exchange, movement and trade. Even the person who is uninformed as to what they are walking past in the shape of a seated figure for sale in a garden centre is a participant in these processes. Buddhism is present in Ontario in many ways, but not everyone who lives here may be aware of that.

Conclusion

In this chapter we have noted the diverse but significant numbers of Buddhists in Ontario. We have examined the types of Buddhism found in the province as seen in the wide range of Buddhist centres and temples. These centres serve the needs of residents of Ontario, both on an individual basis and on a collective basis. We have noted where members of a temple come from an immigrant community, and how that temple has played and continues to play an important role in sustaining a community, demonstrated by the emphasis placed on Buddhist education and formation for the next generation. Temples also serve as resource centres, where community members network and find ways of creating within Ontario a place for themselves. In several instances we have found temples offering assistance in areas such as legal counselling and translation services that would be unusual for a similar religious centre in a community's homeland.

Other Buddhist groups and centres discussed clearly attract people from a wide range of backgrounds. Many are non-Buddhist by birth. These centres offer their participants the chance to directly experience Buddhist teachings through practice, mainly forms of mediation, but also in some cases through the ritual and liturgical traditions the centre in question follows. Often catering to spiritually inclined Canadians who want direct and meaningful contact with different religious activities, these centres offer crucial introductions to the *Buddha dhamma*, however defined. We have suggested that these centres are characteristic of emergent global 'Buddhisms.'

We have looked at other ways Buddhism is present in Ontario. We have observed that there is evidence indicating some interest in Buddhist thought and Buddhist teachings and that information about Buddhism is readily available even where it might not be expected. We have also noted that Buddhism, like other popular religions, has been subject to a certain amount of commodification, with its symbols and imagery and indeed even its most powerful icons virtually rendered meaningless through dissociation from any meaningful context.

We have noted interest in and acceptance of Buddhism, in the sense that Buddhism as a religious system and Buddhists as religious people are accepted as part of Ontario's cultural fabric, as well as accepted in the sense that people, non-Buddhist by birth, have gravitated towards Buddhist teachings and practices and have chosen to follow them. Whether, however, Buddhism has become an integral part of life in Ontario, or whether Buddhism has had any impact, apart from the very real impact it has had on the lives of different individuals, is more difficult to gauge. It has been harder to determine whether anything of Buddhism informs life in general in Ontario or has lent character to the province's identity. Another question is whether any aspect of Buddhism has found its way into writing, fictional or otherwise, produced in Ontario. Scholars such as John McMurtry, a philosopher with the University of Guelph, have integrated Buddhist thought in their work, but whether there are any larger trends is quite uncertain. In other words, has Buddhism made any inroads into popular awareness and vocabulary? It is no longer odd, for example, to hear someone at a bingo hall make a remark about *karma*, but the degree to which Buddhist terminology – words such as *nirvana, bodhisattva* – have found their way into popular usage and popular consciousness remain to be documented.[5] Is Buddhism part of Ontario? Certainly it is present in all kinds of diverse ways. Is it changing Ontario in any way? That is something that remains to be seen.

Notes

1 The Ontario figures compare with the rest of Canada. The 2001 census (see also Bibby 2002: 83) reported 77 per cent of the population of over 29.5 million identifying with themselves as Christian in one form or another. The next largest religious affiliation is with Islam, at nearly 2 per cent of the population, followed in numbers by Jews (1.1 per cent), Buddhists (1 per cent), Hindus (1 per cent), Sikhs (not quite 1 per cent), and other religions (0.3 per cent). Some 16.5 per cent of the population cited no religious affiliation.

2 Ira Rifkin, 'The Accidental Buddhist', *News and Observer* (Raleigh), 7 February 1997, 1E, 4E (cited in Tweed 2002: 20), noted that Helen Tworkov, the editor of the popular Buddhist quarterly, has estimated that half of the publication's 60,000 subscribers do not describe themselves as Buddhist. Examples of encounters with Buddhist material that is not prompted by any interest include workers at a garden

centre who sell statues of the Buddha as ornamental pieces without having any idea of what the statues represent, or someone who picks up a copy of Pema Chödrön's *The Wisdom of No Escape* from a self-help section in a bookstore without ever realizing the author's long-standing connection with a Tibetan Buddhist tradition. Nowhere on the book's cover is that connection made clear. Likewise, diffuse interests in 'Eastern' traditions, including what is perceived to be Buddhist, might be manifest, without an individual being able to sort through the different traditions or the specific contents of any tradition. Recently one of the authors of this article encountered an individual who sported tattoos all over the upper body comprised of phrases in Tibetan, Chinese, Sanskrit script. When asked what the words were saying, the individual responded that being unable to read any of the languages they did not know, but their interest in Eastern traditions, stemming from university courses they had taken, prompted the choice of ornamentation and public display!

3 Material in this section comes from several sources: published information, public information posted on the centres' websites, listing of centres in the directories mentioned above, and from interviews conducted in person, via phone and e-mail in the month of July 2004. A standardized set of ten open-ended questions formed the basis for the interviews. Questions focused on the group's formation in Ontario, membership and history. While our focus was on group history, occasionally personal information proved to be relevant.

4 Estimates in the late 1970s see it showing up in maybe 25 per cent of schools. See Howse (2004). Recent curriculum revisions undertaken in 1999 have made it more difficult for students to fit a world religions course in their schedule even if it is offered at their school.

5 They are making some inroads, as a recent interview heard on the Canadian Broadcasting System showed. The dog of the interviewee had been credited with preventing a man from going on a shooting spree in a Toronto park by approaching him with such friendliness that the man changed his mind. In explaining what had happened, the dog's owner remarked that she and her husband had always thought of this dog as a *bodhisattva*. She went on to offer a very brief definition of the term for the radio audience.

Bibliography

Angulimala: The Buddhist Chaplaincy Organisation (2004) "Introduction to Angulimala." Website located at www.angulimala.org.uk/index.htm

Arrow River Forest Hermitage (2004) "Arrow River Forest Hermitage" and "Ajahn Punnadhammmo." Website located at my.tbaytel.net/arfh/

Bibby, Reginald (2002) *Restless Gods: The Renaissance of Religion in Canada*. Toronto: Stoddart Publishing Co.

Blue Heron Dharma Centre (2004) "Blue Heron Dharma Centre." Information posted on George Klima and Mathieu Ouellet (eds) "Buddhism in South-western Ontario." From *Buddhism in Canada*, online listing of Buddhist sites in Canada. Published by the Buddhist Women's Network. Available online at buddhismcanada.com/sw-ontario.html

BuddhaNet (2004) *BuddhaNet's Buddhist Directory, Americas, Ontario*. Published by Buddha Dharma Education Association. Available online at www.buddhanet.net/americas/can_onta.htm

Buddha Sasana Yeiktha (2004) "Insight (Vipassanā) Meditation." Website of the Buddha Sasana Yeiktha, located at www.buddhasasanayeiktha.ca/

Buddhist Compassion Relief Tzu Chi Foundation Canada (2002) "Ten Years Review." Vancouver, BC: Buddhist Compassion Relief Tzu Chi Foundation Canada. Posted on the organization's website, www.tzuchi.ca

Buddhist Place (2004) Website of the Buddha Place, located at www.buddhistplace.ca/

Butterfield, Stephen (1994) *The Double Mirror: A Skeptical Journey into Buddhist Tantra.* Berkeley, CA: North Atlantic.

Canadian Copper and Brass Association (2001) "World Peace Ten Thousand Buddhas Sarina Stupa Temple – Niagara Falls." *Canadian Copper Magazine*, Issue 47. Available online at www.ccbda.org/pdfs/CCMagazinePDFs/EI47F.PDF

Carus, Paul (1972) *Gospel of Buddhism.* Tuscon, AR: Omen Press.

Chödrön, Pema (1991) *The Wisdom of No Escape and the Path of Loving-Kindness.* Boston, MA: Shambhala.

Coleman, James (2001) *The New Buddhism. The Western Transformation of an Ancient Tradition.* New York: Oxford University Press.

Committee on Religious Education (Ontario) (1969) *Religious Information and Moral Development: The Report of the Committee on Religious Education in the Public Schools of the Province of Ontario 1969.* Toronto: Ontario Department of Education.

Dharma Centre of Canada (2004) Website of the Dharma Centre of Canada, located at www.dharmacentre.org/

Fernando, Tilak S. (2000) "Nalanda – Canada's First Buddhist College." Posted on T. Fernando's London Diary website at www.infolanka.com/org/diary/172.html

Fo Guang Shan Temple (2003) "About Fo Guang Shan Temple of Toronto." Located at the Fo Guang Shan website, at www.fgs.ca/english/about_fgs_toronto.htm

Field, Lloyd (2005) "Buddha in the Boardroom." Public lecture given at the University of Toronto, April 26 2005. Cited on the Centre for Spirituality at Work (Toronto)'s website, www.spiritualityatwork.org/program-calendar.htm

Hanh, Thich Nhat (2001) *Anger: Wisdom for Cooling the Flames.* New York: Riverhead Books.

Hesse, Hermann (1992) *Siddhartha.* New York: Continuum.

Houlder, Kulananda and Houlder, Dominic (2003) *Mindfulness and Money: The Buddhist Path of Abundance.* New York: Broadway Books.

Howse, Jennifer (2004) "Religious Education in Ontario's Public Schools, 1966–2004." Unpublished manuscript.

Karma Kagyu Buddhist Meditation Centre (2004) Website of the Karma Kagyu Buddhist Meditation Centre of Niagara, located at www.kagyu.org/centers/can/can-nia.html

Klima, George and Ouellet, Mathieu (2004a) "Buddhism in Northern and Central Ontario." From *Buddhism in Canada*, online listing of Buddhist sites in Canada. Published by the Buddhist Women's Network. Available online at buddhismcanada.com/heart.html

—— (2004b) "Buddhism in Southwestern Ontario." From *Buddhism in Canada*, online listing of Buddhist sites in Canada. Published by the Buddhist Women's Network. Available online at buddhismcanada.com/sw-ontario.html

—— (2004c) "Buddhism in Eastern Ontario." From *Buddhism in Canada*, online listing of Buddhist sites in Canada. Published by the Buddhist Women's Network. Available online at buddhismcanada.com/e-ontario.html

Kuluta Buddhist Centre (2004) Website of the Kuluta Buddhist Centre of Kingston, located at www.meditateinkingston.org/

Layman, Emma McCloy (1976) *Buddhism in America.* Chicago, IL: Nelson-Hall.

London Vipassanā Meditation Group (2004) "London Vipassanā Meditation Group." Information posted on George Klima and Mathieu Ouellet (eds) "Buddhism in Southwestern Ontario." From *Buddhism in Canada,* online listing of Buddhist sites in Canada. Published by the Buddhist Women's Network. Available online at buddhismcanada.com/sw-ontario.html

McLellan, Janet (1999) *Many Petals of the Lotus: Five Asian Buddhist Communities in Toronto.* Toronto, ON: University of Toronto Press.

Matthews, Bruce (2002) "Buddhism in Canada." In Charles S. Prebish and Martin Baumann (eds) *Westward Dharma. Buddhism beyond Asia.* Berkeley, CA: University of California Press.

Metcalf, Franz (ed.) (2002) *What Would Buddha Do?* Berkeley, CA: Seastone.

Montréal Zen Centre (2004) "Affiliates." Article posted on the Montréal Zen Centre website, located at www.zenMontréal.ca/English/x022affiliates.html

Morreale, Don (1998) *The Complete Guide to Buddhist America.* Boston, MA: Shambhala.

Nalanda College of Buddhist Studies (2004) "Objectives." Statement on the Nalanda College webpage at www.nalandacollege.ca/objectives.php

Numrich, Paul David (1996) *Old Wisdom in the New World: Americanization in Two Immigrant Theravāda Buddhist Temples.* Knoxville, TN: University of Tennessee Press.

Ontario Vipassanā Centre (2004) "Ontario Vipassanā Centre, Dhamma Torana." Website located at www.ontario-dhamma.org/

Ottawa Buddhist Society (2004) "Ottawa Buddhist Society." Website located at www.ottawabuddhistsociety.com/

Palpung Yeshe Chokhor (2004) Website of the Palpung Yeshe Chokhor, located at home.golden.net/~blueherow/schedule.html

Palyul Foundation of Canada (2004) Website of the Palyul Foundation of Canada located at www.palyulcanada.org/

Palyul Namdrölling Foundation Canada (2004) Website of the Palyul Namdrölling Foundation Canada, Chamundi House, located at www.cyberus.ca/~palyul/

Prattis, Ian (2004) "Pine Gate Meditation Hall." Website of the Pine Gate Sangha, located at ianprattis.com/pinegate.htm

Prebish, Charles (1979) *American Buddhism.* North Scituate, MA: Duxbury Press.

Rifkin, Ira (1997) "The Accidental Buddhist," *News and Observer* (Raleigh), 7 February 1997, 1E, 4E.

Riverview Dharma Centre (nd) "Schedule," "Retreats," "Special Events," "Second Annual General Meeting." Website located at www.wrdharmacentre.com

Shambhala International (2004a) Website of the Toronto Shambhala Meditation Centre, located at www.shambhala.org/centers/toronto/

—— (2004b) Website of the Ottawa Shambhala Centre, located at www.shambhalaottawa.ca/index.htm

—— (2004c) "Alliston Dharma Study Group." Information posted on George Klima and Mathieu Ouellet (eds) "Buddhism in Northern and Central Ontario." From *Buddhism in Canada,* online listing of Buddhist sites in Canada. Published by the Buddhist Women's Network. Available online at buddhismcanada.com/heart.html

Soka Gakkai (2004) Website of Soka Gakkai International Canada Ottawa Community Centre, located at sgicanada.org/

Statistics Canada (2001a) "Selected Religions, Provinces and Territories (2001 Census)." Ottawa: Government of Canada. Available online at www.statcan.ca/ english/Pgdb/demo30a.htm

—— (2001b) "2001 Community Profiles." Ottawa: Government of Canada. Available online at www12.statcan.ca/english/profil01/PlaceSearchForm1.cfm

—— (2001c) "Population by Selected Ethnic Origins, Census Metropolitan Areas (2001 Census)." Ottawa: Government of Canada. Available online at www.statcan.ca/english/Pgdb/demo27a.htm

—— (2001d) "Visible Minority Population, Census Metropolitan Areas (2001 Census)." Ottawa: Government of Canada. Available online at www.statcan.ca/ english/Pgdb/demo53a.htm

—— (2001e) "Immigrant Population by Place of Birth, Census Metropolitan Areas (2001 Census)." Ottawa: Government of Canada. Available online at www.statcan.ca/english/Pgdb/demo35a.htm

—— (2001f) "Population by Home Language, by Provinces and Territories and by Census Metropolitan Areas (2001 Census)." Ottawa: Government of Canada. Available online at www12.statcan.ca/english/census01/products/standard/themes/ RetrieveProductTable.cfm

—— (2001g) "Selected Demographic and Cultural Characteristics (104), Selected Religions (35A), Age Groups (6) and Sex (3) for Population, for Canada, Provinces, Territories and Census Metropolitan Areas 1, 2001 Census – 20 per cent Sample Data." Ottawa: Government of Canada. Available online at www12.statcan.ca/ english/census01/products/standard/themes/RetrieveProductTable.cfm

Swick, David (1996) *Thunder and Ocean: Shambhala and Buddhism in Nova Scotia.* Lawrencetown Beach, Portersfield Press.

Theng, Sothea and Ek, Manilene (2004) "Khmer Buddhist Temple of Ontario." Available online at www.khmer-ontario.org/Profile/khmer_Buddhist_Ontario.htm, on the Canadian Cambodian Association of Ontario (CCAO) website.

Trungpa Rinpoche, Chogyam (1991) *Heart of Buddha.* Boston, MA: Shambhala.

Tweed, Thomas (2002) "Who is a Buddhist? Night-stand Buddhists and Other Creatures." In Charles S. Prebish and Martin Baumann (eds) *Westward Dharma: Buddhism beyond Asia.* Berkeley, CA: University of California Press.

Vietnamese Buddhist Youth Association (1999) Website of the Vietnamese Buddhist Youth Association, Ottawa Chapter, located at members.tripod.com/~chanhkien/

Ward, Tim (1991) *What the Buddha Didn't Teach.* Toronto: Somerville House Publishing.

Watada, Terry (1996) *Bukkyo Tozen: A History of Jodo Shinshu Buddhism in Canada, 1905–1995.* Toronto: HpF Press/Toronto Buddhist Church. Excerpts available online on the Thumder Bay Buddhist Fellowship website, at www.members.shaw.ca/ mioko/WhatIsBuddhistFellowship.htm

Wat Lao Veluwanaram (2004) "About Wat Lao Veluwanh." Published by the Wat Lao Veluwanaram of Canada. Available online at www.watlao-veluwanh.com/ about_wat_lao_veluwanh.htm

Wat Ratchadham 2 (2004) "Welcome to Wat Ratchadham 2" and the "Jade Museum." Available online at www.watratchadham2.gq.nu/monks_of_ratchadham2.htm

Waterloo Riverview Dharma Center (2004) Website of the Waterloo Riverview Dharma Center, located at www.wrdharmacentre.com/

White Wind Zen Community (2004) "White Wind Zen Community," "Zen Master Anzan Hoshin," "Long Distance Training Program." Articles posted on website located at www.wwzc.org/

Wideman, Ron *et al.* (1994) "History of Religious Education in Ontario Schools." In *Education About Religion in Ontario Public Elementary Schools*. Government of Ontario: Ministry of Education, Ministry of Training, Colleges, and Universities. Available at www.edu.gov.on.ca/eng/document/curricul/religion/religioe.html

Yeshe Wangpo (2004) Website of Nyingje Companions, Centre for the Development of Meditative Arts and Contemplative Understanding, located at www.nyingjecompanions.ca/Yeshe.html

5

BUDDHISM IN THE GREATER TORONTO AREA

The politics of recognition

Janet McLellan

Introduction

The theoretical framework Charles Taylor developed in his seminal essay 'The Politics of Recognition' (1994: 25–73) serves to explore how social identity is formed through dialogical relations and negotiation of the factors involved in the construction and presentation of image. Within Canada, official policies of multiculturalism encourage ethnic and religious minorities to retain traditional facets of their cultural and linguistic identity. Demonstrating a particular tradition or authentic identity (ethnic, religious, cultural, political) enables a group or collectivity to be accepted as one more component in the diversity that is conceptualized as Canadian multi-culturalism, and allows them to participate in what Andrew Ross (1988) calls the 'politics of difference.' Authenticity is often determined through cultural or religious objectification whereby food, language, religious ceremonies or festivals, clothing, and other facets of tradition become objects which symbolize this identity, and can be observed and participated in by others (Handler 1986: 38–40).

The recognition and/or articulation of distinct ethnic or religious identities provide mechanisms for integration and gaining equitable access to social and political resources, demonstrate a sense of belonging and place within the new multicultural social context and, ideally, contribute towards the development and demonstration of such Canadian values as tolerance and understanding. Social recognition of an ethnic or religious minority particu-larly enables the group or community to engage in 'cultural agency' whereby discourses of identity concerning power, authority, and advantage are actively constructed and contested (Baumann 1996). Karen Leonard notes that the Canadian practice of setting multicultural categories according to nation of origin encourages ethno-religious leaders to essentialize their own particu-lar images of identity to claim recognition, influence decisions, or access scarce resources such as state funds. Sikhs (who constitute only 2 per cent of

India's population today) are the most numerous among Canada's South Asians from India, yet resist being categorized according to their national origin, as do Chinese from Vietnam, Cambodia and Laos, or Ismailis from Uganda (Leonard 2000: 23).

Negotiating the politics of representation and recognition is a dynamic process. According to situational contingencies and determinants of self-interest or need, the process arises simultaneously within a variety of social spaces that include identifiable ethno-religious groups (navigating class, linguistic, generational, gender, national, or other disparate differences among members); intra-religious associations and networks (where doctrinal, linguistic, ethnic, and status distinctions are evident between groups and communities); interfaith contexts (where issues of authenticity and hegemonic dominance overtly emerge); and the larger mainstream context of public and private institutions (educational, political, municipal, medical, social services, employment, media, commerce, civil law). For religious minorities in Canada, identity and representational politics are not only critical to social acceptance and inclusion, but must be mediated through these multiple cultural intersections that are in turn 'actively constructed from competing and conflicting constructions of tradition' (Coombe 1991: 192).

In Toronto Asian Buddhist communities, the process of recreating and redefining religious traditions (i.e., distinct Buddhist identities, beliefs, practices, and institutions) is intimately connected with several concurrent factors. They include, but are not limited to, the image each particular community or group has of itself or of their specific Buddhist tradition (carried over through migration as well as constructed in resettlement); the degree to which prevailing social attitudes of exclusion or tolerance towards religious minorities in Canada are understood; the limitations or advantages of pre-migration experiences and backgrounds; the community or group's capacity and need to articulate identity and/or seek recognition from others; and the different roles which particular religious identities and institutions play within people's lives as first-generation immigrants and refugees as well as their Canadian born-and-raised children. This chapter does not detail the particular beliefs and practices of diverse Buddhist traditions in Toronto (see McLellan 1999), but presents some of the multiple intersections and interconnected dynamics which have shaped Buddhist activities and contributed to the different levels of acceptance and recognition of Buddhism, and of some specific Buddhist groups, in Toronto.

Historical overview of Buddhists in Toronto

Toronto's first Buddhist institution, Toronto Buddhist Church, was founded in the late 1940s by Japanese Canadians (immigrants from Japan and their Canadian-born children and grandchildren) who were forced by the Canadian government to resettle in Eastern Canada following their wartime internment in makeshift camps in northern British Columbia from 1941 to 1945. The forced relocation to Ontario and Québec continued the massive human and civil rights violations to which all Japanese Canadians (including second-generation Canadian citizens) in British Columbia had been subject. This relocation away from British Columbia was one of two 'choices' given to them, the other being repatriation to Japan, a country which most Japanese Canadian citizens had never visited. Japanese Canadians who went to Ontario were not allowed to work, live, or own businesses in Toronto unless they had special permission of the 'Japanese Placement Officer,' and those few who did reside there were restricted from the confines of certain affluent residential areas, unless they were domestic workers (Roy *et al.* 1990: 148; Tanaka 1983: 150). When these restrictions were lifted in 1947, more than 7,000 Japanese Canadians once again relocated from the outlying communities of Port Credit, Windsor, Brantford, Hamilton, London, Kitchener, and Guelph to settle in Toronto.

Although the initial establishment of the Toronto Buddhist Church was viewed by members as a mechanism to bring together a fractured community, the mainstream social climate remained overtly racist and discriminatory towards the presence of Japanese Canadians. Japanese Canadians were refused service in restaurants, denied accommodation and employment, and faced constant pressure to rapidly assimilate and convert to Christianity. In 1951, individuals with Asian origins totalled 0.9 per cent of Toronto's population (Breton *et al.* 1990: 19) and Japanese Canadian Buddhists were easily stigmatized as racial, religious, and cultural minorities. In response to the socially entrenched negative stereotypes of Asians and Buddhists, the Toronto Buddhist Church radically adapted and transformed their traditional Jodo Shinshu organizational patterns to reflect United Church congregational forms. Throughout the 1950s and early 1960s, several processes of religious and cultural educational outreach were initiated, including the rapid assimilation of third-generation (*Sansei*) children, born after internment, through sending them to Christian Sunday Schools or minimizing their Japanese language, cultural, and social retentions, including endogamous marriage. By the 1960s, Japanese Canadians had successfully gained acceptance as a 'model minority' by conforming to mainstream social expectations and stereotypes (Gap Min 1995: 52).

In 1966 the first non-Asian Buddhist group, the Dharma Centre of Canada, was founded in Toronto by a Canadian-born Caucasian who trained initially as a Theravāda monk in Burma during the late 1950s, and subsequently was recognized as a Tibetan *tulku* by His Holiness the 16th Karmapa during a trip to India in the early 1970s. The group established the first meditation retreat centre in Ontario near Kinmount, and continues today, offering courses in Buddhism and other contemplative traditions. Other Buddhist and faith groups from Toronto hold retreats on the Dharma Centre's extensive property, and teachers – both Asian and non-Asian – visit from Burma, India,

Malaysia, Vancouver, Japan, Europe, and New Zealand. The initial members of the Dharma Centre primarily belonged to the non-Asian generation raised in the 1940s through the early 1960s and who became especially interested in Eastern mystical traditions. Similar to the experiences of other non-Asian Buddhists in Toronto, many met Buddhist teachers during overseas travel, and began different kinds of Buddhist practices on their return to Canada. These individuals were the seeds from which most of the non-Asian Buddhist groups in Toronto developed in the late 1960s and early 1970s.

The 1967 changes to the Canadian immigration law removed specific country restrictions and introduced the point system to determine migration eligibility, thus allowing numerous Asian individuals (and their families) to immigrate to Canada. Buddhist immigrants from Korea, Hong Kong, Sri Lanka, Burma, and India immediately began to settle in the Toronto area, increasing in number every year. Most of those accepted through the point system tended to be well-educated professionals from urban backgrounds, and they subsequently sponsored more family members. Tibetans were the first non-European refugees admitted into Canada when a group of 228 individuals and families were scattered across four provinces in eleven localities during 1971. Certain groupings, such as those placed in Lindsay, Ontario, were accompanied by a Tibetan monk. Shortly after arriving in Lindsay, where four families and the monk were placed in one communal house, the monk, Karma Thinley, relocated to Toronto and formed a meditation group of mostly non-Asian students. He continued to retain close connections with the Tibetan communities near Toronto (in Lindsay and Belleville), as well as the small number of Tibetans in Toronto (immigrants as well as those who relocated to Toronto from elsewhere in Canada). During the 1970s and 1980s, other Tibetan monks arrived in Toronto through sponsorship by family members, and by student groups requesting a permanent teacher from one of the monasteries in India.

By the early 1970s, several Theravāda (Sinhalese, Burmese) and Mahāyāna (Chinese, Korean) temples were established. Some of the small groups of non-Asians active in the Vajrayāna and Zen (Japanese and Korean) practice centres developed into temple organizations when permanent teachers settled. In May 1980, the first intra-religious Buddhist celebration of *Vesak* (commemoration of the Buddha's birth, death and *parinirvāna*) was held in Toronto, with participation from over one thousand Buddhists representing fifteen groups, both Asian and non-Asian, from the Ambedkar, Burmese, Chinese, Japanese, Korean, Sinhalese, and Tibetan traditions (McLellan 1999: 31). By 1980, the numbers of Asians in Toronto increased to 2.5 per cent of its total population (Breton *et al.* 1990: 19). The large influx of Indochinese refugees, which began in the early 1980s, significantly contributed to the Buddhist, as well as Asian, presence in Toronto. More than fifty thousand Vietnamese, five thousand Cambodians and seven thousand Lao eventually settled in the Greater Toronto Area. The majority of the Lao and

Cambodians were Theravāda Buddhists. Each of these communities founded a temple, although the Cambodians did not have a permanent monk until 1995. Vietnamese Buddhists tended to be Mahāyāna, sharing a similar Zen/Pure Land tradition, but due to pre-migration divisions at least seven Vietnamese temples and several meditation groups were established in Toronto. In 1987 the co-religious celebration of *Vesak* included twenty-one distinct Buddhist temples and practice groups, rising to twenty-eight in 1990, and thirty-five in 1994. During the 1980s, Buddhism was identified as Canada's fastest growing religion – a distinction now, in 2005, given to Islam.

Substantial immigration from Hong Kong and Taiwan from the mid-1980s throughout the late 1990s, coupled with ongoing family sponsorship and reunification programs from all Asian communities, steadily increased the number of Toronto's Buddhists. During the mid-1990s, immigrants from Hong Kong represented the largest single source of newcomers to Toronto (as well as Canada). They comprised two-thirds of the 350,000 total Chinese population in Toronto, and within ten years had established over thirty distinct temples and Buddhist associations (McLellan 1999: 162). From the late 1990s to the present, China has replaced Hong Kong and Taiwan as the largest annual source of immigrants to Canada. Except for older individuals, religious affiliation is generally low among migrants from China. Ethnic Chinese now comprise almost 25 per cent of Toronto's 4,000,000 people, predominating among the vast array of religious, racial, cultural, linguistic and nationalist plurality (Statistics Canada 2001).

The most recent group of Asian Buddhists in Toronto are the approximately 3,000 Tibetan refugee claimants from Nepal and India who arrived via the United States during 2001 and 2002. Their presence has significantly augmented the small ethnic Tibetan Buddhist community, expanding their social activities (such as birthday celebrations for H.H. the Dalai Lama in July), enhancing political activism (arranging and participating in the 10 March commemoration of the Chinese communist invasion of Tibet), and their capacity for complex community organization (coordinating international events such as the Kalachakra Initiation, held in Toronto during May 2004). At several Vajrayāna temples in Toronto, at least three 'parallel congregations' (Numrich 1996) are affiliated with an ethnic Tibetan teacher: non-Asian practitioners, ethnic Tibetans, and a small group of ethnic Chinese or ethnic Vietnamese. During shared events, teachings are often given in Tibetan with translations into English and Cantonese. Vajrayāna practitioners also include individuals from Mongolia, although ethnic Tibetans represent the majority. Five Vajrayāna temples in the Toronto area have an ethnic Tibetan monk as the head teacher, but the majority of members who attend weekly practices are non-Asian. Two Toronto temples are under the leadership of non-Asian Tibetan monks and nuns (one temple is Gelupa and the other New Kadampa) and have a predominately non-Asian membership, similar to the meditation/practice groups in the Greater Toronto Area led by non-monastic, non-Asian teachers. Tibetan lineages in Toronto include Gelupa, Kargyu, New Kadampa, Nyingma, and Sakya traditions, as well as some syncretic forms found in the Chinese Ling Shen Ching Tze groups.

The Greater Toronto Area now has an estimated 400,000 Buddhists affiliated with more than sixty-five Buddhist temples and associations (McLellan 1999: 13). Although the majority of Buddhists are ethnic Chinese, a variety of teachings, approaches, styles of practice, and traditions is represented. Theravāda Buddhists include immigrants and refugees from Burma, Cambodia, Laos, Sri Lanka and Thailand, as well as some non-Asians. Ambedkar Buddhists from India currently orientate themselves with Bangladeshi-born monks who received Theravāda training in Sri Lanka. Mahāyāna Buddhists from China, Hong Kong, Japan, Korea, Malaysia and Taiwan are primarily immigrants. Most Buddhists from Vietnam arrived as refugees and are Mahāyāna, except for the small numbers of Kampuchea Krom (ethnic Khmer) who are Theravāda. Toronto has several non-Asian practitioners of Japanese Zen, the largest group being the Toronto Zen Centre. In addition to three ethnic Korean temples, there is also the non-Asian Zen Buddhist Temple, founded by Samu Sunim, an ethnic Korean monk.

Some of the Tibetan, Chinese, and Vietnamese temples and groups in Toronto are branches of global transnational organizations which span Europe, North America, Australia, New Zealand, and Asia. They include the Karma Sonam Dorje Ling Temple (connected with Sherab Ling monastery in India, which is part of the Karma Kargyu network, involving large numbers of non-Tibetan practitioners); the Taiwanese-based Buddhist Progress Society of Toronto (Buddhist Light International Association, under Ven. Hsing Yun, with predominately ethnic Chinese membership); the Vietnamese Tiep Hien Order (based in France under Thich Nhat Hanh, with both non-Asian and ethnic Vietnamese members); and the Vietnamese Amida Temple (also in France, under the spiritual authority of Thich Tam Chau, for ethnic-Vietnamese). Two broad categories of Asian Buddhists in Toronto can be identified. One consists of ethnically homogeneous communities, which tend to have less than 5,000 people, and usually just one temple (renovated house or building), include the Koreans, Tibetans, Lao, Sinhalese, Cambodians, Burmese, Ambedkar, Japanese Canadians and Thai. The other category includes the multiple temples and groups associated with the larger Vietnamese (70,000) and Chinese (400,000) communities. The variety of Chinese migration origins (Hong Kong, Taiwan, Vietnam, Lao, Cambodia, mainland China, Singapore, India, Malaysia, and the West Indies), languages and dialects (such as Cantonese, Mandarin, Hakka, Teochew, Taiwanese) give rise to numerous 'sub-ethnicities', as reflected in the temples and associations. Southeast Asian Chinese refugees tend to live within Toronto's city core, their temples being located in renovated buildings; whereas immigrants from Hong Kong or Taiwan live in the more affluent suburbs, with large new temples built in distinct Chinese architectural styles.

The diversity among Buddhists in Toronto, especially between immigrants and refugees, is reflected in the extent to which each group or community is recognized or presents itself to others, and in the ability to recreate and redefine particular beliefs, practices, and institutional organization. The different groups or communities of Buddhists represent a continuum as they work towards public presence, representation, and overall inclusion in a variety of social spheres. Their position demonstrates the kinds and degrees of social capital they utilize and build upon. Social capital is necessary to counter inequalities and barriers to full social participation. Arising within ethno-specific Buddhist communities, intra-Buddhist affiliations and networks, and with individuals associated with, or acting on behalf of, an identifiable group, social capital facilitates the provision of culturally appropriate resettlement needs, enhances educational and employment opportunities, and actively opposes racial or religious discrimination. The presence of low levels of social capital can help explain why certain Buddhist communities in Toronto continue to face difficulties in representation or acceptance.

Social capital

Social capital has been broadly identified as those social structures which make it possible for groups and individuals to achieve particular goals, and to replicate familiar structural relations between people by generating networks of obligations, expectations, and trustworthiness. Whereas certain forms of economic capital can be used to purchase success, the 'dense set of associations' and interactions which arise through social capital are based on trust and reciprocity (Coleman 1990: 316). High degrees of social capital in families or communities have been linked to academic orientation and success among second-generation immigrants and refugees; the promotion of value and behavioural conformity; greater health and well-being; crime prevention and 'walkable' neighbourhoods; career mobility or enhanced economic development; and a variety of supports and constraints that support advantageous aspiration and action (Coleman 1990: 316; Zhou and Bankston 1994; Friedman and Krasckhardt 1997; Sanders et al. 2002; Leyden 2003: 1550).

Among immigrants and refugees, the leadership and community networks which arise through social capital are crucial to establishing social relations within their ethnic/linguistic/culturally specific groups and communities, and with others in the wider social sphere. Within the multicultural, multiracial, and multi-religious context of Toronto, high degrees of social capital are especially effective in negotiating politics of identity and representation. In turn, the politics of identity are crucial to establishing mainstream recognition and respect, and for providing mechanisms for participation in ethnically or religiously identified activities such as festivals, parades, and religious processions. The vast array of ethnic/religious consumerism through music, films, videos, DVDs, food, and cultural items further reflects successful politics of representation. Breton's (1964) notion of 'institutional completeness' is associated with ethnic minority communities who have extensive business, professional and social infrastructures, all of which provide multiple expressions of social capital.

'Bonding', 'bridging' and 'linking' are three broad types of social capital identified by Putnam (2000) and Voyer (2003). Bonding capital functions as a cohesive mechanism within families, groups, communities, and religious institutions, and it especially helps newcomers to maintain and support ethnic and cultural identity, as well as traditional family and homeland values. Churches and temples are 'key locations for mobilizing the social capital necessary for survival' and enable recent immigrants to reterritorialize previously existing social networks, exchange information and financial resources, support the process of legalization, reinforce social hierarchies, construct transnational religious networks, provide alternatives to dominant hegemonic structures and discourses, and engender new meanings within migration (Guest 2003: 195–6). Among Toronto Buddhists, the levels of 'bonding capital' within particular temple communities have effectively contributed to culturally appropriate settlement services, maintaining psychological health (especially among refugees) and the development of transnational connections, and enhancing overall social cohesion.

Bridging social capital extends beyond the particular group or community to connect with others in order to enhance successful and beneficial cooperative activities, such as the annual coreligious celebration of *Vesak* among Toronto Buddhists. Linking capital further expands bridging capital by facilitating 'relations between different social strata in a hierarchy where different groups access power, social status and wealth' (Voyer 2003: 31). For immigrants and ethnic minorities, it is 'linking capital' that helps them to be included in the larger social decision-making process, to participate in politics, and to gain a voice for greater social, economic, or representational opportunities. Bridging and linking capital are the means through which Buddhists connect with non-Buddhists and become recognized. The development of linking social capital initially arose from their coreligious (bridging) activities and facilitated their representation in national interfaith organizations and mainstream media.

Bonding social capital

Among Toronto Asian Buddhists, the presence of a Buddhist temple embodies the development of a community's social capital.[1] The temple responds to the spiritual needs of a particular community, and reifies ethnic, cultural, and national facets of people's identities. For Asian Buddhists, temples also provide venues for numerous secular programs and services, such as culturally appropriate family and mental health counselling; housing and employment networks; senior citizen, children, youth, young adult, and women's programs; skills training through real estate or financial planning seminars; language and cultural heritage programs; vegetarian restaurants; magazines and newsletters; medical clinics; and forums for homeland human rights advocacy. Among the first generation, associational bonds formed in the temples often become the focal point of social interaction and the centre of community activities.

Concern with homeland issues and political allegiances are also sustained and strengthened through the temple and associated religious networks. Visiting clergy (from the homeland or other country in resettlement), the production of DVDs and videos, and internet communication, maintain transnational connections among particular Buddhist groups. Following the weekly service at one local Vietnamese temple, for example, videos of different religious and cultural celebrations that someone filmed while visiting relatives in Vietnam, France or Australia may be shown. As people watch, they keep up a steady conversation, commenting especially when they recognize changes in the rituals or places. Connections through these religious and personal networks help keep people in Toronto up to date concerning floods, famine, or other national disasters, and current social affairs, including social justice and human rights violations, in the home countries. The bonding capital that arises becomes crucial for mobilizing the community to provide aid programs or participate in other forms of activism. Inner-group cohesion is strengthened for those in Toronto and in other overseas communities, including the homeland.

Within the temples, Buddhist memorial and merit-making rituals help to strengthen and support fragile individuals and families in resettlement. One local Vietnamese Buddhist temple, for example, transformed individual memorial practices (*Ky Sieu*) into a weekly practice, in addition to maintaining individual and annual memorial services. Weekly, monthly, and annual memorial rituals significantly contribute to levels of bonding within a Buddhist community by enabling members to share their loss and commemorate the death of loved ones together. Since Asians in general are hesitant to address their mental health concerns outside the family, the presence of Buddhist monks and nuns for counselling or ritual services provides culturally appropriate attention and treatment. If traditional or innovative mechanisms for healing are not available, there are significant negative consequences, not only for the individuals most affected with grief or unresolved trauma, but also for their Canadian-born children. This is especially evident among Cambodians whose pre-migration experiences lead them to suffer extraordinarily high rates of emotional and psychological disorders (McLellan 1999: 150). Until the mid-1990s, the Cambodian Buddhist temple in Toronto had no permanent Cambodian monk to facilitate annual religious observances and rituals, memorial services, and merit-making activities; or to recognize, mediate, and treat the vast array of mental health concerns caused by spirit possession, bereavement, guilt, and atonement needs.

The 'trust, solidarity and social cohesion embedded in the individuals of a community' are necessary assets for newcomer integration, yet are most absent among those who experienced mistrust, fear, and broken relationships (Mehmet *et al.* 2002: 335–57). The horrific genocidal trauma and inhumane living conditions Cambodians experienced under the communist Khmer Rouge from 1975 to late 1979 was followed by mass starvation, terrifying escapes into Thailand, and years of languishing in under-serviced and inhospitable refugee camps. Under the Khmer Rouge regime the entire Cambodian social infrastructure was severely damaged; cultural and religious institutions were destroyed, including the mass killing of Buddhist monks and any lay individual with traditional leadership, or modern educational, and organizational skills. Twenty-five years after resettlement in Toronto, Cambodian Buddhists are still struggling to reaffirm and re-establish their cultural, religious, and community bonds, and a basic trust in one another. Low social capital among Cambodian Buddhists is particularly evident in the absence of a formal Buddhist temple, access to monks, or trusted community leadership. The lack of Buddhist teachings and healing rituals during the crucial early years of Cambodian resettlement in the 1980s intensified their collective sorrow.

Bonding capital is not only important during early periods of resettlement, but also in long-term adaptation, integration, and intergenerational dynamics. Canadian born and raised Asian Buddhist children have undergone rapid acculturation and secularization; they question the relevance of their parents' traditional religious and cultural identities. Children raised in Canada do not easily relate to Buddhist beliefs and practices, especially when their understanding of the ethnic or religious language is limited. Communication with foreign-born *sangha* (monks and nuns) is often restricted; in turn, foreign-born *sangha* have difficulties relating to the attitudes and expectations of the English-speaking younger generation. Buddhist temples with strong social capital (such as those in the Japanese Canadian, Vietnamese, Sinhalese, and Chinese communities) have developed numerous responses to connect with the young people. Some of these responses include weekly Sunday schools; activities geared to youth groups (choirs, summer programs, regular outings); innovative precept-taking or ordination ceremonies, and graduated levels of Buddhist education that result in new Buddhist names or entitlement to wear a specific robe during weekly ceremonies; youth and family meditation retreats; and social activism programs that combine secular and spiritual interests (planting trees on earth day, or picking up litter on city streets).

The strength and effectiveness of a Buddhist temple is most evident in the intermediary and conciliatory roles of its leaders in retaining both youth and *sangha*. In Toronto, the majority of Buddhist temples are purchased and maintained by lay people, most often the community leaders who are also responsible for sponsoring and supporting the *sangha*. Sponsoring a monastic involves complex application forms, immigration fees, airfare, and continual assistance which, depending on the particular Buddhist tradition, can include special provision of meals, visits to other cities, a car, salary, or paid holidays. Foreign-born *sangha* do not easily accommodate to the North American institutional changes, numerous expectations for 'traditional' religious and cultural leadership, or their increased ministerial roles, which may include interfaith participation and social representation. Temples and their lay leaders must have adequate social capital to deal with the kinds of needs and contingencies which arise among members and *sangha*, and to quickly develop innovative programs or responses.

In several Asian Buddhist communities (Burmese, Korean, Japanese, Thai, Chinese, Vietnamese, Sri Lankan), a majority of the lay leaders involved in temple administration and organization are college and university graduates. Their education, levels of employment, and knowledge of Canadian society enhance their ability to address challenges to the temple, such as zoning restrictions, municipal by-laws, or neighbourhood hostility. In comparison, less than 2 per cent of Cambodian refugees in Ontario had completed high school in Cambodia, and 92 per cent could speak neither French nor English (McLellan 1995). After two decades of living in Canada, a large majority of Cambodians are still unfamiliar or insecure in dealing with the bureaucracy in medical, educational, and government institutions at all levels. Cambodians have generalized discomfort communicating with those in official positions, are uncertain regarding their rights as parents or citizens, and have few relations with non-Cambodians beyond employment.

The lack of social capital and limited social networks beyond the community can result in low levels of defense when collective interest is threatened. Low defense mechanisms were especially evident within Lao and Cambodian Buddhist communities when each faced hostile reactions from non-Asian neighbours to the establishment of a Buddhist temple (McLellan 2003; White 2004). The ethno-linguistic isolation among Cambodian and Lao Buddhists (reinforced by pre-migration experiences and cultural aversions to expressing weakness or need) has contributed to the minimal recognition and support given them from other Buddhist communities, intra-faith groups, and mainstream society in general. Responding to discrimination and structural or systemic social barriers with limited social capital significantly lessens the likelihood for positive outcomes. The Cambodian powerlessness to successfully challenge situations of overt inequality has reified their inherent sense of social marginalization and social exclusion.

Following more than twenty-years of financial planning, and the arrival of a permanent monk from Cambodia whose vision and persona provided the community with a cohesive plan to recreate traditional Khmer Buddhist practices and ceremonies, the Cambodian Buddhist Association purchased a large house with extensive property just north of Toronto in the late 1990s. The house, located in a predominately Italian-Catholic neighbourhood, adjoins an empty lot on one side, a house on the other side, and three other properties along the back fence. The newly purchased house immediately became a permanent temple and residence for monks. Municipal zoning by-laws clearly permitted the premises to be used for religious services; but, as soon as neighbours realized that what they had thought was an over-extended Asian family who dressed differently (referring to the monks) was instead a non-Christian religious institution comprised of refugees, open hostilities and opposition arose. A group of individuals whose houses were closest to the temple began a process of bureaucratic harassment. Regular complaints regarding parking, potential by-law violations, and boundary-fence infringements were made to the municipality, while fire-safety and health officials were repeatedly called in to inspect the temple. Legal attempts were initiated to revoke the zoning for a religious institution. Although the Cambodian temple had the support of the local Ontario Member of Parliament's office and officials at the Municipal Board, Cambodian leaders were so intimidated by the local opposition that, to date, the temple is not used for traditional celebrations and festivals.

White (2004) notes similarities in the Lao experience of building a temple in Caledon, a relatively affluent semi-rural region north of Toronto. Municipal zoning for a religious institution had already been established when the Lao purchased the house and seventy-three acres; yet, a group of over fifty area residents formed the Albion Caledon Citizens Trust which began a series of legal challenges to prevent the construction of a Buddhist temple, claiming incompatibility with rural land use, traffic and safety violations, visual infringement, noise pollution, and environmental impact issues. After thousands of dollars of legal fees and revised site plans, approval was given to build a Lao temple, but subject to a variety of restrictive provisos which would not apply to a Christian church (for example, the need to hide the temple behind a row of cedar trees).

These misfortunes of the Lao and Cambodian communities were not only the result of ethnic and religious prejudice, but also of their low levels of social capital which impacted on the degree to which they could represent themselves and receive recognition from others. Neither the Lao nor Cambodians effectively challenged the discourse of oppositions towards them which contained 'culturally and religiously-based constructions of what constitutes a local citizen and the local community, as well as a religious institution' (Dunn 2001: 291). Their ability to articulate need and to advocate for basic social rights is interrelated with their capacity to successfully engage in the politics of recognition, and participate in bridging events with others. As Eck (2001: 373) notes, the absence of shared interaction as coreligionists or in interfaith dialogues limits support mechanisms from stronger communities to help those who are more fragile or in need. Cambodians especially lacked the availability of leaders who could initiate and sustain involvement in co-Buddhist activities or interfaith activities.

Bridging and linking social capital

During the 1980s and early 1990s, considerable interfaith dialogue among most Buddhist groups in Toronto reflected their high levels of bridging social capital. Coreligious activities included the annual celebration of *Vesak*; interfaith lectures featuring local scholars, Buddhist monastics, and lay leaders; and visits to local temples. These activities were organized through the umbrella organizations of the Buddhist Federation of Toronto (from 1979 to 1986), the Toronto Chapter of the Buddhist Council of Canada (1987–89), and the Buddhist Communities of Greater Toronto (1990–94). Until the formation of the Sangha Council of Ontario (1995–present), leadership was provided by lay members and *sangha* representing various Buddhist groups and associations in Toronto. Throughout the 1980s and early 1990s, individuals from different Buddhist backgrounds (country of origin, language, ethnicity, general traditions and specific lineages) volunteered as leaders or as organizers of particular events.

The leadership activities of one individual is especially notable in bringing Buddhist issues and concerns to provincial and municipal arenas, to the media (national and local), to interfaith forums, and in presenting Buddhism and particular Buddhist temples to the general public. Although these activities were supported by the presence and involvement of other Buddhist leaders, Dr Suwanda Sugunasiri was consistently involved in all of the endeavours to develop effective politics of recognition for Buddhism in Toronto since the late 1970s. As co-Vice President of the Sinhalese Buddhist temple, Toronto Maha Vihara, from the mid- to late 1970s, Sugunasiri was involved in dealing with issues regarding adaptation and innovations of Buddhism in Canada. An early example of inter-temple dissension concerned the appropriate place to hold the temple's annual celebration of *Vesak*, one of the most important events in Theravāda Buddhism. Questions arose whether *Vesak* should be held within the small temple space, which would restrict access to the large numbers of Sinhalese who would want to attend, or in a larger 'unsanctified' rented venue. To resolve the issue, Sugunasiri invited a popular Buddhist scholar, Dr Bhante Gunaratana from the Washington Vihara, to give the *dharma* discourse during *Vesak*. The popularity of the guest speaker necessitated a large room being booked at the Ontario Institute for Secondary Education (OISE), which then provided an adequate, if not culturally appropriate, venue to host the Sinhalese-specific *Vesak* ceremony. Another contentious issue concerned language. Most Sinhalese immigrants were well-educated professionals familiar with English. Many, however, were either not comfortable with associating Buddhist beliefs and practices with English or feared loss of the homeland language among their children, and insisted that Sinhalese be used to identify different locations and activities at the Maha Vihara, and that it should also be the language of *dharma* talks. The language issue reflected a common pattern emerging among the Asian

Buddhist groups in Toronto: retaining Asian cultural, linguistic, and national identities in Canada; concern over exposing children to Buddhist teachings in English, yet retaining traditional authenticity; and considering whether provisions should be made for non-Asians to participate in events. Through first-hand experience in grappling with these patterns, Sugunasiri questioned the relationship of culture to Buddhist practices, and the extent to which one could exist without the other. Such questions provided an underlying concern in the creation of the first ecumenical organization of Buddhists in Toronto. The catalyst for a Toronto-based Buddhist federation arose in response to an interfaith service organized by the Japanese-based World Conference on Religion for Peace (WCRP), held in Toronto in October 1979 at the Bloor Street United Church. Reverend Fujikawa (then head minister at the Toronto Buddhist Church) and Sugunasiri were members of the WCRP Toronto branch, yet neither was eligible to be present at the interfaith conference unless they were part of a Buddhist delegation of representative participants. To organize a delegation, a meeting at OISE was held, with fifteen representatives from different Toronto Buddhist groups in attendance. These leaders provided the necessary intra-religious delegation for the interfaith service, and enabled approximately seventy-five Buddhists to participate from their representative communities. In November 1979 a second meeting was held to explore the possibility of a formal organization of Buddhists in Toronto. To develop goals and a constitution, participants from the various Buddhist communities met on a monthly basis. Debates lasted for hours on such key issues as language. By April 1980 the Toronto Buddhist Federation had emerged, with a constitution and government registration. Sugunasiri was the group's first coordinator, and immediately organized the first multi-ethnic *Vesak* at Nathan Phillips Square (City Hall) in May 1980. Additional participating Buddhist communities included the Burmese Association, Gaden Choling and Dharmadhatu (Tibetan), Ontario Zen Centre and the Vietnamese Hoa Nghiem Temple. The youth group of the Hoa Nghiem Temple were especially active in putting decorations around the Square, and creating and installing a thirty-foot picture of the sitting Buddha. A picture of this Buddha painting appeared in the *Toronto Sun* newspaper, the only Toronto-based news media to feature, let along mark, the first *Vesak* ceremony held in North America.

Five *sangha* and 1,000 lay people attended that *Vesak* ceremony (despite intermittent showers, which were perceived as a symbolic 'rain of blessings'). The format of the religious ceremony included a series of chanting and prayers, reflecting both Mahāyāna (Bodhisattva aspiration) and Theravāda (transfer of merit), and an introduction to the Kambutsu ceremony (bathing of the baby Buddha), popular in Vietnam and Japan. Two large Kambutsu statues were placed in bowls of water and people lined up to pour water and chant personal prayers. At the makeshift altar, lay people placed flowers, burned incense, and made food offerings. Following the religious ceremony, cultural presentations included the Tibetan Potala Dance Group (from Lindsay), Vietnamese children who offered flowers (Hoa Nghiem Temple), Sinhalese dancers (Maha Vihara), Ambedkar spiritual music, and Brent Titcomb giving the first performance of the song 'Roll the Dharma Wheel', written by Bhante Punnaji (Maha Vihara). This song became known as the 'Unity Song', and was sung thereafter at every coreligious Buddhist activity to strengthen Buddhist ecumenicism. Participants from each Buddhist community brought different types of food to contribute to the huge communal feast. The overall format of this first coreligious *Vesak* set the tone for the next thirteen years, at which time the Sangha Council of Ontario assumed leadership over the Buddhist communities of Greater Toronto. For whatever reasons, the name of the essentially religious and cultural event of *Vesak* was thereafter changed to a 'peace day commemoration', but important media exposure during the 1980s allowed presentations by Buddhist community representatives about specific issues and concerns of being Buddhist in the Canadian context. Asian and non-Asian Buddhists alike were profiled to indicate the inherent diversity of Buddhism in Toronto. The English language format, however, made it difficult for many recent immigrants and refugees to become involved, thus inhibiting their representation.

Buddhist involvement in interfaith meetings encouraged the diverse religious groups to officially request the Canadian Radio and Television Commission to establish a Canadian Inter-faith Network. Through their joint efforts, 'Vision TV' emerged, with two programming divisions, 'Cornerstone' and 'Mosaic'. 'Mosaic' programming enabled different faith communities to buy air time for their specific programs, whereas 'Cornerstone' was funded by the station. Due to a lack of financial resources to buy air time, and possibly lack of interest, there were no Buddhist programs on 'Mosaic'. 'Cornerstone', however, featured programs such as 'The Long March', and films on Sri Lanka and on the Dalai Lama, thus increasing public exposure to Buddhism. Participation in the Canadian Inter-faith Coalition seemed to suggest that a national organization of Buddhists be established. In 1986, the Buddhist Council of Canada (BCC) was founded, but so strong was the cultural commitment to each form of Buddhism within it that the Council could never really bring to birth a common sense of religious identity. The Council soon fell apart and has not been replaced with anything similar at a national level. Nonetheless, in the late 1980s, Toronto's diverse *sangha* members continued to give free, widely advertised public lectures, including such key personalities as the Korean monk Samu Sunim (Zen Buddhist Temple), Bhante Punnaji (Toronto Maha Vihara), Bishop Sunoda (Buddhist Churches or Canada), and Zazep Tulku (Gaden Choling). Later events included 'Meet the Teachers' and 'Dharma on Wheels' which introduced different Buddhist teachers and temples to the Toronto public. Participating temples and groups included Gaden Choling, Hoa Nghiem, Toronto Maha Vihara, Dharma Dhatu, Zen Buddhist Temple and Hong Fa. Their biggest challenge was that few immigrant Buddhist *sangha* in Toronto spoke English or felt comfortable enough to participate, despite the public expectation for Asian-born teachers. In 1990, Venerable Samu Sunim of the Zen Buddhist Temple initiated a series of co-Buddhist activities in Toronto. He organized the Conference on Buddhism in Canada, July 8–14, 1990, which brought together Buddhist *sangha* and lay leaders from temples, monasteries, and centres across Canada, as well as academics from Canadian universities. The event was held at his temple in Toronto, but jointly sponsored by Hoa Nghiem Temple, Tai Bay Temple, Tam Bao Temple (in Montréal), Manshu Yuen, the Buddhist Council of Toronto and the Toronto Buddhist Church. The several themes presented at this conference included life stories of some Asian-born *sangha* now living in Canada, experiences of lay Buddhists, the development of Buddhist groups and movements in Canada, and social issues facing Buddhists. The Toronto conference was modelled after the July 1987 Conference on World Buddhism in North America, held at Samu Sunim's Zen Buddhist Temple in Ann Arbor, Michigan.

In an interesting educational development, in 2000 Suwanda Sugunasiri obtained provincial government approval for what became known as the Nalanda College of Buddhist Studies. Commitments were secured from several Toronto-area academics to be available to teach a variety of courses. Although the number of full-time students has remained small, the objectives are important. Other initiatives include development of a *Canadian Journal of Buddhist Studies*, and a 2005 conference on 'Canadian Buddhism: State of the Art and Future Directions', ostensibly to celebrate one hundred years of Buddhism in Canada.

Summary

The strong social bridging capital among Buddhist leaders from the different cultural, linguistic and doctrinal traditions in Toronto facilitated the first multi-ethnic celebration of *Vesak* beginning in May 1980 (the first in North America), and led to ever greater forms of social and political recognition and representation. An interesting development among Buddhist groups in Toronto is that, as particular temple groups and communities increased numerically and attained favourable social, political, and economic conditions of recognition and representation, their involvement with other Buddhist groups and communities in coreligious activities decreased. Particular temples and groups enhanced their own bridging and linking activities apart from the intra-Buddhist context, identifying themselves instead as distinct facets within the larger Buddhist diversity. This pattern is most evident among the larger Chinese temples in Toronto. Due to their numerical dominance in Toronto since the early 1990s, Chinese temples do not require the support of other Buddhist groups and communities to establish presence or representation. Temples from a variety of traditions now advertise their particular identities and programs in ethnic magazines, radio, TV, and on English internet websites. Different educational forums are held to encourage the participation of non-Asians and may feature guest *sangha* speaking on specific facets of the particular tradition, a series of lectures on general Buddhist beliefs and practices by visiting scholars, or a meditation retreat. Some temples operate restaurants as an informal introduction to their particular tradition, providing vegetarian food and well-placed advertisements featuring events. The larger temples encourage non-Asians (especially municipal and provincial politicians!) to participate in traditional rituals, ceremonies, and their particular New Year celebrations, and tend to represent themselves during multicultural or multifaith events.

Chinese temples, Sinhalese temples, and the Toronto Buddhist Church annually support local charity walks (sponsored by the United Way), participate in food drives, blood banks and interfaith projects concerned with the homeless. The Toronto chapter of Buddha's Light International Association (BLIA) has been featured in Toronto newspapers (English and Chinese) doing these activities, as has the Han Shan Sih Buddhist Society of North York, when they funded a large endowment to York University to support students with environmental concerns. These activities are similar to Chen's contention that Buddhist temples in the United States engage in the politics of recognition by cultivating public acceptance through the cultivation of merit and socially engaged beneficial actions (Chen 2003: 67). To date, Buddhist activities in Toronto have received nothing but positive recognition from the media, and despite instances of neighbourhood hostility, Buddhist institutions have never been targeted with the kinds of hate messages or vandalism that Jewish, Sikh, Hindu and Muslim places of worship have experienced in Toronto and elsewhere in Ontario.

Certain Buddhist temples in Toronto, however, are consistently called upon to host educational visits by high school or university groups, participate in multifaith forums, or provide feedback on issues concerned with Canadian politics. The high level of bridging and linking social capital necessary for these kinds of social and political representation is directly related to the presence of bilingual (English and homeland/ethnic language) individuals in organizational and religious leadership roles. Their capabilities are in contrast to the linguistic and cultural barriers in some other Buddhist temples which inhibit responses to initial telephone contact, meeting informally with others, or participating in events which would increase bridging and linking capacities. It is unfortunate that those individuals, groups, and temples with the highest levels of social capital did not cultivate direct involvement and support in helping those with the least opportunities and abilities.[2]

Particular historical waves of arrival, pre-migration identity status and experiences, language, education, and employment have contributed to a hierarchy among Buddhists in Toronto. Those with high degrees of social and economic capital are successful in the politics of recognition and representation. Their organizational and leadership coordination, cooperation, and expertise in articulating or negotiating discourses of identity facilitate plans, programs and activities for their particular religious institutions, as well as in the larger ethnic or mainstream community. Those with low social capital continue to demonstrate particular issues of accommodation and adaptation, and have difficulties in mediating social hostility, or enhancing interfaith activities. The economic wealth and social capital of Asian Buddhist immigrants can be correlated with their identity as independent 'point' (a standard used by the government for purposes of immigration) or business class migrants, but high levels of social capital can also be found among refugee communities whose close-knit bonds with one another (transnationally or locally) support successful social/political representation. For those with weak bridging and linking capital or few networks developed beyond a particular ethnic community, ultimately the 'the warmth of welcome' and support given them by others becomes critical to developing a sense of inclusion (Kunz 2003: 34). Maintaining an isolationist orientation may well reflect strategies to limit 'aversive contacts with segregationist or exclusionist members of the host majority while seeking protection and solace within their own immigrant community' (Bourhis and Montreuil 2003: 41). Perhaps the next decade of Buddhist activities will demonstrate that those with greater social competencies and strong networks of social capital will develop enabling structures to embrace all Buddhist groups and communities, and act accordingly when unequal conflicts over recognition and rights arise.

Notes

1 Although ethnic Tibetans have not yet established a temple, their extensive transnational networks and linkages provide a similar foundation for support. Global relations among Tibetans in Canada have provided strong bonding capital since 1971. The transnational connections are especially sustained through the Dalai Lama, the internationally recognized political and religious leader of the Tibetans, and Dharamsala (seat of the Tibetan government-in-exile). Bonding capital is evident in the consistent religious leadership with its strong cultural and ethnic reification. Extending to the generations born in Canada, the global framework of Tibetans provides purpose in exile, and maintains highly active political advocacy. The extensive bonding capital enables Tibetans in Toronto to develop connections with the large numbers of non-Tibetan, primarily Caucasian, practitioners affiliated with Tibetan monks, engaged in Vajrayāna practices, or who support Tibetan independence. These connections enhance the Tibetan community's bridging and linking capital, of which numerous examples were seen during the May 2004 Kalacharka ceremony in Toronto.

2 There are exceptions. For several decades, Michael Kerr has been outstanding in his attempts to advocate for equitable opportunities for Indochinese refugees, first in Southeast Asian refugee camps, and then in Toronto. Through his efforts, culturally appropriate healthcare was made available, sponsorship opportunities were identified and supported, resettlement and general social services were increased, and advocacy on particular issues was given. In too many instances, however, his efforts were not supported by other Buddhist leaders.

Bibliography

Baumann, Gerd (1996) *Contesting Culture: Discourses of Identity in Multi-Ethnic London*. New York: Cambridge University Press.

Bourhis, Richard and Montreuil, Annie (2003) "Exploring Receiving Society Attitudes Towards Immigration and Ethnocultural Diversity," *Canadian Issues (Themes Canadiens)*, April, 39–41.

Breton, Raymond (1964) "Institutional Completeness of Ethnic Communities and the Personal Relations of Immigrants," *The American Journal of Sociology*, 193–205.

Breton, Raymond, Isajiw, Wsevolod W., Kalbach, Wallen and Reitz, Jeffrey (eds) (1990) *Ethnic Identity and Equality: Varieties of Experience in a Canadian City*. Toronto, ON: University of Toronto Press.

Chen, Carolyn (2003) "Cultivating Acceptance by Cultivating Merit: The Public Engagement of a Chinese Buddhist Temple in American Society," in Jane Naomi Iwamura and Paul Spickard (eds) *Revealing the Sacred in Asian and Pacific America*. New York: Routledge.

Coleman, J. S. (1990) *Foundations of Social Theory*. Cambridge, MA: Harvard University Press.

Coombe, Rosemary (1991) "Encountering the Postmodern: New Directions in Cultural Anthropology," *Canadian Review of Sociology and Anthropology*, 28(2): 188–205.

Dunn, Kevin (2001) "Presentations of Islam in the politics of mosque development in Sydney," *Tijdschrift voor Economische en Sociale Geographe*, 92(3): 291–308.

Eck, Diana (2001) *A New Religious America*. San Francisco, CA: HarperCollins.

Friedman, Raymond and Krasckhardt, David (1997) "Social Capital and Career Mobility," *Journal of Applied Behavioral Science*, 33(3): 316–34.

Gap Min, Pyong and Ha Kim, Jung (eds) (2002) *Religions in Asian America*. Walnut Creek, CA: Altamira Press.

Guest, Kenneth J. (2003) *God in Chinatown: Religion and Survival in New York's Evolving Immigrant Community*. New York: New York University Press.

Handler, Richard (1986) "Authenticity," *Anthropology Today*, 2(1): 38–40.

Kunz, Jean Lock (2003) "Social Capital: A Key Dimension of Immigrant Integration," *Canadian Issues (Themes Canadiens)*, April, 33–4.

Leonard, Karen (2000) "State, Culture, and Religion: Political Action and Representation among South Asians in North America," *Diaspora*, 9(1): 21–37.

Leyden, Kevin (2003) "Social Capital and the Built Environment: The Importance of Walkable Neighborhoods," *American Journal of Public Health*, 93(9): 1546–51.

McLellan, Janet (1995) *Cambodian Refugees in Ontario: An Evaluation of Resettlement and Adaptation*. Toronto, ON: York Lanes Press.

—— (1999) *Many Petals of the Lotus: Five Asian Buddhist Communities in Toronto*. Toronto, ON: University of Toronto Press.

—— (2003) "Continuities and Change in Religious Identities, Beliefs and Practices among Cambodians in Ontario," paper given at the Canadia Society for the Study of Religion (CSSR) conference, 28–31 May, Halifax, NS.

Mehmet, Ozay, Tahiroglu, M. and Li, Eric A. L. (2002) "Social Capital Formation in Large-Scale Development Projects," *Canadian Journal of Development Studies*, 23(2): 335–57.

Numrich, Paul David (1996) *Old Wisdom in the New World: Americanization in Two Immigrant Theravāda Buddhist Temples*. Knoxville, TN: University of Tennessee Press.

Putnam, Robert (2000) *Bowling Alone: The Collapse and Revival of American Community*. New York: Simon & Schuster.

Ross, Andrew (ed.) (1988) *Universal Abandon? The Politics of Postmodernism*. Minneapolis, MN: University of Minneapolis Press.

Roy, Patricia, Granatstein, J. L., Iino, Masako and Takamura, Hiroko (1990) *Mutual Hostages: Canadians and Japanese during the Second World War*. Toronto, ON: University of Toronto Press.

Sanders, Jimy, Nee, Victor and Sernau, Scott (2002) "Asian Immigrants' Reliance on Social Ties in a Multiethnic Labor Market," *Social Forces*, 81(1): 281–314.

Statistics Canada (2001) *2001 Census* (www.statcan.ca).

Tanaka, Toyo (1983) *Nikkei Legacy: The Story of Japanese Canadians from Settlement to Today*. Toronto, ON: NC Press.

Taylor, Charles (1994) "The Politics of Recognition" in Amy Gutmann (ed.) *Multiculturalism: Examining the Politics of Recognition*. Princeton, NJ: Princeton University Press.

Van Esterik, Penny (1992) *Taking Refuge: Lao Buddhists in North America*. Arizona State University Press, co-published with Centre for Refugee Studies, York University, Toronto: York Lanes Press.

Voyer, Jean-Pierre (2003) "Diversity Without Divisiveness: A Role for Social Capital?," *Canadian Diversité*, 2(1): Spring, 31–2.

White, Marybeth (2004) "Multiculturalism: The Conversation with the 'Other': A Case Study of Wat Lao Veluwanaram," presented at the CSSR, Winnipeg, 28 May–1 June.

Zhou, Min and Bankston, Carl (1994) "Social Capital and the Adaptation of the Second Generation: The Case of Vietnamese Youth in New Orleans," *International Migration Review*, 28(4): 821–84.

6

LAO BUDDHISM IN TORONTO

A case study of community relations

Marybeth White

This chapter will examine the experience of the Greater Toronto Area Lao refugees in establishing their Buddhist temple, Wat Lao Veluwanaram in Caledon, a small rural town outside of Toronto. The previous chapter presents a theoretical model for understanding the dynamics of Buddhist communities in Toronto through the politics of recognition and representation. Similarly, this chapter utilizes Charles Taylor's notions concerning the 'politics of recognition'; however, rather than presenting a theoretical model, this chapter offers a case study of one community's engagement with the 'politics of recognition' in order to examine the validity of Taylor's position. In his article 'The Politics of Recognition', Charles Taylor examines the liberal democratic culture in North America and questions the current political and legal structure's ability to offer the realization of cultural harmony. Taylor is primarily concerned with 'the rigidities of procedural liberalism' fostering an environment which is 'inhospitable to difference' because of the universal axiom of equality and the conflicting desire for the 'survival' of a culture which is distinct from that of the hegemony (Taylor 1994: 61). This case study will dilate on the ideal of cultural harmony, as it applies to the Lao Buddhist in Toronto, within the context of such key features as group identity, cultural expression, multiculturalism, and power. First, a brief account of the Lao's arrival in Canada will be set down in order to show the connection between group identity and their refugee experience, and to demonstrate the relevance of a temple in their community.

Recreation of a community: group identity, ritual and the importance of the temple

Groups of Laotian refugees were able to escape the unstable political conditions of Laos in the late 1970s, making their way to refugee camps in Thailand. Over 10,000 Laotians found asylum in Canada during the two year period of 1979 to 1980 (Gordon 1990: 16). Many of the refugees settled in the Toronto area and joined cultural groups established by Laotian immigrants prior to the large influx of refugees. The newly organized multiculturalism policies established by the Canadian government in the 1970s assisted secular groups in promoting cultural but not religious endeavors.

Unlike Buddhist immigrants who make a conscious choice to move to another country, refugees are forced to flee their homeland without planning in advance where they are going or how they will survive. This has a poignant affect on individual and group identity (McLellan 1999: 22). Both collectively and personally there are varying degrees of identity crisis as people deal with the sudden loss of their way of life.

It is significant that Buddhism has emerged as one of the central features of Lao refugee ethnic identity, a source of conversation through which group and individual identity and motivation can be reflected on (Berger 1969: 17; Krulfeld 1999 [1994]: 101). Berger purports 'conversation' is the key to providing notions of identity and world construction and examines the effect on identity after the loss of conversation with a significant 'other', such as a social milieu, as in the case of refugees. The diaspora community's connections to their homeland, other diaspora groups and the new host country are essential in recreating their self-identity. In effect the identity crisis experienced by the Lao refugees ushered in an opportunity to become more self-reflective, discerning the core and peripheral aspects of their religion, the majority of which are Theravāda Buddhists. This process was intensified when their experience as Buddhist refugees was juxtaposed with the Christian refugee camps in Thailand. Many of the camps were operated by Christian denominations, in turn 'engaged in subtle and overt attempts of proselytization' (McLellan 1999: 124; also see Van Esterik 1992: 18–20). Also, 65 per cent of private sponsorships were Christian (Van Esterik 1992: 27), with the result that some refugees converted outright or maintained dual religiosity, participating in both Buddhist and Christian ceremonies. There are many reasons for conversion: some felt Christianity was the religion of North America, therefore conversion was appropriate; others saw a cultural gain in becoming Christian, while for others it was a sense of obligation to the sponsors which brought them to engage in, or convert to Christianity.[1] The identity crisis experienced by the Laotian society left them searching for ways to adapt to life outside Laos in countries heavily influenced by Christianity. The internal and external pressures to convert posed a challenge for refugees in recreating their traditional religion.

The distress brought on by the abrupt 'identity crisis' experienced by so many refugees can clearly be reduced by participation in a religious community. There is a link between religion and mental health among those who are resettling in a foreign land, and recreating a religio-cultural community (Van Esterik 1992: 35). This sentiment is echoed by Edward

Canda in his article 'Buddhism as a Support System for Southeast Asian Refugees.' Canda's research finds that many of the social services mandated to provide aid to refugees are lacking in knowledge of both the 'functions of the temple' and the workings of the Buddhist tradition itself (Canda 1992: 63). Furthermore, there is an 'apathy' on behalf of social service workers toward understanding the importance of religion in the resettlement process (Canda 1992: 63).[2] As Canda makes clear, societies following the Theravāda tradition, such as the Lao, turn to the religious expert as the primary source of relief in their suffering.[3] He suggests an improvement in the services provided by government programs could be gained by initiating a training program 'between Buddhist monks and social workers to encourage mutual understanding and collaboration' (Canda 1992: 65). This is in concert with the ideal of a multicultural or pluralistic society which values difference.

During the 'recreation process' of group identity, ritual practices are imbued with new meaning. For example, in North America, Lao refugees have instilled new meanings into traditional rituals such as the *Baci-Sou Khuan*[4] ritual in order to foster a 'new identity' (Van Esterik 1999: 65; also see Padgett 2002: 209). The *Baci-Sou Khuan* ritual now focuses on healing the wounds of the refugee experience by symbolically regrouping the community. Another activity which altered in significance following the Lao refugee experience is the 'merit-making' associated with the formation of a temple. In Laos, the temple is not only a place to worship and make merit, but also a centre to be utilized as 'a school, village-affairs meeting hall, guesthouse, and dispensary' (LeBar and Suddard [1960] 1967: 70). It is at the temple where one could obtain counseling, seek advice on spiritual or worldly matters, and bring merit-making gifts. In short, the Laotian temple was the hub of community life, particularly in rural areas, which comprise most of Laos. In North America the temple continues to be of major importance to the community but for differing reasons. The physical centrality of the temple in everyday life is not possible within the North American lifestyle (Van Esterik 1999: 64). Frequently, as is the case with Wat Lao Veluwanaram, the temple is not within walking distance. The daily exchange between the laity and monks, as it occurred in the villages of Laos, does not easily exist in Canada. However, the temple's centrality is still prevalent in the regrouping of the community and acts as an important religio-cultural centre, where the Lao can maintain their culture in a new land. The spiritual aspect of patronizing a new temple in a diaspora, which accommodates the essential function for the refugees of bringing the community together for Buddhist and cultural celebrations, networking and feasting, is now a central feature. By establishing and supporting a temple, group cohesion is enhanced, and it is believed that the most highly regarded kind of merit for the Laotian people is generated (Zhou *et al.* 2002: 53). The struggle to arrive at the point where this group had the financial ability as well as sufficient Canadian cultural understanding to purchase land and negotiate the construction of a temple requires a certain level of social capital and group cohesion.

The temple as voice: ethnicity and translation

The temple in a diaspora community plays two crucial roles. First, it provides sanctuary for a group, a place where the community can heal individual and communal wounds. Ruth Krulfeld echos the findings of both Canda and Van Esterik when she notes that it is the Lao monks who are best able to help community members 'in overcoming their grief, and to deal with their stress . . . [rather than the] agencies intended to aid them' (Krulfeld [1994] 1999: 106). Second, it acts as a visible marker of a community and gives that community voice. This new-found voice is bilingual, speaking to the interior workings of the ethnic component as well as the intercommunication between the community and the larger society in which they live.

The importance of the temple as a sacred space embodying the religio-cultural aspects of a community cannot be overstated, particularly among groups of people that have been uprooted from the markers which maintain their group identity (Matthews 2002: 124; also see Zhou *et al.* 2002: 64). At this crossroads of identity, where one is in some ways no longer Lao, not yet Canadian, yet somehow both, the temple offers a 'flexible template' upon which the community can work out their new identity, accepting and/ or rejecting aspects of their old ways and the new ways at hand. Padgett refers to the immigrant temple as the 'translating temple' in his research on the Thai Wat Mongkolratanaram. There is no single mold of Thai Buddhism, just as there is no uniform brand of Lao Buddhism, and most importantly the recreation is not simply a hybrid of the two (Van Esterik 1992: 133), for it 'represents neither old nor new . . . It manifests the work of the translators themselves' (Padgett 2002: 212). Through this hermeneutical process, a community's notions of 'self' congeal. The temple then becomes a visible marker, the physical manifestation of the voice of a community. The Lao of the Greater Toronto Area had successfully negotiated this process of group recreation and self-identity, culminating in the purchase of land in Caledon with the intent to erect a temple, representing their ethnic religious community.

The physicality of a temple brings the issue of difference to the fore. For the Lao community of the Greater Toronto Area who wanted to build their temple in Caledon, there were seventy area non-Lao families who supported their endeavour and signed a petition to this end, perceiving Wat Lao Veluwanaram (Veluwanh) as an asset to their community. But other residents perceived the temple as a threat to the existing community. As Seager suggests in his recounting of an Illinois community's struggles, the temple was seen by some area residents as the 'Laotian's unwillingness to assimilate' (Seager 1999: 141). Why does this occur in countries such as Canada and the United States, where notions of multiculturalism and pluralism are fostered? These questions will be explored following the case study.

The Greater Toronto Area Lao community: a case study

In spite of a lack of tangible government support for religious endeavors in both Canada and the United States, immigrant and refugee Buddhist groups establish temples. In the case of the Greater Toronto Area Lao community, the importance of the temple in its manifold meanings is evident in their willingness to commence saving toward its realization shortly after their arrival in 1979. Many of the Lao refugees came from a modest background, coming to Canada as 'boat people, working as general labour, making minimum wages' (Bounmy Sihaphom, 30 October 2000 *Toronto Star* interview). The purchase of land, almost twenty years later, implicitly marks the transition of this group's desire for internal cohesion to the external establishment of their group as a legitimate player at the multicultural table – seventy-three acres of land in Caledon, purchased in November of 1997, with frontage along two roads, one of which is a major artery. The monks took up residence in the farmhouse, and while the temple was constructed, the living room was utilized as a shrine room. The actual incorporation of Wat Lao Veluwanaram[5] occurred in February 1997, when the Lao community started to actively look for a temple site. The rear of the property straddles the Oak Ridges Moraine and the Niagara Escarpment, and is designated as an Escarpment Natural Area. The remaining property is deemed an Escarpment Protection Area (EPA), resulting in stringent guidelines for any construction or changes in the geography of the land.

In April of 1998 both the Toronto and Regional Conservation Authority (TRCA) and the Niagara Escarpment Commission (NEC) approved minor building proposals, with the exception of a soccer field, which invited further questions. The Town of Caledon expressed concerns about the long-term plans of the new owners. Because of the EPA designation, the land can never be rezoned as institutional, although under the rural designation, small-scale institutional use is permitted. The town council recommended Wat Lao Veluwanaram submit a comprehensive site plan to reflect their future plans for the property. Accordingly, the Laotian community organized an informal gathering to meet their new neighbours. Flyers were delivered to rural mailboxes and the mayor and town councilors were invited. Many neighbours attended, as did the mayor and several councilors. Bounmy Sihaphom, the president of Wat Lao Veluwanaram, reflected on the gathering's success in establishing connections with their new neighbours and answered many questions about the Buddhist tradition and their ceremonies. But relationships became strained in July 1998 when the town office received letters from some of the neighbours who were frustrated and concerned about excessive noise during a large gathering to celebrate the beginning of the Buddhist

'Lenten' season.[6] The event had been staged outdoors due to the large number of people attending, amplifiers had been set up and different games were played, such as *sepak takraw*, a Lao game which is similar to soccer. Although similar to a large church family picnic, complete with sack races, the concerns extended beyond mere noise to the water table's ability to deal with hundreds of people congregating on the property for a two-day event. There were questions concerning traffic and zoning by-laws; but the largest emerging concern was the distinction between a social gathering and a religious gathering.

The town council called a meeting to address the area residents' concerns over zoning by-laws. In Caledon, rural zoning allows for places of religious worship. The neighbours were primarily concerned as to the definition of 'religious activity' versus 'cultural activity', yet environmental and traffic issues became pressing subjects of debate. Wat Lao Veluwanaram was asked to provide a comprehensive site plan with architectural renderings for the proposed temple construction. Because of the environmental sensitivity of the property numerous levels of government were involved: the TRCA, the NEC, the Region of Peel, and the Town of Caledon. The former two are responsible for the environmental aspects of the property, while the latter two oversee the zoning, traffic and parking issues. In order to submit a comprehensive site plan, Wat Lao Veluwanaram hired various engineering and consulting companies to complete the numerous necessary studies, such as an Environmental Impact Study, Management Plan, hydro-geological analysis, and plans for storm water run-off, landscape and parking, archeological assessment and sewage disposal. The Region of Peel and Town of Caledon completed infrastructure reports and assessed traffic conditions and road tolerances for their particular jurisdictions. While the various consulting and governing bodies were conducting their studies over the next year a stream of letters from disgruntled and frustrated neighbours continued to arrive at town hall. Although noise was no longer the main issue, the letters express concern over environmental issues as well as questions of the perceived 'church's' constituency. Speaking from a hegemonic Christian North American perspective, they expressed concern that the temple was not like a 'regular' or 'traditional' church, nor were the practitioners acting in accord with North American stereotypes of popular Buddhism, such as quiet meditation practice.[7] The authenticity of the religious group was directly linked with the tax exemption granted to religious organizations. Letters to the town complained that the tax base would be eroded as religious groups purchase property in Caledon and questioned how the validity and authenticity of these religious groups were legitimated.

The Town of Caledon called a meeting in November 1999 to address the neighbours' concerns, but the meeting fell ten days shy of amassing the completed environment and traffic surveys. As a result the Town was not able to provide the residents with concrete results from the various studies.

Consequently the meeting showed the exasperation in the voices of those neighbours who attended with statements such as, 'Who are these people?' 'Why can't they go to an industrial area?' 'We can't deal with these people!' The recurrent theme underlying the voiced environmental and traffic concerns was the unease with cultural differences and changes to their relatively affluent country lifestyle that might result from the arrival of a different ethnic religion. In the ten days following the meeting with the residents, the TRCA, Traffic Operations, the Town's Infrastructure group and the Region of Peel sent reports to the Town of Caledon indicating that there were no difficulties with the application in their respective departments. The site plan was approved with the proviso that numerous conditions be met, such as prohibiting any sales at community events, no camping or storing of buses on the property, and Wat Lao Veluwanaram was to cover the expense of 'no-parking' signs necessary along the access road, as well as planting a wall of cedars so as to minimize the view of the temple from the roadway. The application was passed to the NEC, which had the final say in all regional land site plan proposals. At this juncture the area residents retained a lawyer. With the threat of legal action and fifty annoyed residents at the first town council meeting in January 2000, the Town of Caledon decided to defer the NEC meeting until all information could be re-evaluated and an independent traffic study completed at the opponent's expense. Given the professional nature of those conducting the initial surveys, which were now to be redone, and the provisos which stipulated that no camping could occur on a 73-acre property, it is evident that Taylor's charge – that procedural liberalism fails to recognize difference, but continues to empower the dominant group – appears to be valid. As reported in the 12 February 2000 edition of the local paper, *The Enterprise*, the Town of Caledon council determined that the original studies were conducted properly and forwarded the application to the NEC for final approval. The area residents, however, vowed to 'fight this day and night' (*The Enterprise*, 12 January 2000: 1). Forty-three people formed the Albion Caledon Citizens Trust (ACCT) and offered to purchase Wat Lao Veluwanaram, claiming the professional studies were faulty. According to Lao spokesperson Bounmy Sihaphom, the community felt frustrated and some questioned the wisdom in proceeding. Financial concerns were another issue with which the community had to grapple. With the money for the construction of the temple spent on legal fees it would take many years for the community to replenish the funds. The Greater Toronto Area Lao were bolstered financially and emotionally through their relationship with other Lao diaspora communities, in particular the Washington DC area community.

In this regard, Padgett acknowledges the significance of the transnational diaspora community in shaping the orientation of immigrant religious communities (Padgett 2002: 203–4). The transnational diaspora communities communicate with each other and provide a 'space' for the notion of an ideal or 'imagined community' (Anderson 1983: 4). This was manifested in the Caledon situation with the Laotian community in dialog with the Caledon residents and Canadian levels of bureaucracy, as well as the homeland contact with friends, relatives and religious officials, and finally with other diaspora Lao Buddhists who have similar experiences, albeit in differing countries. Although some wished to retreat, the Lao community, represented by their lawyer, met with Albion Caledon Citizens Trust at the Ontario Municipal Board office in May of 2000.

The final hearing was held at the Office of Consolidated Hearings, which is a joint board comprised of the OMB and the Environmental Assessment and Appeals Board. It ran from 18 September to 6 December of 2000, with the final decision being released on 30 April 2001. The decision rendered gave Wat Lao Veluwanaram permission to proceed with the construction of the temple, provided they meet 31 conditions outlined by the Office of Consolidated Hearings. In the preamble of the final report, the Office of Consolidated Hearings acknowledged the rights of the Lao community to practice the 'devotional and cultural holidays associated with the Buddhist religion and their Laotian culture' (Government of Ontario Document 2001: 2 – this wording offers an example of government recognition of Canada's commitment to multiculturalism by ensuring the continuation of ethnicity among various cultures living within Canadian society). The Office of Consolidated Hearings also acknowledged the broader function of religion when it stated '. . . and like many denominations there will also be some associated social and institutional uses of the building' (Government of Ontario Document 2001: 10). This focused on the underlying concern of those who were opposed to Wat Lao Veluwanaram – the ethnic differences in how the Laotian Buddhist community celebrate their religion as embedded within their culture. Laotian Buddhists hold some events which unite the collective memories of the Lao, such as the Lao New Year in April. As indicated above, many letters in opposition to the construction of the Lao Buddhist temple in Caledon questioned the authenticity of this community's Buddhist practice, as their practices did not match the previously held assumptions such citizens had of the Buddhist tradition.

The Lao endured a considerable amount of hardship through their experience as a refugee community, having regrouped and recreated their identity and religion. When faced with opposition from their neighbours in the Caledon temple struggle, they required both tenacity and financial resources. During the final hearings, the environmental concerns raised by objectors who pushed for secondary peer reviews and independent studies were not carried forward into the hearing. This left the issue of cultural difference front and centre. The struggle for a religio-ethnic community's recognition is decided in courts of law, in this case only after that cultural community was able to provide for their own defense and had the financial ability to do so; but while the government ideal of multiculturalism was upheld after four years of legal proceedings, the provisos issued by both the Office of Consolidated Hearings and the Town of Caledon indicated an underlying favouring of the hegemonic culture.

Multiculturalism

It could be argued that while Canadian federal multicultural policy addresses ethnicity it does not address religiosity. Many ethnic-based religious groups must compete with one another for limited 'power and resources' made available through government funding, but only to cultural, not religious, organizations (Matthews 2002: 131). Rather than recognizing an ethnic community's cultural and religious collective difference together, the religious aspect is left out of the equation. This is what Taylor refers to as 'difference-blindness' (Taylor 1994: 40). Paradoxically, society is asked simultaneously to ignore the differences, upholding the universal principal of equality, and to appreciate the uniqueness of each culture.

The notion that existing multiculturalism policies stifle ethnic communities is expressed by Phayvanh Phoumindr in assessing Australian multicultural policies. The author contends that the necessity to adhere to a dominant discourse, leaving community differences aside, is a form of government 'control' (Phoumindr 1995: 8), where one is free to be different but for political recognition must kowtow to a majority's preconceived notions of Buddhism and European Christian cultural hegemony. Something is reflected in the Caledon temple affair. To obtain political recognition the Lao community must remain a unified voice and adapt to the expectations of the dominant culture. One of the conditions for the approval of the site plan is that the temple conform to the natural landscape in such a way as to blend into the land, both aesthetically and physically. To further emphasize the point, a row of cedars must be planted to shield the temple from the view of neighbours and motorists along the major artery. While the Office of Consolidated Hearings upheld the Laotian community's right to practice their religion based on multicultural ideology, the practical outcome is that the temple must hide so as not to disturb the hegemonic culture.

Peter Li's assessment of current multicultural practice in Canada, like Phayvanh Phoumindr's on Australian policy, perceives multiculturalism as an ideal only (Li 1999: 169). Yet parts of the current Multicultural Act (1988) are supposed to bolster cultural group cohesion and agency. Unfortunately these policies were compromised in 1993 when the Department of Race Relations and Multicultural Affairs was divided into the Department of Citizenship and Immigration and the Department of Canadian Heritage respectively. This effectively removed programs of multiculturalism from immigration and refugee contexts, realigning connotations of multiculturalism with notions of heritage. Public policy on multicultural issues shifted from inter-group dialogue and enhancing the development of communities to the more traditionally focused mindset of heritage, such as language. It now speaks to the issues of rights, ownership and a dominant heritage. Li claims this downgrading of multiculturalism – from immigration needs to something more reflective of mere cultural legacy – is a feature of what amounts to racism, something favouring of a more assimilative stance, a response to the large influx of immigrants that marked the times (Li 1999: 158). There was no provision of effective programs to assist the negotiations which must inevitably take place when two different cultures interact.

Racism: fear of the other, loss of power

Wat Lao Veluwanaram is one of many temples throughout North America which have had to fight for their cultural difference in courts of law. Repeatedly they have made concessions to appease the cultural hegemony milieu in which they find themselves. Seager states that it is the 'local zoning boards, which often serve as the immigrant's first encounters with American bureaucracy' (Seager 1999: 142; see also Krulfeld 1992; Eck [2001] 2002: 296).[8] Eck notes that 'the first response to difference is often suspicion and fear' and that religious difference is often 'conflated with race' (Eck [2001] 2002: 301).

Multicultural ideals can be seen as divisive. Ronald Skeldon states that 'nation states can feel challenged by diasporas' (Skeldon 1997: 218). His concern is that diaspora groups are encouraged to maintain their difference through continued ties with the homeland, at the expense of forming new ties with their host country. The notion that multiculturalism is a nationally divisive force whereby the new immigrants are not integrating with their new country, as Skeldon maintains, is not supported by data, indeed arguably the 'opposite is occurring' (Tepper 1997: 53). Rather than dividing the country into enclaves of ethnic groups, multiculturalism fosters Canadian identity and citizenship. Wat Lao Veluwanaram's Buonmy Sihaphom supports this view. Arriving as a refugee, he now is committed to remaining in Canada and greatly admires the country's policies of multiculturalism, which enable his community to retain their cultural traditions.

In order to receive political recognition many ethnic communities strive to be, in Pyong Gap Min's words, 'model minorities' (Gap Min 1995b: 52). However, this recognition comes with a price as the group must maintain their model minority status, which entails performing a role acceptable to the dominant culture, or, as Alan Simmons suggests, 'racism is based on "othering"' (Simmons 1997: 30). The role to be performed is the stereotype of 'Indian-ness', 'Chinese-ness' or 'Japanese-ness', which has been determined through a largely Caucasian and Christian European lens. Whenever the inferior/minority status is threatened by the success of ethnic groups, consequently shifting the stereotypes, some in the dominant culture will react with hostility as they fear the viability of their own culture is threatened (Simmons 1997: 35).

Racism is exacerbated when resources are perceived to be in short supply. During the mid-1980s, just after the arrival of thousands of Asian refugees and immigrants, there was an economic slowdown and minor recession in Canada. What had been an outpouring of support and accommodation toward refugee groups in certain circumstances turned into a backlash kind of racism which steadily increased through to the late 1990s (Tepper 1997: 59–62) as groups vied for 'power, resources and cultural dominance' (Simmons 1997: 30). Immigrants were blamed as competition for jobs increased and refugees resented for receiving assistance from government programs (Rumbaut 1995: 233). (Both of the above points are brought forward in the documentary *Blue Collar and Buddha*, which interviews labourers in Rockford, Illinois to solicit their reaction to the Lao community during an economic slow down.)

Conclusion

Pluralism and multiculturalism are two-edged swords. These concepts can be viewed as either divisive, unifying or both simultaneously. As Eck notes, pluralism is not equated with diversity; rather than tolerating 'difference' it is a relationship with 'difference' (Eck [2001] 2002: 70–2). The key lies in the concept of relationship. Establishing effective policies which foster relationship provides a means for reaching out to the ideal of equality. Eck avers that delegitimatizing a religion is a form of destructive religious prejudice as the 'other's' religion is not recognized as having any 'value' (Eck [2001] 2002: 301). Several of the letters addressed to the Town of Caledon's office attempted to delegitimize the Lao Buddhist tradition by indicating that it did not appear to be a recognizable and legitimate form of Buddhism. The attempt to undermine the legitimacy of a tradition would bring about far reaching implications, such as the loss of tax relief for religious institutions, the loss of recognition within the political and multicultural arena, and the incapability of participating in interfaith dialogues or building a place of worship. The power of the dominant culture is immense should programs not be in place to negotiate differences in cultural and religious practices.

Although environmental and traffic issues were the concerns expressed to the Town of Caledon Council Chambers and the Office of Consolidated Hearings, the underlying concern was the issue of cultural, social and recreational usage for what was deemed a religious institution. As Zhou makes clear, 'the temple is intended to preserve Laotian culture' (Zhou *et al.* 2002: 57). Given the historical arrangement whereby religion and ethnicity overlap, it becomes clear that 'Buddhism is an important culture-specific support system for Asian immigrants and refugees' (McLellan 1999: 217).

Li, Matthews, and Phoumindr imply that current notions of multiculturalism and pluralism paradoxically raise issues of segregation, competition and the privatization of culture, or separation of culture and state. This paradox is because of the theoretical nature of the policies. Neither Australia nor Canada offer practical programs which instill active engagement and relationship building between cultures. As a result cultures, like religions (Berger 1969: 130), are deemed private affairs where diversity is reductive rather than relational, isolating religious and cultural groups and leaving the hegemonic culture unchallenged. Consequently those groups with larger numbers are better able to compete for resources, while those groups that have been marginalized are less able to compete for power, and political recognition.[9]

By establishing a temple in Caledon, the Lao community of the Toronto area are presenting a visible identification marker to their existing community, giving voice to the old traditions and new contextual milieu in order to arrive at a collective meaning that resonates within their membership. This recreation of identity is an ongoing process, especially for the refugee, providing the drive to reconceptualize their identity in relation to the new culture, homeland, and to other diaspora groups. The Laotian community and the Caledon residents continue to recreate their identity by virtue of interacting with each other. The community of Wat Lao Veluwanaram have taken a momentous step in establishing their temple and their voice within the multi-cultural arena. The visible marker of the temple now demands recognition as a legitimate religious and ethnic phenomenon. As this paper indicates, the response to this ultimate political recognition was a mixture of animosity and welcome. The opponents had the financial and legal wherewithall to delay the project for four years, a timely and costly delay for the Lao community. Ultimately those opposed to the temple had no legal grounds to do so, but their opposition almost exhausted the social capital accumulated by the Laotian community. The effort to establish Wat Lao Veluwanaram demonstrates the dominance of the white Christian culture in mainstream Canada, and the struggle of a differing religio-ethnic group to gain recognition within a country that purportedly advocates multiculturalism.

Notes

1 The video *Blue Collar and Buddha* (1989) provides some excellent footage of interviews with Laotian refugees who address these various reasons for embracing Christianity.

2 An example of this lack of recognition can be seen in physician Matthew Suh's article 'Psychiatric Problems of Immigrants and Refugees' (1980) in which he never makes reference to the notion of religious specialists as a viable alternative to the mental health profession in assisting immigrants and refugees in overcoming their mental anguish.

3 It is particularly telling that the Canadian government did not sponsor Lao monks, as they were not considered skilled labour; rather they were privately sponsored (Van Esterik 1992: 57). This would seem to bolster the notion that religious specialists were not considered essential to multiculturalism ideals as ethnicity is thought to be areligious.

4 The Baci-Sou Khuan ritual traditionally recalls the 32 souls believed to reside in a human being. It is a 'refreshing' or 'regrouping' act which has symbolically altered within the North American context to reflect the refugee experience and the regrouping of both the community and the individual.
5 The name Veluwanaram is the same as that of the first temple in which the Buddha resided in India following his enlightenment. It means 'bamboo', from which the Indian temple was most likely constructed.
6 This is the commencement of the rain-retreat in traditional Theravāda Buddhist practice. The countries of Southeast Asia experience heavy monsoons between July and October. Historically the monks would withdraw from the community to the forest.
7 Similar complaints are expressed in the material collected in the 'Pluralism Project' and reported in Diana Eck's book *A New Religious America* (Eck [2001] 2002: 330); see also the Vietnamese 'Bixby Temple' story.
8 Diana Eck's book *A New Religious America* ([2001] 2002) has many examples of disputes, such as the Hsi Lai Temple's five-year court case. Of particular note is a section entitled 'Not in this Neighbourhood'.
9 For example, by converting to Christianity, the Hmong gained the ability to compete for political recognition, which they would garner as a small marginalized culture of non-Buddhist Lao (see Winland 1992: 96–119).

Bibliography

Anderson, Benedict (1983) *Imagined Communities: Reflections on the Spread of Nationalism*. London: Verso.
Berger, Peter L. (1969) *The Sacred Canopy: Elements of a Sociological Theory of Religion*. New York: Doubleday.
Blue Collar and Buddha (1989) Producer Taggert Siegel. Film Makers Library: 57mins. Canadian Multiculturalism Act C-18.7: 1988. www.pch.gc.ca/progs/multi/policy/act_e.cfm
Canda, Edward R. (1992) "Buddhism as a Support System for Southeast Asian Refugees," *Social Work*, 37(1): 61–7.
Donaldson, Ian (2004) "Identity, Intersections of Diversity and the Multiculturalism Program," *Canadian Diversity*, 3(1): 14–16.
Eck, Diana ([2001] 2002) *A New Religious America*. San Francisco, CA: HarperCollins.
Gap Min, Pyong (1995a) "An Overview of Asian Americans," in Pyong Gap Min (ed.) *Asian Americans: Contemporary Trends and Issues*. Thousand Oaks, CA: Sage Publications.
—— (1995b) "Major Issues Relating to Experiences," in Pyong Gap Min (ed.) *Asian Americans: Contemporary Trends and Issues*. Thousand Oaks, CA: Sage Publications.
Gordon, Napat Sirisumbhand (1990) "Women's Role in Adaptive Strategies Among Laotian Refugee Families in the Toronto Area." York, ON: North York Faculty of Environmental Studies, York University.
Government of Ontario Document (2001) Office of Consolidated Hearings, Toronto Case No. 00-021.
Krulfeld, Ruth (1992) "Cognitive Mapping and Ethnic Identity: Changing Concepts of Nationalism and Community in the Laotian Diaspora," in Pamela DeVoe (ed.) *Selected Papers on Refugee Issues*. Washington, DC: American Anthropological Association.

—— ([1994] 1999) "Buddhism, Maintenance and Change: Reinterpreting Gender in a Lao Refugee Community," in Linda Camino and Ruth Krulfeld (eds) *Reconstructing Lives, Recapturing Meaning: Refugee Identity, Gender, and Culture Change.* Singapore: Gordon & Breach.

Kurien, Prema (1998) "Becoming American by Becoming Hindu: Indian Americans Take Their Place at the Multicultural Table," in Steven Warner and Judith G. Wittner (eds) *Gatherings in Diaspora: Religious Communities and the New Immigration.* Philadelphia, PA: Temple University Press.

LeBar, Frank and Suddard, Adrienne ([1960] 1967) *Laos: Its People, Its Society, Its Culture.* New Haven, CT: HRAF.

Li, Peter S. (1999) "The Multicultural Debate," in Peter Li (ed.) *Race and Ethnic Relations in Canada.* Oxford: Oxford University Press.

Matthews, Bruce (2002) "Buddhism in Canada," in Martin Baumann and Charles Prebish (eds) *Westward Dharma.* Berkeley, CA: University of California.

McLellan, Janet (1999) *Many Petals of the Lotus*: Five Asian Buddhist Communities in Toronto. Toronto, ON: University of Toronto Press.

Numrich, Paul (1996) *Old Wisdom in the New World: Americanization in Two Immigrant Theravāda Buddhist Temples.* Knoxville, TN: University of Tennessee Press.

Padgett, Douglas (2002) "The Translating Temple," in Martin Baumann and Charles Prebish (eds) *Westward Dharma.* Berkeley, CA: University of California.

Phoumindr, Phayvanh (1995) "Multiculturalism, Social Control and the Lao Community in Australia," *Lao Study Review* 1. www.global.lao.net/laostudy/multicom.htm

Rajah, Ananda (1990) "Orientalism, Commensurability, and the Construction of Identity: A Comment on the Notion of Lao Identity," *Sojourn*, 5(1): 308–22.

Royal, Peter (1980) "Laos: The Prince and the Barb," in Elliot Tepper (ed.) *Southeast Asian Exodus: From Tradition to Resettlement.* Ottawa, ON: Canadian Asian Studies Association.

Rumbaut, Ruben G. (1995) "Vietnamese, Laotian and Cambodian Americans," in Pyong Gap Min (ed.) *Asian Americans: Contemporary Trends and Issues.* Thousand Oaks, CA: Sage Publications.

Said, Edward (1978) *Orientalism.* New York: Vintage.

Seager, Richard (1999) *Buddhism in America.* New York: Columbia University.

Simmons, Alan (1997) "Globalization and Backlash Racism in the 1990's: The Case of Asian Immigration to Canada," in Eleanor Laquianr, Aprodicio Laquian and Terry McGee (eds) *Silent Debate: Asian and Immigration Racism in Canada.* Vancouver, BC: University of British Colombia Press.

Skeldon, Ronald (1997) "From Multiculturalism to Diaspora: Changing Identities in the Context of Asian Migration," in Eleanor Laquian, Aprodicio Laquian and Terry McGee (eds) *Silent Debate: Asian and Immigration Racism in Canada.* Vancouver, BC: University of British Colombia.

Suh, Matthew (1980) "Psychiatric Problems of Immigrants and Refugees," in Elliot Tepper (ed.) *Southeast Asian Exodus: From Tradition to Resettlement.* Ottawa, ON: Canadian Asian Studies Association.

Taylor, Charles (1994) "The Politics of Recognition," in Amy Gutmann (ed.) *Multiculturalism: Examining the Politics of Recognition.* Princeton, NJ: Princeton University Press.

Tepper, Elliot L. (1997) "Multiculturalism and Racism: An Evaluation," in Eleanor Laquian, Aprodicio Laquian and Terry McGee (eds) *Silent Debate: Asian and Immigration Racism in Canada.* Vancouver, BC: University of British Colombia.

Van Esterick, Penny (1992) *Taking Refuge: Lao Buddhists in North America.* Arizona State University Press.

—— (1999) "Ritual and the Performance of Buddhist Identity among Lao Buddhists in North America," in Duncan Williams and Charles Prebish (eds) *American Buddhism.* Surrey: Curzon.

Winland, Daphne (1992) "The Role of Religious Affiliation in Refugee Resettlement: The Case of the Hmong," *Canadian Ethnic Studies*, 24: 96–119.

Zhou, Min, Bankston, Carl L. III and Kim, Rebecca Y. (2002) "Rebuilding Spiritual Lives in the New Land: Religious Practices among Southeast Asian Refugees in the United States," in Pyong Gap Min and Jung Ha Kim (eds) *Religions in Asian America: Building Faith Communities.* Walnut Creek, CA: AltaMira.

7

BUDDHISM IN QUÉBEC

Louis-Jacques Dorais

The first Buddhist worshippers in Québec were most probably found among the Chinese immigrants who started to move from British Columbia to eastern Canada as early as the late 1880s. Most of them settled in Montréal (the city had only 33 Chinese residents in 1891 but 888 in 1901; cf. Chan 1991: 28); a few also went to smaller places such as Québec City, Sherbrooke and Hull (Dorais 1996: 5). The Chinese were followed later on by small numbers of Japanese and other Asian immigrants, who also included some Buddhists. It is difficult to assess – or even approximate – the number of practising Buddhists during this time. Presbyterian and Roman Catholic inland missions were particularly active among Asian Québecers, and many of them converted to Christianity, at least nominally. According to Helly (1987: 282), though, out of a total of 496 children born in Montréal between 1898 and 1951 from one or two Chinese parents, 268 (54 per cent) were not christened at birth. Their families' religious beliefs thus presumably included some Buddhist elements.

As late as 1970, only two Buddhist temples – one Chinese and one Japanese[1] – operated in Montréal, and none in the rest of the province. Buddhism in Québec really started to develop a few years after the last restrictions on Asian immigration to Canada were lifted in 1967. Successive waves of Chinese and Korean migrants, Tibetan, Indochinese and Sri Lankan refugees, and Japanese executives, as well as investor immigrants and restaurant chefs from Hong Kong, brought to our shores tens of thousands of Buddhists and Confucian Buddhists (this is how the Canadian census refers to practitioners of a Chinese blend of Confucianism, Taoism and Buddhism), who founded a rapidly growing number of temples and religious organizations. Their influence – and the general evolution of culture in late twentieth-century North America – also contributed to a renewed interest in Buddhism on the part of non-Asian Québecers, who visited temples and got into Zen and other forms of meditation in increasing numbers.[2] According to Canadian census data, the number of Buddhists living in Québec increased exponentially over a period of five decades, jumping from 378 in 1951 and 548 in 1961 to 1,490 in 1971, 12,005 in 1981, 31,640 in 1991, and 41,380 in 2001.

George Klima's Buddhismcanada.com website lists a total of 52 Buddhist temples and meditation centres found in Québec in 2001. The majority (36) were in Montréal and its suburbs, but 16 of them stood in outlying regions: six in Québec City (the capital of the province and its second largest metropolitan area); four in the Laurentians (just north of Montréal); four in the Eastern Townships (to the southeast of Montréal); and one each in Chicoutimi (along the Saguenay River) and Rimouski (on the lower south shore of the Saint Lawrence River). Significantly enough, 26 of these worship and meditation places were operated and frequented by francophone or anglophone non-Asian Québecers,[3] and six more had mixed Québecer-Asian congregations. This means that more than half of Québec's Buddhist centres belonged to the so-called Western tradition (see McLellan 1998: 231) and/or catered to a totality or majority of non-Asians.[4] In terms of number of adherents, however, Western Buddhists only accounted for some 8 per cent (3,500 individuals) of Québec's total, more than 90 per cent of the province's Buddhists being of Asian origin or ancestry. In 2004, Buddhist temples with a predominantly Asian congregation were distributed as follows: Vietnamese, seven (in Montréal); Vietnamese and Chinese, two (one each in Montréal and the Laurentians); Chinese, five (in Montréal); Lao, three (two in Montréal; one in the Laurentians); Khmer, two (in Montréal); Japanese, one (in Montréal). To these should be added the already mentioned 'mixed worship' centres. Four of them (all in Montréal) catered to both Tibetans and non-Tibetans,[5] and two (one in Québec City, another in the Eastern Townships) had a mixed Vietnamese and non-Asian congregation.

Sri Lankans and Koreans are notably absent from this data, although from a census perspective 8,475 of the former and 4,475 of the latter were living in Québec in 2001.[6] It is not known if they operate their own Buddhist temples (presumably in Montréal) or frequent other worship places. Significantly, Theravāda monks from the Sinhalese diaspora on occasion visit some of Québec's Vietnamese Buddhist temples, even if these belong to the Mahāyāna tradition.

The vast majority of Buddhist groups found in Québec are Mahāyāna, only nine out of 52 being Theravāda (three of these are Lao, two Khmer, one southern Vietnamese, and three Western). Among Mahāyāna Buddhist centres, ten belong to the Vajrayāna Tibetan tradition, the balance being mostly Pure Land and/or Zen.[7]

The 26 Buddhist groups whose followers are totally or preponderantly non-Asian generally practice various types of 'Western' Buddhism, however defined. Although these forms of worship and meditation differ from Asian Buddhism, they can be traced back to lineages originating in Asia. According to the Buddhismcanada.com website, a digest of these groups in Québec in 2001 included such Mahāyāna groups as those affiliated with Japanese Zen (13 groups, five in Montréal; four in Québec City; two in the Eastern Townships; one in the Laurentians; one in Rimouski); Soka Gakkai (two groups, one each in Montréal and Québec City); Gelupa (Tibetan, two groups, one each in Montréal and Chicoutimi);[8] Shambala (Tibetan, one group in Montréal); Kagyu (Tibetan, one group in Montréal); Rigpa (Tibetan, one group in Montréal); Tiep Hien (Vietnamese), three groups (in Montréal, though technically this is not classified as Western). In the Theravāda tradition, several groups have outreach to a Western devotional audience. These include Burmese Vipassanā (one group in the Eastern Townships); the International Buddhist Meditation Centre of Canada (IBMCC, one group in the Laurentians); and Friends of the Western Buddhist Order (one group in Montréal).

As can be seen, the preferred Buddhist tradition among Western Québecers is Zen meditation, which accounts for exactly half of all 26 preponderantly non-Asian groups. Zen is followed by various Vajrayāna Tibetan lineages, with a total of five groups, Tiep Hien Order (three groups), Theravāda meditation centres (three groups), and the Soka Gakkai association (two groups). Twelve of these non-Asian Buddhist centres lie outside the Montréal area.[9]

Vietnamese Buddhism

As an interesting case study, let us now direct our attention towards the religious organizations, beliefs and activities of Vietnamese Buddhists in Québec, who accounted for 30 per cent of the provincial total of Buddhist adherents in 2001. As elsewhere in Canada, most Vietnamese came to Québec either as refugees, between 1975 and the early 1990s (with a peak in 1979–82), or through family reunification programs. In contrast with other Canadian provinces, though, Québec already harboured, before 1975, a small (ca. 1,200 individuals) but active community of Vietnamese students and recent graduates who lived for the most part in Montréal and Québec City. When the first wave of refugees fleeing the extension of communist rule to South Vietnam started reaching Canada in mid-1975, 65 per cent of them resettled in Québec because they had relatives residing there. It is these students and first wave refugees who established the very first Vietnamese Canadian pagoda[10] at Brossard (now part of Longueuil, on the south shore of the Saint Lawrence River across from Montréal), in 1975.

In 2001, according to census data, 28,310 Vietnamese Canadians were living in the province of Québec. They accounted for 18.7 per cent of the 151,425 Canadian residents who had declared a unique or multiple Vietnamese ethnic origin to census takers. About 75 per cent of them followed the principles of *Tam Giao*, the 'Three Religions,' this intimate blend of Taoist cosmology, Confucian social ethics (which includes ancestor veneration), and Buddhist teachings on karma and reincarnation, that characterizes Vietnamese (and Chinese) philosophical and religious thinking.[11]

As Vietnamese are prone to mention, Buddhism was the first non-East Asian religious philosophy to enter Vietnam, in the second century CE. Vietnam then belonged to China,[12] and thus borrowed the Mahāyāna tradition which predominates in lands influenced by Chinese civilization.[13] From the thirteenth century on, however, Vietnamese kings found that Confucian philosophy was superior to Buddhism as far as ruling the state and constructing national unity were concerned. By way of consequence, Buddhism was progressively relegated to the rank of popular belief, without much formal training for monks, nuns, and lay persons. Paradoxically, French colonialism (1883–1954) and the Vietnam War (1954–75) precipitated a Buddhist renewal. After the demise of Confucianism as official ideology (but not as private family ethics) and model for state organization, Buddhism progressively came to symbolize a Vietnamese cultural identity put in jeopardy by the intrusion of the West. This new consciousness encouraged religious leaders to strengthen the theological and organizational bases of Buddhism. Drawing their inspiration from similar movements that were appearing all over Asia, they founded associations for Buddhist studies in Saigon (1931), Hue (1932) and Hanoi (1934).

After the installation of a communist regime in North Vietnam in 1954, Buddhism was persecuted in that part of the country. This situation extended to South Vietnam in 1975. It was only after 1990 that conditions improved, when the *Doi Moi* policy of economic and social reform was implemented. Even now, however, monks are still occasionally harassed, jailed, or assigned to forced residence.

In the south, Buddhism pursued its development after 1954, despite problems when Roman Catholic president Ngo Dinh Diem was in power (1955–63). In 1975, South Vietnamese Buddhism had become an important religious, social and educational force. It comprised three main groups, whose political positions regarding American involvement in Vietnam may have been at variance, but who were able to present a united front when necessary. It was this mix of beliefs and practices, at least nominally shared by a majority of the South Vietnamese population, that refugees – including some Buddhist monks and nuns – brought to Québec and the rest of Canada.

During the summer of 1975, a dozen refugees from Vietnam recently resettled in Montréal met together in order to establish a Vietnamese Buddhist community in Canada.[14] Most of them were men and women in their sixties and early seventies, and they had already been active on the religious scene when living in Vietnam. In September 1975, they founded the Lien Hoa (i.e. Lotus Flower) Group of Buddhist Adepts. Because their financial means did not enable them to build and maintain a pagoda, they had to be satisfied with a non-permanent prayer hall (*niem phat duong*). The principal of a school in Brossard, the town of residence of some influential adepts, lent a classroom in which an altar of the Buddha was laid out every Sunday, in front of which *sutras* were recited.

A problem arose during the 1976 summer holidays. The school closed and the Buddhists had no more access to their prayer hall. It was first decided to meet in the home of the president (a woman) of the newly established Vietnamese Buddhist Association in Canada, a formalization of the Lien Hoa Group. On Vu Lan (Filial Devotion) Day, however (8 August 1976), participants were so numerous that most of them had to stand outside the house. People then realized that it was time to have their own temple, and a committee was formed to collect donations, loans, and subscriptions. The sums thus accumulated enabled the Vietnamese Buddhist Association to buy a large lot in Brossard, in a residential area with direct bus link to a Montréal subway station. The temple was built within two months, from September to November 1977.[15] Statues of the Buddha were installed, and the Lien Hoa pagoda was formally inaugurated on 10 December by Venerable Thich Tam Chau, leader of one of the three main Buddhist groups active in South Vietnam before 1975, who was then residing in France. A few years later, Ven. Tam Chau moved to Montréal, where he took charge of the Brossard temple. With the progressive aging of its congregation, the Lien Hoa pagoda started playing an increasingly active role as purveyor of funeral services. In 1982, with the support of an association of Vietnamese Canadian senior citizens, the pagoda was granted a concession of 500 lots in Montréal's Eastern Cemetery. These were to be used by Vietnamese residents from the Montréal area, without consideration of religious affiliation. A huge granite monument was erected, bearing the inscription: 'Vietnamese Cemetery of Montréal.' That same year, the pagoda built a mausoleum to preserve the ashes of its deceased adepts who preferred to be cremated.

In the meanwhile, two members of the Vietnamese Buddhist clergy, Ven. Thich Thien Nghi and his niece Ven. Quang Oanh, had arrived in Montréal in June 1980, sponsored by the Lien Hoa congregation.[16] Ven. Thien Nghi had led another of South Vietnam's pre-1975 Buddhist factions, one based in Saigon in contrast with Thich Tam Chau's Hue-based group (in central Vietnam). Thich Thien Nghi and his niece first settled at Lien Hoa, but they left after three months because they felt that the temple was run by the laity and that they were not allowed enough leadership. As shall be seen later on, this type of conflict – ending in a schism – between clerics and laity, both claiming control over a temple's administration and material resources, is a recurring pattern among Montréal's (and other Canadian–Vietnamese Buddhist) congregations. The proliferation of Vietnamese Canadian pagodas during the 1980s is due in large part to such a process.

With the financial support of a group of adepts who had followed them when they left Lien Hoa, Ven. Thien Nghi and his niece rented an apartment in downtown Montréal which they transformed into a prayer hall. They also founded a second Vietnamese Canadian Buddhist group, the Community of Vietnamese Buddhists in Canada, thus perpetuating in a way the division between Thich Tam Chau's and Thich Thien Nghi's former South Vietnamese factions. The Community collected enough funds to purchase, in late 1981, a former synagogue in the Côte-des-Neiges area of Montréal, then heavily populated by Vietnamese, Cambodian and Laotian refugees. According to Soucy (1994: 25, note 8), it was believed that 'the building's former status of being a synagogue was beneficial, as the building therefore had already been put to sacred use.' The Tam Bao (Three Jewels) pagoda was inaugurated in June 1982. From then on, Tam Bao was known – to both ethnic and Chinese Vietnamese[17] – as an active centre for training Buddhist clergy and educating laity. In August 1983, Ven. Tam Chau ordained a monk and a nun, the first Vietnamese Buddhist clerics to receive ordination in North America. Five years later, Tam Bao pagoda established the Great Pine Forest Monastery in the Laurentian Mountains northwest of Montréal, in order to house an institute of Buddhist teaching, a library and a retreat centre.[18] In 1994, twelve novice monks and nuns were receiving their initial training at Tam Bao, before being sent to colleges and universities to complete degrees in religious studies.

The conflict and divisive process already mentioned affected the Tam Bao pagoda during its early years. In 1982, part of the congregation decided to leave. They wished that the material and financial administration of the temple be answerable to a committee of lay persons, the role of the clergy being strictly limited to spiritual matters. In March 1983, these secessionists founded the Quan Am[19] Buddhist Society and opened a chapel in a private apartment. They immediately started collecting funds for a new temple, which was built (in the Côte-des-Neiges area) and inaugurated a year and a half later. In 1986, a young Vietnamese monk then residing in Europe accepted the position as spiritual leader of the Quan Am pagoda, but conflict emerged again in 1987 and the monk left Quan Am in order to establish a new temple (Thuyen Ton), first in a residential apartment and subsequently in a separate building of the north-central part of Montréal.[20]

Another administrative conflict occurred at the Lien Hoa pagoda in 1985, when Ven. Thich Tam Chau left the temple and bought an old house in eastern downtown Montréal, where he established To Dinh Tu Quang (*Tu Quang* Ancestral Home). The mere name of the new foundation (*To Dinh* rather than *Chua*, 'pagoda') showed that for Ven. Tam Chau, Tu Quang was more than just a temple. He rather envisioned it as a global centre for developing traditional Vietnamese identity and spirituality.

More recent Vietnamese Buddhist pagodas in Montréal include Linh Thuu Thien Vien, founded in 1995 by Ven. Thich Quand Due,[21] as well as Tu Vien Huyen Khong, and the Bat Nha Thien Vien Theravāda temple. At the end of the 1980s, a group of Vietnamese intellectuals living in Montréal, who belonged to various local Buddhist congregations, established a study group devoted to the practice of *Thien* (Zen) meditation, according to the tradition of the Tiep Hien [Interbeing] Order, founded and directed by Ven.

Thich Nhat Hanh (who resides in France), a master of modern Buddhism. This group, called the Maple Buddhist Society, bought a lot at Saint-Étienne-de-Bolton, in Québec's Eastern Townships, where a large communal house (Lang Cay Phong, 'Maple Village') was inaugurated in 1989. Since then, retreats and meditation courses have been organized more or less on a regular basis, for both Vietnamese and non-Vietnamese adepts (the Tiep Hien Order operates three other meditation centres in Montréal).[22] Outside of the Montréal area, the only Vietnamese Buddhist congregation in the province is Québec City's Bo De (Banyan Tree) pagoda. In the fall of 1986, local Vietnamese started meeting every two weeks on Sundays in a downtown school hall in order to recite *sutras*. It took six years to collect sufficient funds to buy an old house in Beauport, an eastern suburb of Québec City, where a permanent temple was established in 1993. The Bo De pagoda never had a residing monk (it is formally headed by Ven. Thich Vien Dieu of the Thuyen Ton temple in Montréal), but since 2000, a Vietnamese Canadian trilingual nun has moved in, and she presides over most ceremonies. Québec City's Vietnamese Buddhist community is relatively small (it does not exceed 800 individuals), and only about thirty of them visit and support the pagoda on a regular basis. In order to survive, the Bo De temple thus had to enlarge its congregation by opening its doors to the general public. Right from the beginning, it attracted non-Vietnamese adepts in increasing numbers. At the same time, it became a major community centre for the area's Vietnamese Québecers, whatever their religious affiliation, who now gather there by the hundreds at least three times a year: for *Vesak* (Buddha's anniversary) in May, Vu Lan (Filial Devotion Day) in August, and Tet (Lunar New Year) in January or February. There may have been some misunderstandings at first between Vietnamese and non-Vietnamese adepts, the former feeling that 'their' temple was 'invaded' by 'strangers', but these problems seem to have been levelled out, and no parallel congregations or separate groups worshipping at the same place were formed. The type of Buddhism practised at Bo De has by no means become Westernized, however. The weekly Saturday morning services, as well as daily prayers, are conducted in Vietnamese, according to the Vietnamese Mahāyāna Pure Land ritual, and this includes preaching in the language of Vietnam. In fact, both Vietnamese and non-Vietnamese participate in the same Vietnamese ceremonies (hence the lack of parallel congregations), but in the course of that ceremony, the monk or nun may give a brief summary in French of what he/she has just said in his/her Vietnamese sermon. Besides that, however, the pagoda offers various activities, usually at night, specifically aimed at a French-speaking audience: 'full-consciousness' meditation; Tibetan meditation; classes by Buddhist masters representing different traditions (Vajrayāna, Theravāda, Zen).[23] Moreover, many non-Vietnamese of various faith backgrounds participate in the already mentioned *Vesak*, Vu Lan, and Tet celebrations.

Formal Buddhist organizations

As seen in the preceding section, most – if not all – Vietnamese Buddhist temples operating in Québec stem directly or indirectly, through a process of schism and division, from one original source: the Lien Hoa pagoda founded in 1975. Several temples in other Canadian cities (Ottawa, Toronto and Vancouver for instance) also trace their ultimate origin to Lien Hoa. Despite their proliferation (some forty Vietnamese Buddhist centres may now be found in Canada), Canadian – and other diasporic – Vietnamese pagodas do not operate in an anarchical way. Since 1979, efforts have been attempted to unify Buddhists living outside of Vietnam. This has resulted in the emergence of a number of transnational Vietnamese Buddhist networks, four of which operate in Québec and the rest of Canada: the World Vietnamese Unified Buddhist Order; the Union of Vietnamese Buddhist Churches in Canada; the Linh Son World Buddhist Congregation; and the Tiep Hien Order (Boisvert 2002).

In 1979, eighteen Vietnamese Buddhist clerics met in Washington, DC, where they founded the International Order of the Vietnamese Buddhist Sangha. Ven. Thich Tam Chau was elected as its Supreme Patriarch. The stated objectives of this organization were to coordinate the activities of Vietnamese Buddhists abroad, facilitate the religious training of monks and adepts, and work at the dissemination of Buddhist teachings. The Sangha also pledged to fight against the violation of human rights – more especially religious rights – in Vietnam, and to bring an active support to Vietnamese refugees. To reinforce Buddhist unity, a second meeting was held in November 1984 at the Lien Hoa pagoda in Brossard. Sixty delegates attended, representing fourteen Vietnamese Buddhist associations from the diaspora, four of them Canadian, seven American, and three French. After three days of discussion, it was decided to establish the World Vietnamese Unified Buddhist Order, which continued being presided by Ven. Thich Tam Chau (then head monk at Lien Hoa). The Order set itself two principal goals: to find a practical way to unify Vietnamese Buddhist associations around the world and develop cooperation among them; and to promote Buddhist teachings in accordance with the nationalist and democratic spirit of Vietnam.

The World Vietnamese Unified Buddhist Order now has affiliate pagodas in Montréal, Ottawa, Toronto, the United States, and various European countries. According to its members, Buddhism operates within a social, cultural and political context of opposition to the current communist regime in Vietnam. This is one reason why, as already mentioned, the Order's headquarters, Montréal's Tu Quang temple, is defined as a *To Dinh* (Ancestral Home) rather than a *chua* (pagoda). According to Boisvert (2002), monks trained at Tu Quang are not encouraged to study in secular environments. Together with clerics from other pagodas belonging to the Order, they must attend an annual monsoon retreat at Rawdon, near Montréal, where the

To Dinh owns a house. None of them – in Montréal at least – speaks any English or French.

Despite the Order's efforts towards unification, several Buddhist associations did not join it. As previously mentioned, at least three different Buddhist groups (one of them headed by Ven. Thich Tam Chau) had existed in pre-1975 South Vietnam, and Vietnamese Buddhists never recognized any central authority. This pattern was exported abroad. In August 1983, Ven. Thich Thien Nghi, the leader of another former South Vietnamese Buddhist faction, founded the General Vietnamese Buddhist Association in Canada, which later became the Unified Vietnamese Buddhist Congregation of Canada, also known as the Union of Vietnamese Buddhist Churches in Canada. Based at the Tam Bao pagoda, the Union maintains links with some fifteen temples throughout Canada, in Montréal, Toronto, Winnipeg, and a few other cities.[24] It caters to both ethnic and Chinese Vietnamese. Its four main objectives are: first, to disseminate religious doctrine; second, to support persecuted Buddhist adepts in Vietnam; third, to supervise a network of temples in Canada according to the Union's ways; and fourth, to train Vietnamese monks and nuns in order to fulfil the religious needs of Vietnamese communities within Canada and to educate young third-generation Vietnamese Canadian Buddhists. As already mentioned, Tam Bao and the Union encourage formal college-level education for their clerics-in-training, and most of these speak English and/or French (Boisvert 2002).

A third Vietnamese Buddhist network operating in Québec is the Linh Son (Vulture Peak) World Buddhist Congregation. Based in France, where it was founded by Ven. Thich Huyen Vi, it offers a somewhat ecumenical approach to Buddhism. According to Boisvert (2002), its executive board includes Pure Land, Vajrayāna, and Theravāda Buddhists from various ethnic backgrounds. Montréal's Linh Thuu Thien Vien temple, which opened in 1995, is attached to the Congregation. Besides Sunday services in Vietnamese, it offers meditation classes in English and French. The fourth Vietnamese Buddhist transnational network is the Tiep Hien ('Interbeing') Order, also known as the Unified Buddhist Church. Founded and headed by Ven. Thich Nhat Hanh (also a Buddhist leader in pre-1975 South Vietnam), it is based in Plum Village (Village des Pruniers), in southwestern France, but it operates several satellite centres in Europe and North America, including the already mentioned Maple Village (Lang Cay Phong) in the Eastern Townships, as well as meditation centres in Montréal. The Order emphasizes meditation rather than ritual and for this reason, several Vietnamese consider Tiep Hien as 'watered-down Buddhism' (Boisvert 2002). The preferred type of meditation is *Thien* (Zen), but Thich Nhat Hanh insists on joy, relaxation and flexibility rather than on the rigid formality often associated with Zen. All of Tiep Hien religious teachers, whether lay people or monks, are considered as belonging to the *sangha*, another point of divergence with common Vietnamese Buddhism (McLellan 1999: 232, note 6).

Québec's Tiep Hien meditation centres target both Vietnamese and non-Vietnamese, who generally participate separately in meditation retreats. Some of these are ministered to in Vietnamese, others in English or French. Vietnamese members of the Order usually go to other Montréal pagodas for ritual celebrations, though some ceremonies, including weddings, were celebrated at Maple Village up until 2003. According to McLellan (1999: 214), Tiep Hien is more global and transnational than most other forms of Buddhism, though its 'religious tradition remains grounded in culturally specific norms and organizational structures that reflect a particularized Vietnamese Buddhist culture.'

The vernacular Vietnamese Buddhist tradition

The culturally specific Vietnamese religious tradition mentioned by McLellan is based, of course, on common Mahāyāna Buddhist practices, teachings and beliefs which need not be described here. However, it may be interesting to expose parts of these: the way they are retold and re-enacted by Vietnamese Québecers.[25] All of Québec's (and, presumably, most other diasporic locations) Vietnamese pagodas present a more or less similar look. A relatively vast prayer hall built – out of respect – on the uppermost floor, or at least on a level higher than the ground, contains several altars, including a high altar supporting statues representing the principal entities of the Buddhist pantheon. These can either be characters belonging to the original Buddhist tradition, or Chinese and Vietnamese spirits and deities which the adepts' devotion added to the pantheon in a more or less remote past. The first category includes Buddhas (*Phat*) who have escaped the circle of reincarnations and reached *nirvāna* – or, at least, who have been illuminated – as well as *bodhisattvas* (*Bo-tat*) who will reach illumination and *nirvāna* during their next existence or at the end of their present life. At the centre of the high altar one always finds Buddha Sakyamuni (*Thich Ca Mau Ni Phat*),[26] the historical Buddha, the Indian prince Siddhartha Gautama. For most Vietnamese Buddhists, their faith can be summarized as follows: as long as one does not realize that the world as perceived is ephemeral, one will go through successive reincarnations.[27] The nature of reincarnation (divine, human, animal) is a function of the merits accumulated during one's latest existence – this is one's karma (*kiet-ma*). It is only once one has been illuminated, i.e. has reached perfect consciousness through renouncing desire, that one can escape the cycle of life and suffering to dissolve into non-being, *nirvāna* (*Niet-ban*). As soon as he had been illuminated, Buddha Thich Ca Mau Ni started preaching Truth. Disciples gathered around him and constituted the first monastic community, or *sangha* (*Cong doan Phat giao*). It is only when he was sure that his teachings would be transmitted to the world that the Buddha departed existence for a last time and reached *nirvāna*. In Vietnamese Canadian pagodas, to the right of Thich Ca Mau Ni (when facing his statue), on the same altar or, more generally, on a separate altar, one finds the statue of the feminine Bodhisattva Quan The Am[28] or, in abridged form, Quan Am (Guan Yin in Chinese, Kannon in Japanese). 'She who hears the screams of those suffering below.' Popular legend tells that Quan Am was a young woman who took refuge in a pagoda disguised as a monk, because she had been unjustly suspected of having killed her husband. A girl living in the neighbourhood fell in love with her, thinking that Quan Am was a male novice. After having been repelled, the girl consoled herself with a local boy who made her pregnant. By way of revenge, she accused Quan Am of being the father of her baby. Full of compassion for the child, Quan Am adopted it and raised it rather than confronting the girl. It is only after her death that truth was finally discovered. Because of her merits, Quan Am was thence venerated as a *bodhisattva*, the 'Mother of Mercy.'

Assisting Buddha A Di Da (see below) in his vow to bring salvation to all beings, Quan Am can, it is believed, take 32 different forms to accomplish her task. She has donated 14 virtues to humanity. Her effigies represent her under one of her 32 forms. In many Buddhist temples of the Vietnamese diaspora (Brossard's Lien Hoa pagoda for instance), she is venerated under the guise of Quan Am Nam Hai (Quan Am of the South Sea), in which, standing on a lotus, she floats on the waters of the South China Sea. Buddhists have great confidence in the immense powers and unlimited mercy of Quan Am. She responds immediately to those who invoke her. Adepts pray to her when in danger or in pain, or when they wish to have a child. She was thus invoked by boat people during storms or when attacked by pirates, and is seen as a merciful and caring mother, shared by all human beings.[29] This is why her popularity far exceeds that of any other *bodhisattva*. To the left of Thich Ca Mau Ni (when facing the altar), one finds the statue of Bodhisattva Dia Tang Bo Tat (Ksittigarbha). Like Quan Am, he is a *bodhisattva* of mercy. He possesses the power to save souls which, because of their evil deeds, must suffer in Hell while waiting for a distant reincarnation. Dia Tang Bo Tat is, thus, considered as the King of Hell. He vowed not to enter Nirvana as long as the subterranean world would not have been emptied of souls. He is represented with a toque on his head, holding a metal stick in his right hand and a jewel in his left. The stick symbolizes his strong will and the jewel his intelligence. For vernacular Buddhism, though, Dia Tang uses the former to break Hell's door open (in order to free humanity), and the latter to give light to liberated souls and show them the way. At a deeper level, Dia Tang symbolizes the radiance of the spirit, because he has been delivered through illumination (the diamond) and the exercise of a strong will (the stick).

This *bodhisattva* is always figured on funeral altars[30] and in mausoleums. Thich Ca Mau Ni has put him in charge of watching over the souls of the deceased, in order to assist them and bring them from darkness to light. He is asked to help people escaping the cycle of rebirth or, at least, having an easy reincarnation. His support is especially solicited during the first 49 days after death, the period during which, many believe, the soul is awaiting its judgement.

A fourth character plays an important part in the Buddhist pantheon: Buddha Amitabha (A Di Da Phat), the 'Buddha Without Quantity,' an allusion to his infinite power. He is a former human sovereign who has now become King of Heaven. He resides to the west of the universe, in his paradise called Tinh Do ('Pure Land'). This paradise is distant of thousands and thousands of 'Buddhist Lands' (*Phat Do*) from our world, which means that the distance between Heaven and Buddhist adepts depends essentially on the 'religious heart' of the latter. If they possess a pious heart and an illuminated spirit, paradise is already within them.

Pure Land is said to be fashioned out of precious stones and auriferous sands, and strewn with flowers and fountains. Celestial music is heard and beautiful birds can be seen. All of its inhabitants are skilful at discussing Buddhist doctrine. Desire, attachment, birth, illness, old age and death are totally unknown in Pure Land. In principle, this paradise is reserved for *boddhisattvas*, the quasi-illuminated beings who are awaiting final deliverance and entry into *nirvāna*, but A Di Da is ready to welcome anyone appealing to him with a pure heart. He has even vowed not to enter *nirvāna* himself as long as all beings who have asked to access Pure Land will not have been hearkened to. This is why he is frequently prayed to. In Vietnam's older pagodas, A Di Da stands at the centre of the high altar. In modern temples, however, as well as in those of the diaspora, this position belongs to Sākyamuni (Thich Ca Mau Ni). This way of doing things is more in conformation with the original tradition, which venerates primarily the historical founder of Buddhism. In Québec's pagodas, the effigy of A Di Da is not included among the three principal statues. It is rather found on a secondary altar along a side wall or, if on the high altar, at the feet of Thich Ca's statue, in a smaller size. It sometimes appears in both of these positions.

Other characters may be represented in Buddhist temples: Ho Phap, the guardian of teaching; La Han, the guardian of the altar, and others. However, the pagodas of the diaspora, at least in Québec, are much less richly endowed with statues and effigies than those in Vietnam. In the homeland, a typical high altar may exhibit up to thirty different statues, without taking into account effigies standing on secondary altars. Sometimes, these statues and effigies represent characters who have nothing to do with Buddhism, such as the Jade Emperor – the supreme deity of popular Taoism – or the Polar Star.

In the Mahāyāna tradition, *sangha* – monks and nuns – are the only ones to practise the Buddhist way in all its fullness, because they live in poverty, chastity, meditation and prayer, and abstain from eating meat. As lay people are concerned, if they have faith, practise compassion and show some degree of moral discipline, salvation will be obtained by taking refuge in the Buddhas and *bodhisattvas*. Various schools of thought have developed through the centuries to explain how salvation can be reached. Three of these are present in Québec: Tinh Do, Thien, and Mat Tong. The Tinh Do (Pure Land) school, also called Amidism because of the prominent role played by Buddha Amitabha (A Di Da), is the most important. Vernacular Vietnamese Buddhism as it is practised by older people, especially women, stems from this school. Its doctrine is very simple. It is based on A Di Da's eighth (out of 48) vow for saving the world: 'Those who will have invoked me ten times will be admitted to my paradise.' The invocation most frequently heard is *Nam Mo A Di Da Phat* ('Hail, Buddha A Di Da').

This invocation is included in most prayers uttered by adepts. During some services, it must be repeated 108 times. It can be recited in four different ways: by invoking the name of A Di Da, in order to think about him; by murmuring the formula in one's mind (if this murmuring generates a sound, one must become conscious of the source and arrival point of this sound); by imagining that A Di Da is facing one and that one is sitting on a lotus; and by invoking A Di Da with one's own deepest concentration, because it is 'mind-only' which constitutes the absolute and eternal truth. When the adept has reached the fourth stage, his or her nature becomes lost in A Di Da's, and the Tinh Do paradise lies within his/her heart. Conscious repetition of the *Nam Mo A Di Da Phat* formula is more than a simple prayer. It leads to an inner state of peace which can produce positive effects: forgetting about daily troubles; not having time to think about evil; preserving a serene mind; being admitted to the Pure Land paradise after one's death. To be really efficient, though, the invocation to the Buddha must be uttered with faith. It is essential that the adept believe in A Di Da's limitless power, in the existence of his paradise, and in the usefulness of prayer. He or she must also consciously express the wish to enter the Tinh Do paradise directly after death.

The Tinh Do school thus offers a path towards salvation which is accessible to everyone, is easy to understand, and whose practice is simple. This explains its popularity. Faith in a Buddha saviour, who generously offers his support to lead one towards paradisiac happiness, is very attractive to Vietnamese Buddhists. According to tradition, and as shown by his name, Buddha A Di Da ('Without Quantity') possesses unlimited powers. This is why he is also invoked under appellations which define some of these powers: *Vo luong to Phat* ('Buddha of Immense Longevity'), *Vo luong cong Duc Phat* ('Buddha of Immense Virtue'), *Vo luong quang Phat* ('Buddha of Immense Light').

The Thien – or Meditation – school, better known in the West under its Japanese name of Zen, attracts a number of Vietnamese from Québec. It is particularly appealing to highly educated individuals, intellectuals, and younger people in general. This school teaches that salvation is primarily based on personal initiative. In order to be illuminated, adepts must practise meditation frequently and regularly. This consists in trying to reach full consciousness – which opens the path towards knowledge – through various respiratory and contemplative techniques. Buddhist meditation provokes beneficial effects, physical (on the circulation of fluxes of energy) as well as mental (a serenity of mind that helps to fight stress, solitude and anxiety). As already indicated, Thien is the favourite meditation technique of the Tiep Hien Order. Several pagodas also tend to combine the practice of Tinh Do with that of Thien. The former is aimed at the general population, while the latter appeals to educated individuals and to young people.

A third Buddhist school to be found among Québec Vietnamese is Mat Tong, or Tantric Buddhism. It teaches that the universe is filled with cosmic energies that man can put into use. In such a context, the Buddha himself is a 'Cosmic Body,' an 'Ultimate Reality' from which emanates a light which radiates over the world: 'Man's salvation consists in reaching, through sacred actions, identification and union with the Corpus of Buddha's Law' (Nguyen 1981: 334, my translation). It is principally through the use of ritual performance (mantras, visualization) that one can enter into contact with cosmic energy and fulfil one's wishes, illumination in particular. Tantric meditation consists in erasing all consciousness of one's ego to visualize a Buddha with which one becomes identified in thought. This identification enables one to get access to the qualities of mind characterized by that particular manifestation of Buddha being visualized or invoked.[31]

Practically speaking, on chosen occasions (such as the Lunar New Year or the feast day of Buddha Duoc Su Phat, 'Master of Remedies'), the adepts of Tantric Buddhism utter mantras (*phu*) in Sanskrit, which may be found in prayer books or given during a blessing ceremony.[32] Monks also perform mudras (*bat an*, 'sacred gestures'), while reciting mantras during some ceremonies.

Buddhist ceremonies and festivals in Québec

Besides individual prostration and offerings of incense, Buddhist ceremonies essentially consist of prayers chanted by monks, nuns, and adepts. These prayers are partly unintelligible to the lay people – and to some clergy too – because not a few of them are in Sanskrit.[33] Prayer ceremonies are generally followed by a homily during which a monk explains Buddhist Law, or *dharma* (*Dat-ma*). *Dharma* is transcribed and discussed in Vietnamese and Chinese books (the Buddhist Scriptures) kept in the temple. In most of Québec's pagodas, a daily memorial prayer is offered to the deceased. Many Buddhists entrust temples with wooden tablets bearing the name and photograph of their deceased relatives, so that these may be protected by the Buddha. These tablets are laid on a side altar, in the main prayer hall or in a separate room. Every day, at noon and in the evening, a monk or nun offers incense and prayers to help these people with their reincarnation.

In most pagodas of the diaspora, the main service is held on Sunday – or, in a few temples, on Saturday – the only day of the week when adepts have time enough to devote themselves to religious activities. This service, where chanted prayers alternate with homilies, can last for several hours. It is briefly interrupted around noon for a vegetarian meal taken in common.[34] Special ceremonies are held on the first and fourteenth days of each month according to the Chinese lunar calendar. Prayers and practice then deal with abstinence, and adepts are expected to fast or, at least, to adopt a vegetarian diet.

Many festivals (e.g., the Birth of Buddha Thich Ca Mau Ni; the Celebration of Bodhisattva Quan Am) are the occasion of special prayer services. Most temples add to their religious calendar a number of festivals inspired by Vietnamese tradition and without any direct link with Buddhism, such as Tet, the Lunar New Year in late January or early February; the anniversary of the Trung Sisters, two heroines of the first century CE (sixth day of the second lunar month); the anniversary of King Hung, ancestor of the Vietnamese people (tenth day of the third month); Vu Lan, the Buddhist celebration of the Dead, which also celebrates filial devotion (fifteenth day of the seventh month); and the Mid-Autumn festival for children (*Tet Trung Thu*), on the fifteenth day of the eighth month.

Some events of family life can also be celebrated at the pagoda: weddings, memorial services for the recently deceased, and death anniversaries. More formal Buddhist weddings are a recent custom that seems to have appeared in the diaspora.[35] After a ceremony during which the monk reminds the bride and groom of their conjugal responsibilities, the guests share in a vegetarian meal. On the occasion of memorial services and death anniversaries, prayers are offered asking A Di Da to welcome the deceased in his Pure Land. The funerals themselves are not held in the pagoda but at the home of the deceased – or, increasingly, in a funeral parlour – and at the cemetery, where the officiating monk chants prayers for the dead.

Some devotional practices are restricted to a smaller number of adepts. This is the case with *Tinh Do*. Every Sunday during late afternoon, in several of Montréal's pagodas, devotees line up before the altar of A Di Da. Each of them holds with both hands a paper lotus flower on which his or her Buddhist name is inscribed. The officiating monk or nun then recites the 48 vows of A Di Da. Adepts respond and prostrate themselves, after which everybody forms a file, headed by the monk or nun, and walk around the hall repeating the formula *Nam Mo A Di Da Phat*, in order to get access to the Pure Land paradise. At the beginning of each month, in a few temples, small groups of adepts may practise *Tho bat quan trai*. During twenty-four hours they live like a cleric: praying, reflection of the Buddhist scripture, in silence and isolation from the outside. Once a year, a ten-day retreat (*An cu*), at the rate of a few hours a day, also gives the laity an opportunity to taste religious life.

Buddhism can also be practised at home. Numerous houses and apartments harbour a small altar with an effigy of Quan Am or A Di Da, to which offerings of incense, fruits and prayers are made. Some people, especially older women, recite the Buddhist service daily at home. Such a practice is common during the 49 or 100 days following the death of a close relative, if one cannot make regular visits to the temple. Many individuals – women in particular – wear a medal or a statuette representing a being from the Buddhist pantheon, most often Quan Am. A kind of rosary is also used, whose 108 beads help in counting invocations.

Social and cultural activities

Besides celebrating services and teaching Buddhism, pagodas generally play an important social, cultural, and even political part within Québec's Vietnamese community. Far from just being worship places, they also operate as ethnic centres which contribute to the preservation of Vietnamese identity abroad. This role is explicitly mentioned in the charter of some Buddhist organizations. That of the Vietnamese Buddhist Association of Canada, for instance, stipulates that the objectives of the Lien Hoa pagoda, besides venerating the Three Precious Jewels (the Buddha, the Dharma and the Sangha), consist in perpetuating ancestors' worship, symbolizing traditional Vietnamese culture, and encouraging comprehension and compassion among compatriots. In a similar way, the Quan Am Buddhist Society has defined two objectives: teaching Buddhism, and working towards the preservation and promotion of Vietnamese culture. This explains why, as mentioned in the preceding section, Québec's temples often combine both Buddhist and traditional Vietnamese festivals and ceremonies. In this way, they fulfil some of the functions which, in Vietnam, were – and still are in some locations – attributed to the *Dinh*, the communal house found in towns and villages, where the cult of local heroes and spirits was celebrated.[36]

This interest in social and cultural concerns becomes manifest in several ways. On many occasions, the Lien Hoa pagoda has witnessed the accession of some of its members to Canadian citizenship. In the presence of a federal judge, they swore allegiance to the Queen of Britain and Canada, their right hand on the *Dieu Phap Lien Hoa* Buddhist prayer book. Lien Hoa's congregation also persuaded the Brossard municipal council to change the name of Place Sahara, one of the town's streets, to Place Saigon! Several Buddhist temples work in collaboration with local associations of Vietnamese senior citizens, thus serving as community centres for elderly Vietnamese people who live in the area. Some pagodas do not hesitate to organize more overtly political activities, such as the annual commemoration of 30 April 1975, when communist forces entered Saigon, or 10 December, the International Day for Human Rights. A pre-1975 South Vietnamese patriotic anthem may be sung at the beginning of important celebrations (*Vesak* for instance).

Many activities, mostly held on Saturdays and Sundays, are directed to young adepts. These include religious undertakings such as the teaching of Buddhism, but also cultural activities: Vietnamese language courses; lectures on the geography and history of Vietnam; traditional dance and music and so on. A number of Montréal's pagodas have formed their own troops of Boy Scouts and Girl Guides, as well as other groups for children and youngsters. Excursions and summer camps are organized, and young people are offered the opportunity to take part in various community activities, including the publishing of a number of religious and cultural newsletters and magazines.

Conclusion

One among various Buddhist traditions present in the province of Québec, Vietnamese Mahāyāna Buddhism – like most other immigrant religious traditions – plays a double role: it enables its adepts to connect with a spiritual universe and a world view with which they are familiar, while giving them the opportunity to express an ethnic identity they often perceive as jeopardized by emigration. Even if identification between Buddhism and ancestral culture is not as developed in Vietnam and the diaspora as it is among the Lao, Khmer, or Tibetans, the activities of most of Québec's Vietnamese pagodas go far beyond strict Buddhist teachings and practices – for example, the relatively high number of specifically Vietnamese festivals celebrated in pagodas, or the emphasis laid on ancestor veneration and filial devotion. Some temples like the Lien Hoa pagoda and To Dinh Tu Quang operate partially as traditional communal houses (*dinh*), thus fulfilling functions answerable to both Buddhism and the basic family religion. This presents a strong contrast with Vietnam, where the Buddhist temple (*chua*) and the communal house are completely separate institutions.

The role of pagodas in relation to identity also shows up in the various cultural and social activities that occur under their aegis. For most overseas Vietnamese Buddhists, the preservation of ancestral values and culture, among children in particular, seems inseparable from religious practice. In a context of immigration, the religion, language and culture of Vietnam constitute a whole whose elements strengthen each other. Hence the classes in Vietnamese language, history, and geography offered by a number of pagodas in Montréal; the stated objectives aiming at preserving ancestral culture; and the other activities (music, religious dancing, camping, publishing) which simultaneously reinforce Buddhist faith and Vietnamese identity.[37] Hence, too, the social services offered to senior adepts (meetings of the elderly; funeral services), which facilitate their integration to Canada and Québec.

The expression of ethnic identity also becomes manifest at another level, that of the reproduction overseas of some economic, political and social characters specific to Vietnamese society. The religious life of Québec's

Vietnamese Buddhists offers a good reflection of their original milieu. For instance, each of Montréal's pagodas appears to cater to the needs of a well-defined segment of the Vietnamese population. One temple has the reputation of being mostly frequented by rich people; another by more recent – and poorer – immigrants, especially by Chinese from Vietnam; a third one allegedly attracts intellectuals and professionals.[38] Rumour asserts that this or that pagoda is mostly visited by defenders of one or another political tendency. As already mentioned – and as noted by McLellan (1998: 237) in Toronto – the transnational Vietnamese Buddhist networks operating in Canada continue regional, political and doctrinal divisions which were established in Vietnam during the 1960s. All this is perfectly normal. The religious life of any immigrant group reproduces the social morphology of the national community from which it originates.

Finally, as outlined by Boisvert (2002), Vietnamese Buddhism in Québec shows some changes by comparison with what it was in Vietnam. Ceremonies are shorter. The role of women is not exactly the same, their sphere of activity being wider than in Vietnam. They still fill domestic duties to temples (preparing vegetarian meals for instance), but they also teach Vietnamese language and culture to the young. At Montréal's Tam Bao pagoda, a nun conducts meditation classes and sits on the board of directors.

Because monks and nuns are not numerous enough, they are sought for counselling and giving services rather than spending their time on learning and teaching. This causes a problem, according to Boisvert, because few of them have formal education and speak English or French, and they do not really know about Western culture. The situation is changing, though, and increasing globalization among overseas Vietnamese Buddhists – since 1975, Vietnam has not been a reference any more in religious matters – might lead to a higher degree of integration into the host society. At the same time, it might encourage a growing number of non-immigrants to join their Vietnamese Canadian compatriots in a type of Buddhism that would be both Vietnamese in form and universal in content.

Notes

1 This temple belonged – and still belongs – to the Japanese Canadian Buddhist Churches of Canada, which follow the Jodō Shinshū tradition. According to Fradette (2002), the congregation has been in operation since 1948. It should be noted that in the late 1960s and early 1970s, a few Zen meditation groups were to be found in Québec, and Tibetan Buddhist masters already visited the province on a more or less regular basis.

2 As early as the 1920s, a few non-Asian Québecers (most of them – if not all – anglophone Montréalers) had converted to Buddhism (Castel 2003). According to Bouchard (2002: 38), current interest for this religion in francophone Québec results from a fragmentation of a religious market no longer monopolized by the Roman Catholic Church, and where spirituality has become a private phenomenon with an open content.

3 In three cases, though, the centre's spiritual head was Tibetan, and in another Vietnamese.

4 Two of the mixed groups – both with a strong Vietnamese component – do not belong to the Western tradition.

5 One of these had a predominantly Vietnamese and Chinese congregration. The others mostly catered to non-Asians. It is worth noticing that in the mid-1980s, a young Western boy living in Québec was officially recognized to be the reincarnation of a Tibetan lama (Alain Bouchard, personal communication, October 2003). This might have helped Tibetan Buddhism take root in the province.

6 In 1991, however, only 4 per cent of Québec's Koreans claimed to be Buddhists (Castel 2003), and a majority of Sri Lankans may have been Tamil Hindus. Thai and Burmese are not mentioned either in the consulted data, but these groups are under-represented in Québec (there were no more than 975 Thai and 80 Burmese Quebecers in 2001).

7 In terms of proportions of adherents in 2001, Theravāda Buddhists accounted for 32 per cent of Québec's total, Mahāyāna for 59 per cent, Vajrayāna for 1 per cent, and converted (Western) Buddhists for 8 per cent (Castel 2003). Members of the last group, however, generally claimed adherence to one of the first three traditions.

8 The Tibetan monk heading the Chicoutimi temple moved to Québec City in 2002.

9 In Québec, there is no central association or federation that would enable Buddhists from various traditions to collaborate among themselves. An inter-Buddhist *Vesak* (anniversary of the Buddha) celebration was held in Montréal in the year 2000, but it has not been repeated since (Hori 2003).

10 Buddhist temples are called *chua* in Vietnamese, but they are generally referred to as *pagodes* in French, and 'pagodas' in English, though strictly speaking, the word 'pagoda' only applies to the belfry of a Chinese-style Buddhist temple.

11 Other Vietnamese Québecers being Roman Catholic, Protestant, or Caodaist (a syncretic religion born in Vietnam in 1925).

12 Vietnam was occupied by China for over 1,000 years (111 BCE to 939 CE), hence the strong Confucian and Taoist components of Vietnamese religious philosophy.

13 Some southern Vietnamese adopted the Theravāda tradition several centuries later, after Vietnam had conquered the Mekong Delta, whose original population was Khmer.

14 This description of Vietnamese Buddhism in Québec is drawn for the most part from Dorais and Nguyen (1990), and Dorais *et al.* (1992).

15 After extensive renovations, its floor area was almost doubled in 1981.

16 They had left Vietnam in 1979 and lived for about a year in the Pulau Bidong refugee camp. They were the first Vietnamese Buddhist clerics to come to Canada (Soucy 1994). According to a declaration by Ven. Thien Nghi (quoted in McLellan 1999: 232–3: note 8), Lien Hoa's spiritual leader (then residing in France), Ven. Thich Tam Chau, first refused that Thich Thien Nghi be sponsored, but he finally accepted when the latter threatened to solicit sponsorship from a Christian organization.

17 Ven. Thien Nghi lived in Taiwan for seven years and he speaks and reads Chinese fluently.

18 In the summer of 2003, ten monks and nuns were living at the Great Pine Forest Monastery (Dai Tong Lam Tam Bao Son). The site comprised a temple, living quarters for the clerics and retreating visitors, a Buddhist library of some 5,000 volumes, and huge outdoor statues depicting the life of the Buddha and other scenes.

19 Quan Am (Guan Yin), the 'Mother of Mercy,' is the most popular Mahayāna *bodhisattva.*

20 In 1990, Chinese Vietnamese members of the Quan Am congregation established their own temple (Hoa Nghiem) in downtown Montréal. It is not known if this temple is still in operation; it is not listed in the Buddhismcanada.com website. A temple of the same name exists in Toronto (McLellan 1999: 222).

21 A monk originally trained by Ven. Thich Thien Nghi at Tam Bao, who, according to Boisvert (2002), had later joined the Linh Son World Buddhist Congregation, is based in France.

22 Two more Vietnamese centres remotely linked with Buddhism, both of them in Montréal, are not taken into account here: the Ching Hai Quan Am meditation group, whose adepts venerate a self-proclaimed Chinese Vietnamese living *bodhisattva* who resides in Taiwan (see Supreme Master Ching Hai 2001), and the Len Dong Tho Mau temple, where a traditional Vietnamese possession cult – whose adepts consider themselves Buddhists (a statue of the Buddha stands in uppermost position on the altar) – is celebrated (see Dorais and Nguyen 1998).

23 Several times a year, Tibetan monks – including one who can preach in French – are invited to take part in Bo De's ceremonies. Elsewhere, too, Vietnamese pagodas have developed more or less regular links with the Tibetan tradition. During its passage through Québec in fall 2003, for instance, a world-touring Tibetan-led exhibition of sacred Buddhist relics was hosted in a Montréal Vietnamese temple.

24 It also 'maintains institutional religious connections with organizations in the United States, Europe, Australia, and Vietnam' (McLellan 1998: 237). Membership in the Union may be at variance from one year to another, because affiliation and disaffiliation are common phenomena.

25 As was the case with the preceding sections, data are chiefly drawn from Dorais and Nguyen (1990) and Dorais *et al.* (1992).

26 The noun 'Thich' in Thich Ca Mau Ni is understood as Sakyamuni's family name. This is why all Vietnamese monks adopt a name starting with Thich, to show that they belong to the Buddha's family.

27 Some Buddhists believe that reincarnation (which may be preceded by a punishing transit through Hell) occurs many decades after death. In the meanwhile, the 'soul' (hon) resides in a sort of limbo from which it is called back to earth whenever the deceased is worshipped by his or her descendants. Others think that reincarnation occurs much more rapidly, but that the 'soul' of the reincarnated individual subsists in some way and may, thus, be worshipped all the same. This shows that within Tam Giao, conciliation between Buddhist, Confucian, and Taoist beliefs is not uncommon.

28 Quan The Am is the equivalent of the Indian Bodhisattva Avalokiteœvara ('Who has unlimited hearing'), whom Tibetans call Chenresig.

29 Testimonies of Vietnamese boat people saved by Quan Am can be found in Dorais *et al.* (1992: 65–8); see also Farber and Fields (1987). A photo of the Mother of Mercy appearing on a dragon in the South China Sea – allegedly taken by a German journalist in 1982 – is reproduced in Dorais *et al.* (1992: facing p. 68).

30 Most of Québec's Vietnamese Buddhist temples have an altar (in the main prayer hall – along a side wall – or in a separate room) with the photos of deceased adepts. The temple's clergy offer daily prayer for the happy desincarnation and reincarnation of these 'souls'.

31 Many Vietnamese Buddhists seem to believe that identification will give them direct access to the supernatural powers allegedly owned by the manifestation of Buddha they visualize.

32 These words are unintelligible to the non-initiated. They include expressions such as: Yet De, Yet De, Ba la yet De.
33 These texts have been adapted to Vietnamese phonetics and orthography, so that they can be read and chanted without difficulty.
34 Rumour has it that in Montréal, some adepts choose the pagoda they regularly visit on the basis of the good reputation of the vegetarian meals prepared there.
35 In Vietnam, the bride and groom prostrate themselves before the ancestral altar of the groom's family, after which a banquet is served in the groom's parental home or in a restaurant. Only Christian weddings are solemnized in church.
36 This is manifest in the name of Montréal's Tu Quang pagoda, which is called To Dinh (ancestors' communal house) rather than Chua (Buddhist temple).
37 It would be interesting to study the impact of Buddhism on the preservation of language and culture among young Vietnamese Canadians. For instance, do youngsters who visit pagodas on a regular basis show a higher degree of fluency in Vietnamese than those who do not?
38 Pagodas also tend to attract people originating from provinces and regions in Vietnam which are the same as those of the temple's principal donors. In many pagodas, the names of these donors are on public display. At the Great Pine Forest Monastery, for instance, beside each of the giant outdoor statues, a board lists in four languages (Vietnamese, Chinese, French and English) the identity of the donor, the cost of the statue, the country (usually Thailand) where it was made, its year of erection, and what the statue represents.

Bibliography

Boisvert, Mathieu (2002) "Vietnamese Buddhism in Montréal. 'When does the Hermit crab stop being a crab?'" Paper read at the American Academy of Religion meetings, Ottawa, April.

Bouchard, Alain (2002) "Un Bouddha au sirop d'érable?," *Cahiers de spiritualité ignatienne*, no. 102: 33–41.

Castel, Frédéric (2003) "La croissance des communautés bouddhistes au Québec (1945–2001). Diversification ethnique et confessionnelle". Paper read at Le Québec à l'heure du bouddhisme conference, Québec, Université Laval, October.

Chan, Kwok Bun (1991) *Smoke and Fire. The Chinese in Montréal*. Hong Kong: The Chinese University Press.

Dorais, Louis-Jacques (1989) "Religion and Refugee Adaptation: The Vietnamese in Montréal," *Canadian Ethnic Studies*, 21(1).

—— (1996) "Asian Communities in Québec," in *Aspects de l'immigration asiatique au Québec* (Louis-Jacques Dorais). Québec: Université Laval, Laboratoire de recherches anthropologiques (Document de recherche no. 11).

—— (2000) *The Cambodians, Laotians and Vietnamese in Canada*. Ottawa, ON: The Canadian Historical Association (Canada's Ethnic Group Series, booklet no. 28).

—— and Nguyen, Huy (1990) *Fleur de lotus et feuille d'érable. La vie religieuse des Vietnamiens du Québec*. Québec: Université Laval, Laboratoire de recherches anthropologiques (Document de recherche no. 7).

—— and Nguyen, Huy (1998) "Le Tho Mâu, un chamanisme vietnamien?," *Anthropologie et Sociétés*, 22(2).

—— and Pilon, Lise (1988) *Les communautés cambodgienne et laotienne de Québec*. Québec: Université Laval, Laboratoire de recherches anthropologiques (Document de recherche no. 5).

——, Gaudette, Piene and Nguyen, Huy (1992) *Religion et adaptation: Les réfugiés vietnamiens au Canada*, unpublished research report. Québec: Université Laval, Département d'anthropologie.

Farber, Don and Fields, Rick (1987) *Taking Refuge in L.A. Life in a Vietnamese Buddhist Temple*. New York: Aperture Foundation.

Fradette, Daniel (2002) "Le bouddhisme au Québec. Une présence réelle, mais difficile à cerner," *Cahiers de spiritualité ignatienne*, no. 102.

Gheddo, Piero (1970) *The Cross and the Bo-Tree. Catholics and Buddhists in Vietnam*. New York: Sheed and Ward.

Helly, Denise (1987) *Les Chinois à Montréal 1877–1951*. Québec: Institut québécois de recherche sur la culture.

Hori, George Victor (2003) "The First *Vesak* in Québec". Paper read at *Le Québec à l'heure du bouddhisme* conference, Université Laval, Québec, October.

McLellan, Janet (1987) "Religion and Ethnicity. The Role of Buddhism in Maintaining Ethnic Identity among Tibetans in Lindsay, Ontario," *Canadian Ethnic Studies* 19(1).

—— (1998) "Buddhist Identities in Toronto: The Interplay of Local, National and Global Contexts," *Social Compass*, 45(2).

—— (1999) *Many Petals of the Lotus. Five Asian Buddhist Communities in Toronto*, Toronto, ON: University of Toronto Press.

Nguyen, Huy Lai (1981) *La tradition religieuse, spirituelle et sociale au Vietnam*. Paris: Beauchesne.

Soucy, Alexander (1994) "Gender and Division of Labour in a Vietnamese Canadian Buddhist Pagoda," MA thesis, Montréal: Concordia University.

Supreme Master Ching Hai (2001) *The Key of Immediate Enlightenment*. Taipei: The International Supreme Master Ching Hai Meditation Associations Publishing Co.

Thich Nhat Hanh (1967) *Vietnam: Lotus in a Sea of Fire*, New York: Hill and Wang.

Vu, Thai Van (2001) "L'enseignement du moine Thich Tâm Chau à Montréal," M.A. thesis, Montréal: Université du Québec à Montréal.

8

BLURRED BOUNDARIES

Buddhist communities in the Greater
Montréal region

Mathieu Boisvert, Manuel Litalien and
François Thibeault

When Buddhism originated in North India in the sixth century BCE, it was rapidly exported from its original cultural locality to new places, in Asia and beyond. Over many centuries, followers of various Buddhist traditions negotiated new expressions of the faith, doctrines and practices depending on their specific context. Buddhist communities in Canada are not alienated from this age-old process, and they continually need to redefine themselves in terms of the society in which they are now rooted. The primary goal of this chapter is to look at some manifestations of Buddhism in the greater Montréal region, and to underline the fact that it is composed of dynamic traditions that are anything but static – yet by no means does this chapter intend to provide a complete descriptive account of the various communities in Montréal.

Buddhism in Montréal was first introduced by Chinese immigrants who moved from British Columbia to Québec around the 1880s (Helly 1987: 37). Since then, the composition of the Montréal Buddhist community has greatly changed, primarily because of Indochina's political situation in the 1970s. This resulted in the migration of a large number of Sino-Vietnamese refugees to Canada. A few decades later, other political circumstances – such as the events of Tiananmen Square in 1989, or Hong Kong's reversion to China in 1997 – were responsible for stimulating Chinese immigration to Canada. Between 1990 and 1997, nearly 450,000 Chinese immigrants entered Canada (Chuenyan Lai *et al.* 2005: 91).

Québec's Chinese community of approximately 63,000 Chinese in 2001 is largely settled in Montréal. About two-thirds of them are immigrants. According to the 2001 Canadian census, 8,890 of these declared they were Buddhists. However, arguably this information is misleading, if only because the categories from which to choose in the census are arguably an over-simplification of the Chinese religious beliefs. Traditional practices performed by many Chinese families, in China or abroad, are an amalgam of Buddhist, Taoist and Confucian rituals and world-views – a particular kind of religious pluralism known as *san-jiao*. In fact, Taoist rituals, Confucianism beliefs and age-old practices are often observed in an environment tinted by Buddhist iconography and doctrine (Chan 1991: 186: Chuenyan Lai *et al.* 2005: 91). In the 2001 Canadian Census neither the category of *san-jiao*, nor 'Confucianism' were present (the former category of Confucianism was abandoned because it was scarcely used by the respondents). This situation shows the potential inaccuracy of categories to determine specific religious orientations of a group. There is also another variable: Chinese born and raised in China during the Cultural Revolution (1966–76) sometimes perceive themselves as having no religious affiliation. This auto-perception tends to be shared by some Chinese living abroad as well. Yet, their actual practices tend to suggest otherwise. In sum, Canadians of Chinese origin who did not identify themselves as exclusively Buddhists or Taoists are wrongly classified as having no religious affiliation, a category that does not reflect their religious reality. The actual number from Chinese descent practicing Buddhism is therefore much higher than suggested by the census. This is corroborated by the various Montréal Chinese institutions, which are overtly Buddhist and cater almost exclusively to those of Chinese lineage.

In this regard, the International Buddhist Progress Society of Montréal (IBPS), associated with the Fo Guang Shan International Order from Taiwan, is by far the biggest Buddhist Chinese temple in the city. Founded in 1991, the main center located on Rue Jean-Talon has two nuns operating the program with the help of lay volunteers.[1] The center aims to help new immigrants and the Montréal Chinese community as a whole to better understand their host society. Like other Chinese Buddhist temples in Montréal, its membership is from various regions, notably Southeast Asia, Taiwan and China. The nuns have both missionary and ministerial objectives. For example, they offer Buddhism classes in the Chinese language, organize religious ceremonies and Chinese 'cultural' activities. Funding for the Society comes from its Montréal members, but also from time to time from the Fo Guang Shan International Order in Taiwan.

The Montréal Chinese Buddhist Society (MCBS) is another important Chinese Buddhist temple in the city core. Located in the heart of Chinatown on St-Laurent Boulevard, it was founded in 1989 by two laymen. MCBS has no permanent monk or nun in residence. Approximately twice a year, however, Rev. Ngo Tuck from the Vietnamese Ching Kwok temple in Toronto is invited to offer Buddhist lectures. Approximately thirty people attend regular weekend services. Yet, on special events or traditional celebrations, the confined apartment that serves as its center can hardly support the hundreds of participants. Collaboration with the Montréal Vietnamese Buddhist communities is therefore frequent in order to host bigger ceremonies. Thus the Thûye Tôn Pagoda and the Tam Bào Pagoda, both Vietnamese institutions, often organize specific events to cater to the Chinese Buddhist communities of Montréal. For example, exclusive Chinese annual celebrations are held at the large Vietnamese Great Pine Forest Monastery in Harrington, Québec, affiliated with Tam Bào. The fact that Rev. Thich Pho Tinh – the nun in charge of Tam Bào temple in Montréal – has received her monastic training in Taiwan facilitates such exchanges. This is understandable since MCBS has a majority of Sino-Vietnamese practitioners, sharing a linguistic and religious culture close to that of migrants from the People's Republic of China, Taiwan and Hong Kong. It is also worth noting that the MCBS has shared its space with the Tzu Chi practitioners (see below) before these had any formal location. Cooperation between these two communities reveals the integration efforts between the different Montréal Chinese Buddhist communities that hold allegiance to different 'Grandmasters', and practice distinct religious rituals. The MCBS has also had four practitioners who became nuns. They are now located in Toronto's Ching Kwok temple, catering to Mandarin, Cantonese and Vietnamese-speaking communities.

Montréal Chan Hai Lei Zang Temple, belonging to the True Buddha School, an international Buddhist institution based in the USA, was founded in 1990 and is affiliated with the Association Des Bénévoles Huaguang (the two organizations want to be seen as quite separate, however). At the Chan Hai Lei Zang Temple, the majority of the members are immigrants from mainland China, with a small percentage from Taiwan and Vietnam. Its Grandmaster, Sheng-Yen Lu of Seattle, Washington (a syncretistic figure with links to the Chinese and Tibetan Buddhist traditions as well as with Taoism), is considered by his devotees to be a living Buddha. The organization offers ceremonial rituals and recommends the performance of *chi kong* exercises for health. Devotional offerings to Grandmaster Sheng-Yen Lu, to various Buddhist deities and to ancestors are regularly performed (Chan 1991: 189).

As for the Association Des Bénévoles Huaguang, whose members are Chinese from Mainland China, with a small percentage from Taiwan, Hong Kong and Southeast Asia, its primary function is to provide an infrastructure to implant and offer the various programs supported by the Ministère des Relations avec les Citoyens et Immigration (MRCI) of the province. It offers private classes as well in languages (French, English, Chinese) and even such subjects as mathematics. The association registered as a non-political and non-profit organization in 1995, and is funded in part by both a provincial government subsidization, and by donations from individuals and various organizations. Closely affiliated with the Montréal Chinese Hospital, the Association recently bought a building on Rue St-Denis with the objective of constructing a 'Huaguang Senior Age Home'. This facility will include a temple suitable for both residents and the larger community.

Another important organization is the Montréal Buddhist Compassion Relief Tzu Chi Foundation, whose main objectives are charity, medicine, education and culture. Montréal currently acts as a *Bureau de liaison* between other Tzu Chi centres in Vancouver and Toronto. It has more than four million members around the world, and approximately 5,000 in Canada, with 350 in Montréal. Ninety per cent of their members are from Taiwan, while others are from mainland China, Hong Kong and Southeast Asia.

We now turn to the Cambodians in Montréal, who have collectively gone through an immigration process very similar to that of the Vietnamese. Many first arrived as university students in the 1950s; a second cohort came as refugees in the 1970s and, later on, as immigrants brought to Canada with the help of the family reunification plan.[2] The specific conditions in Cambodia from which the Cambodian refugees escaped (for instance, the Khmer Rouge regime in the mid-1970s and the Vietnamese-backed government that over-threw it), has clearly had a deep impact on community self-identity. This, along with the distinctive Theravāda Buddhism of the Cambodian majority, has differentiated them from the Vietnamese and the Chinese.

From only 200 Cambodians residing in Canada in 1974 (about 150 stayed in Montréal), their number in Canada increased to over 7,000 during the 1975–82 period and, following the 1982 Canadian family reunification pro-gram, reached over 18,000 in 1991 (Dorais 2000: 7–10). According to the 2001 Canadian census, with over 10,000 Cambodians, the Province of Québec hosts the largest Khmer Cambodian community in Canada, of which more than 9,000 reside in Montréal.

Amongst the five Khmer Buddhist temples in Canada listed by Janet McLellan, Montréal's Khmer Pagoda of Canada (KPC) is the largest and best supported Khmer Buddhist institution, currently led by Hok Savann, an elderly monk (1999: 142). It is not uncommon to see Laotian or Thai monks who reside in Montréal invited to the Khmer Buddhist temple in order that the number of monks might legitimize specific rituals on special occasions. Many white-garbed and mostly aged women (following the ten Buddhist precepts) take care of the holy precincts. The temple as such caters to an exclusively ethnic community (composed of around 300 families). Major events of the Cambodian civic and Buddhist calendars are celeb-rated, and Khmer language classes offered on the weekends for young boys and girls. Funds are now being raised in order to buy land in Laval (just north of Montréal), on which a new pagoda, likely very Cambodian in its architectural style, will be built. A new Cambodian pagoda was also inaugurated in the summer of 2004 in Rivière-des-Prairies (East of Montréal). Many Theravāda monks of differing origins (Laotian, Thai), and coming from as far as California, participated in the opening ceremony. Two young Cambodian men had also taken temporary monastic vows for the duration of the weekend-long festivities.[3]

Contrasting with the rather large Chinese and Cambodian commun-ities of Montréal – both of which cater almost exclusively to Chinese and Cambodians – the Tibetans constitute a minor ethno-religious community

145

of approximately 200 persons. Yet the presence of Tibetan Buddhism is strongly felt in the city. Most Tibetans arrived in Montréal as refugees in 1971 and natural increase in Canada has been the primary factor for the growth of the population to the present. Tibetans have rapidly organized themselves in order to preserve their language and culture, and to promote awareness of the situation in Tibet since China's invasion in 1951. Two major Tibetan organizations have been established in Montréal. The Tibetan Cultural Association is mainly responsible for organizing cultural activities, such as celebration of the Tibetan New Year, that cater to both Tibetan and 'tibetanophiles' (this later category encompass both non-Tibetans practicing some form of Tibetan Buddhism, and Westerners sympathetic to the political situation of Tibet). On the other hand, the Canada Tibet Committee (CTC) is solely dedicated to promoting the political liberation of Tibet. The CTC is an antenna of an international network based in New York. The four Tibetan temples in the Montréal area cater to both Tibetan and non-Tibetan peoples interested in Vajrayāna Buddhism.

In *Prisoners of Shangri-la* (1998), Donald S. Lopez argues that the popularity of Tibetan Buddhism in the West is due in part to certain misconceptions about the tradition. Some of these are responsible for the Manichean perception that is generally imposed on the two parties involved in the Sino-Tibetan conflict. This contributes to a growing reverence towards Tibet, its culture and religion. These factors contribute as well to the manufacturing of a 'Western' interpretation and definition of Tibetan Buddhism (and arguably even affect the vision that Tibetans-in-exile have of their own tradition).

In Montréal, there are far more non-Tibetans practicing Tibetan Buddhism than Tibetans. Nonetheless, the Tibetan practice of recognizing reincarnated *lama* (*tulku*) may be responsible for deconstructing traditional boundaries between Tibetan and non-Tibetan devotees. Over the past centuries, reincarnations of *lama* are said to have occurred within Tibetan or neighbouring territories. In the last two decades, however, a number of non-Tibetans have been recognized as *tulku*. Spanish, American and Québécois children have been attributed the title of *tulku* by the tradition. A documentary has been produced on Elijah Ary, a Montréaler recognized as a *tulku* at the age of four, who spent six years of training in a Tibetan monastery in South India between the age of fourteen and twenty, as well as a thought-provoking autobiographical account in Sumi Loundon's book, *Blue Jean Buddha* (2001). Recognition of *tulku* outside the Tibetan ethnic community may be a strategy for seeking support outside Tibet against China (just as the recognition of the Third Dalai Lama by Altan Khan in 1578 has been interpreted as a formal Tibeto-Mongol *front commun* against China).

The participation of many Caucasians within various Montréal Buddhist movements points to how the notion of ethnicity is challenged as a typological tool to classify Western Buddhist traditions.[4] Albert Bastenier defines ethnicity as the 'social identification of oneself and others in order to estab-lish a positioning into organised social groups' (Bastenier 1998: 198, our translation). Therefore, a sense of attachment (based on an complex amalgam of common characteristics such as culture, language, religion, a shared history, etc.) binds individuals into the same ethnic group as different factors (e.g., economic, political) influence a particular society at a particular time, thus implying that ethnic groups are social constructions (Bramadat and Seljak 2005: 8). Thus defined, ethnicity opens up a field of inquiry into both 'ethnic' and 'convert' Buddhist traditions that can shed light on many of their under-lying social and religious dynamics.

The Japan-based Sōka Gakkai International (SGI) has branches through-out the world, including the SGI-Canada (officially founded in 1976) to which belongs two centres in the province of Québec, one each in Montréal and Québec City. Categorized as a religious sect in France because of its polit-ical and economic implications in Japan (Chelli and Hourmant 2000: 90), the SGI is somehow one of the most populous Buddhist organizations in Europe (Baumann 2002: 92). Even though the body of directors of the SGI is Japanese, Québecois followers of the SGI-Canada are mainly non-Asian converts (Boisvert in Bramadat and Seljak 2005: 83). Despite this 'two-folded' ethnic identity inside the SGI-Canada, the psychosociological research made by Chelli and Hourmant (2000) on SGI French followers seems to show that a common set of religious and social values unites Asians and non-Asians within the movement. Consequently, as far as the SGI can be seen as a homogeneous movement, its ethnic composition does not account fully for the religious dynamics that distinguish it from a 'parallel congregation', consisting of two ethnic groups pursuing, under one roof, 'largely separate and substantively distinct expressions of a common religious affiliation' (Numrich, quoted by Prebish 1999: 62–3).

Arguably such a parallel congregation could be found in S. N. Goenka's Vipassanā Tradition that reached the eastern part of North America in the late 1970s. A Vipassanā Meditation Centre was established in 1999 in the Eastern Townships, in Sutton City.[5] More than eight hundred 'students' visited the centre in 2003, which has now reached its maximum capacity (i.e. fifty students per ten-day silent meditation retreat). Originating from Burmese Theravāda Buddhism, the S. N. Goenka Vipassanā Tradition – with hundreds of centres throughout the five continents – attracts people from various religious, ethnic and cultural backgrounds. In Québec, special ten-day courses are offered for Vietnamese and Khmer Buddhist immigrants. Some of the latter have completed a few *vipassanā* courses while continuing to participate in the religious activities of the Khmer Pagoda of Canada. Consequently, different interpretations about the nature of the Buddhism represented in the *vipassanā* tradition have developed. Non-Asian converts appear convinced that they practice a pure form of *dhamma* unaffected by cultural and traditional beliefs. This causes a certain identifiable cleavage between Montréal's ethnic Buddhist temples and the *vipassanā* centres (Boisvert in Bramadat and Seljak 2005: 83).

In another example pertinent to Montréal, the New Kadampa Tradition (NKT), initially based in England, shows many aspects of the complex implantation processes of Buddhism in the West. Under the spiritual leadership of Gueshe Kelsang Gyatso (who founded the NKT in 1991), more than eight hundred affiliated NKT centres throughout 36 countries pursue a common set of Buddhist and spiritual goals, in the line of the Kadampa Vajrayāna teachings. In Montréal, the Kankala Buddhist Centre[6] (which does not identify itself as a 'Tibetan Buddhist' centre) is frequented by around 300 individuals, almost exclusively francophone and from non-Buddhist origins. Its numerous activities include daily guided meditations, weekend retreats, weekly teachings, and also intensive practice and study programs (in which are involved around sixty regular practitioners). Kankala's simply fashioned inner halls, including statues and paintings of Buddhas and *bodhisattvas*, cannot be guessed from the building's conventional external appearance. Gen Kelsang Drenpa, a Québec-born woman who converted to Buddhism in the early 1990s, (she was ordained as a nun in 2001) founded the centre in 1994, and has since become its main resident teacher. Broadly, and in the light of the work of Obadia (1999, 2000), the Kankala Centre shows how Asian Buddhist native institutions are complexly re-established outside Asia in order to suit a majority of converts, while taking root in, and developing from, traditional structures.

In sum, it could be said that the so-called 'convert' Buddhist groups are ethnically defined on the basis that they are bound to a degree by a common sense of religious belonging based on specific historical and social conditions. Many Buddhist centres in Montréal are composed of people identified with distinct ethnic origins, but are in turn linked to a wider network of centres belonging to a kind of Buddhism that is not exactly 'ethnic' nor 'convert'. Such a theoretical opposition between ethnic and convert Buddhism appears thus to be rooted in a wider conceptual field of ethnicity, from which neither immigrants nor converts may entirely escape.

Buddhism is no longer confined to Asia where congregations were relatively distinct and reflected local culture. Different Buddhist traditions are now represented in cities such as Montréal, and the 'global village' is forcing the different Buddhist communities to interact with one another in ways that were never seen before. For instance, important links are now well established between the Chinese Buddhist communities and Vietnamese temples. This type of exchange, where two distinct ethnic communities share a ritual space, and sometimes even teachers and clergy, indicates there is dialogue between the various factions. The same might even be said about ethnic and convert Buddhists. Thus two or even more seemingly distinct categories of Buddhists interact, negotiate and redefine what they think Buddhism ought to be. Boundaries between Buddhist groups may at times become blurred, but arguably this natural process of transformation is necessary to the process of redefining the various expressions of Buddhism in its new environment – and the example of Montréal brings this phenomenon very much to the fore.

Notes

1 Ven. Man Hung became responsible for the Montréal IBPS in 1992. The other nun, Ven. Miao Da, has been newly ordained in Taiwan. She is Sino-Vietnamese and has lived in Québec for more than twenty years.
2 See L.-J. Dorais's chapter, 'Buddhism in Québec,' in this book.
3 Regarding the traditional ceremony of ordination of young boys into the Burmese, Thai, Laotian and Cambodian monastic communities, see Boisvert 2000.
4 For in-depth discussions about the typology of Buddhism and Buddhists in the West, see Prebish and Tanaka 1998; Lenoir 1999; Obadia 1999, 2000; Prebish 1999; Williams and Queens 1999; Baumann 2000.
5 Ontario and British Columbia both host one *vipassanā* centre.
6 Affiliated to Kankala and the NKT, centres were started in Québec City, Trois-Rivières and Joliette (a centre in Sherbrooke is planned in the near future). Elsewhere in Canada, six centres are to be found in Ontario, one in Alberta and one in British Columbia.

Bibliography

Barth, Frederik (1969) *Ethnic Groups and Boundaries: The Social Organization of Cultural Difference*. Boston: Little, Brown.

Bastenier, Albert (1998) "L'incidence du facteur religieux dans la 'conscience ethnique' des immigrés marocains en Belgique," *Social Compass*, 45(2).

Baumann, Martin (2000) "Le bouddhisme theravāda en Europe: histoire, typologie et rencontre entre un bouddhisme moderniste et traditionnaliste," *Recherches sociologiques*, XXXI(3): 7–31.

—— (2002) "Buddhism in Europe: Past, Present, Prospects," in Charles S. Prebish and Martin Baumann (eds) *Westward Dharma: Buddhism beyond Asia*. Berkeley, CA: University of California Press.

Boisvert, Mathieu (2000) "A Socio-cultural Analysis of the Burmese Shin pyu Ceremony," *Journal of Beliefs and Values*, 21(2): 203–11.

Bramadat, Paul et Seljak, David (eds) (2005) *Religion and Ethnicity in Canada*. Toronto, ON: Pearson Education.

Brook, Timothy (1993) "Rethinking Syncretism: The Unity of Their Joint Worship in Later Imperial China," *Journal of Chinese Religions*, 21 (Fall).

Chan, Kwok Bun (1991) "In Lieu of Family," in K. B. Chan, *Smoke and Fire. The Chinese in Montréal*. Hong Kong: The Chinese University Press.

Chelli, Norbert and Hourmant, Louis (2000) "Orientations axiologiques dans le bouddhisme du mouvement Soka Gakkaï en France," *Recherches sociologiques*, XXXI(3): 89–102.

Cormier, Louis (2001) "Tibétains au Québec: Profil d'une communauté bouddhique," MA Thesis, UQÀM.

Dorais, Louis-Jacques (2000) *Les Cambodgiens, Laotiens et Vietnamiens au Canada*. Ottawa, ON: Société Historique du Canada.

Helly, Denise (1987) *Les Chinois à Montréal 1877–1951.* Québec: Institut Québécois de Recherche sur la Culture.

Lai, Chuenyan, Paper, David, Paper, Jordan, Paper, Chuang and Chuang, Li (2005) "The Chinese in Canada: Their Unrecognized Religion," in Paul Bramadat et David Seljak (eds) *Religion and Ethnicity in Canada.* Toronto, ON: Pearson Education.

Lenoir, Frédéric (1999) *Le bouddhisme en France.* Paris: Fayard.

Lopez, Donald S. Jr. (1998) *Prisoners of Shangri-La: Tibetan Buddhism and the West.* Chicago, IL: University of Chicago Press.

Loundon, Sumi (2001) *Blue Jean Buddha: Voices of Young Buddhists.* Summerville, MA: Wisdom Publications.

Mackenzie, Vicki (1996) *Reincarnation: The Boy Lama.* Boston, MA: Wisdom Publications.

McLellan, Janet (1999) *Many Petals of the Lotus. Five Asian Buddhist Communities in Toronto.* Toronto, ON: University of Toronto Press.

Obadia, Lionel (1999) *Bouddhisme et Occident. La diffusion du bouddhisme tibétain en France.* (Religion et sciences humaines). Paris: L'Harmattan.

——(2000) "Une tradition au-delà de la modernité: l'institutionnalisation du bouddhisme tibétain en France," *Recherches sociologiques,* XXXI(3).

Paper, Chuang Li and Paper, Jordan (1995) "Chinese Religion, Population, and the Environment," in Harold Coward (ed.) *Population, Consumption, and the Environment: Religious and Secular Responses.* Albany, NY: State University of New York Press.

Poulin, Marcel (1994) "Memories of a Previous Life," Montréal, QC: Thuk Kar Productions [documentary].

Prebish, Charles S. (1999) *Luminous Passage: The Practice and Study of Buddhism in America.* Berkeley, CA: University of California Press.

Prebish, Charles S. and Martin Baumann (eds) (2002) *Westward Dharma: Buddhism beyond Asia.* Berkeley, CA: University of California Press.

Prebish, Charles S. and Kenneth K. Tanaka (eds) (1998) *The Faces of Buddhism in America.* Berkeley, CA: University of California Press.

Williams, Duncan Ryuken and Queen, Christopher S. (1999) *American Buddhism: Methods and Findings in Recent Scholarship.* Richmond, Surrey Curzon.

9

BUDDHISM IN ATLANTIC CANADA

Bruce Matthews

Atlantic Canada is comprised of New Brunswick, Prince Edward Island, Nova Scotia and Newfoundland. Of the four provinces, Nova Scotia has the most substantial Buddhist representation, but the number of practicing Buddhists in the Atlantic region in 2004 would still only be about 2000 or 0.5 per cent of the total population (for sake of comparison, the Jewish population is about the same).[1] Buddhism in Atlantic Canada is a relatively new phenomenon. It is largely associated with Shambhala International and some smaller Zen meditation centres. Ethnic Buddhism is present among Chinese, Vietnamese and Sri Lankan communities, but is not found outside of the principal metropolis of Halifax. By way of method, this chapter first reviews the background and continuing significance of ethnic Buddhism. It then focuses on Buddhist organizations that have Eastern roots but which cater almost entirely to Western devotees.

Turning first to the Buddhism of specific ethnic communities, Chinese Buddhists have the longest association with the cities and towns, though the only temples are found in two centres in Nova Scotia. The principal centre is Ji Jing Si (Solemn Silence Temple), a converted Wesleyan chapel in central Halifax. Though completely nondescript and perhaps deliberately somewhat shabby from the outside (there is no English sign to indicate what the building is, the windows are opaque and all doors securely locked), the interior of the temple is completely renovated and exquisitely appointed. Major financial gifts continue to support this beautiful edifice. Upon entry, a delicate screen, huge temple bell, Wei-t'o and another guardian figure divide a foyer from the meditation and worship hall. A towering, finely crafted golden Shakyamuni image dominates the temple's sanctuary. Pictures of Bodhidharma and the Patriarch Grandmaster Hsu Yun (1839–1959) grace the library, which features extensive works in Chinese and English. The great Hsu Yun was one of the reformers who brought a balance to the contemporary devotional Pure Land practices by focusing on meditation; a blend of Pure Land devotion and Chan is not unusual in Chinese Buddhism, and the Halifax temple is a good example illustrating the fusion of the two ways of being Buddhist. There is also an attractive smaller meditation room and garden presided over by an image of Kuan Yin, and a 'memory hall' for spirit tablets featuring a graceful image of Ti-ts'ang P'u-sa (Earth Store Bodhisattva or Ksitigarbha). The temple has an interesting history. Cantonese-speaking Chinese immigrants have lived in Halifax for over a century, some prospering greatly in the restaurant business. Later Chinese arrivals have usually been better educated and for historical reasons often Christian, marking a sociological division within the community. There is some suggestion that the Chinese temple represents a working-class rather than professional-class immigrant population. For many years, that community has been led by an itinerant monk, Yun Feng Shih-fu (Rev. Cloud Peak), but he would not stay unless there was a permanent residence. The temple, established in 1994, is an attempt by the dozen or so foremost Chinese families to keep Shih-fu in Halifax, though, more often than not, he is either in Ottawa (where he is associated with another congregation) or in China (where he is said to be building a new *sangha* just three hours outside of Shanghai). The temple offers devotional services (chanting and meditation) on Sundays and Tuesdays, and has occasional visiting teachers (for example in 2004, for several weeks, Rev. Quan Ping from Santavana Forest hermitage, Kotakinabalu, Sabah). The temple has the occasional Western devotee, but does not promote itself as a centre for non-Chinese worshippers.

Elsewhere, the Eastern Sea Temple Buddhist Association operates from an old farm on a dramatic hillside facing the ocean at St Margaret's Bay, an hour's drive from Halifax. The resident monk, Rev. Jian Ming, ministers to a few Cantonese-speaking Chinese families from Halifax, but most of his efforts are focused on Chinese Buddhists from Toronto's Cham Shan Temple who come to the farm on retreat. A meditation and devotional hall, with sleeping accommodation for a dozen pilgrims on another storey, has been constructed on site. Although a Kuan Yin image dominates the meditation centre, devotional ritual is secondary to meditation and instruction. Week-long retreat sessions occur during the summer, with Sunday services throughout the year. Jian Ming lives as close to a 'forest monk' lifestyle as is possible, though he also travels weekly to Halifax in the centre's car to teach in private houses. He is also a *taijiquan* (Tai Chi Ch'uan) master. Originally from Saigon, from which Jian Ming managed to escape in 1972, this interesting, multilingual erudite monk trained as a civil engineer in Germany. Ordained in a small Chinese Buddhist temple (Tai Bay) in Toronto in 1991, he came to Nova Scotia three years later to establish this mission. It has no local outreach or specific interest in attracting Westerners. This by itself is telling, as Jian Ming has the talents to teach Buddhism in excellent English. He considers his role to be ethnically focused, though he would agree to teach Buddhist philosophy to Westerners who deliberately sought him out – but few know of his presence.

A relatively recent migration of Sri Lankan, Laotian, Thai and Burmese Buddhist families to Halifax, combined with a dozen or so South and Southeast Asian university students from Halifax's three universities, provides a community of about one hundred Theravāda practitioners.[2] This is still too small to make possible a self-supporting *vihara*. By consequence, the community meet on Poya days once a month in a private home, though it is important to note that they are planning a *dhamma* school for Sunday morning children's instruction. Twice a year, the Sinhala community invite a *bhikkhu* from Ottawa to come to Halifax for ritual events. Of special interest, however, is the annual invitation from Shambhala International's temple (Karma Dzong) to celebrate *Vesak*, the all-encompassing commemoration of the Buddha's enlightenment and demise (*parinibbana*). This single event brings the faithful of the three Buddhist *yanas* or 'vehicles' together in a unique gathering of an otherwise fragmented *sasana* into a collective whole for one day.

A second aspect of Buddhism in Atlantic Canada is associated with sects and schools that have an Asian origin, but whose outreach in the Atlantic region is largely Western. Rinzai Zen Buddhism of the Korean tradition is represented in Halifax with a small meditation group, the Zen Community of Halifax, under the instruction of Samso Sylvia McCormick. Samso McCormick, a bright, friendly woman of middle age with part Mi'kmaq heritage, studied with Ven. Samu Sunim's Buddhist Society for Compassionate Wisdom. She lived in the Society's Toronto temple from 1993 for the better part of five years, and was ordained in 1995. There she learned how to fashion the hard round meditation cushion (*zafu*) as a religious discipline, and she still produces these for Buddhist groups. Her mentor, Sunim, knows of the existence of the Halifax outreach, but Samso McCormick's group is independent from his organization. Nonetheless, Sunim's influence is everywhere apparent in Samso McCormick's teaching and meditation agenda. Originally from Chinju City, South Korea, Sunim has been active in the West since 1967, and sponsors temples in Chicago, Ann Arbor, and Mexico City. Samso McCormick follows a format of instruction and devotion based primarily on weekly meetings for study, sitting meditation, quiet chanting (the shrine room is in an apartment building), prostrations and walking, all under her guidance. She does her own advertising, especially in Halifax's several universities, and finds most of her new practitioners from these sources. Of interest is her attempt to introduce Korean Zen in the city of Moncton, New Brunswick prior to coming to Halifax in 1998. Despite her efforts, Moncton proved a difficult place to introduce Rinzai Zen, and yielded too few followers to constitute a viable community. Even now, Samso McCormick avers that it will take seven years before a Buddhist outreach such as the one she fosters has roots. Halifax has been more promising, partly because of its more cosmopolitan population and because of the presence of Shambala International (Vajradhatu) since 1979. It is an interesting example of how the general public in Halifax has accepted the presence of Buddhism as part of the religious landscape of the city, though it is also clear that few would make much of a distinction between the different kinds of Buddhism.

Elsewhere, there are Soto Zen communities in two Nova Scotia locations. The Wolfville Zazenkai ('gathering together for zazen') is a branch of the White Wind (Hakukaze) Zen Centre of Ottawa (Honzan Dainen-ji). White Wind Zen's spiritual leader is Zen Master Anzan Hoshin, of the Dogen tradition associated with Joshu Dainen, who in turn came to Canada in the early 1970s. The Wolfville zendo, attractively situated in a rural setting among sweeping hills, was established in 1990 under the lay monk (*shraman*) Zenki Anagarika Michael Hope-Simpson, otherwise a consultant to various non-governmental overseas development agencies. There are few practising members or 'formal students' (*deshai*), but the zendo provides opportunities to experience 'sitting practice' twice weekly. White Wind has an extensive 'long-distance' training program based in part on recorded *teisho* and dharma talks, and either telephone or electronic interviews (*daisan*) with Anzan Hoshin at the Ottawa temple. Perhaps the outreach of the Soto tradition in Nova Scotia can in one sense best be reflected in the personal observation of a botanist who leads the biodiversity program for the Government of Nova Scotia, and who has found equilibrium and succour in this form of Buddhism. Sherman Boates notes:

> I am a keen scientist, conservation biologist and government bureaucrat with a passion for nature; very serious about addressing the extinction of species and the degradation of air, water and ecosystems. Early in the 1990s, I met my teacher and the practice of Zen. Since that time everything has been more interesting and fun. More importantly, I see how much I have been missing; the blue of sky, the earthy smell of a peat bog, the sheer joy of parenting, the importance of saying hello to the grocery clerk, and the possibility that we can save the earth. Stopping thinking and talking about stuff and just getting on with the simple and radical practice of *zazen* has become the most important thing I do.

On the other hand, the Atlantic Soto Zen Centre at White's Lake in Shad Bay, Nova Scotia, is affiliated with the much larger and older Atlanta Soto Zen Centre in Georgia. Jim Smith (So Tess Shin), a local elementary school teacher, trained with Zenkai Taiun Michael Elliston roshi in Atlanta, and moved to Canada in 1981. He has been active in Buddhist life for many years and supervises a zendo in his house for a small community of regular practitioners, practicing sitting, and recitations of the Heart or Diamond Sutras in English and phonetic Japanese. A central altar focuses on an image of Ho Tai, a Maitreya figure whose emphasis is on the possible immediacy of enlightenment. The connection with Atlanta is an important one, and Elliston Roshi usually visits White's Lake on an annual basis for one-on-one interviews (*dokusan*), and holds *dharma* discussions by speaker phone with the community once a month. Smith takes individuals through ceremonies to formalize their association (*zaika tokuda* – 'receiving the precepts'), but further steps to achieve 'disciple' and 'priest' status are at the discretion of Elliston Roshi.

Halifax and St John's, Newfoundland also have associations identified with Thich Nhat Hanh's Vietnamese Zen or Mindfulness Community. The *sangha* in Halifax ('Waves and Water') is the more established of the two, under the leadership of Bethan Lloyd, ordained in 2000 as a lay member of the tradition's Tiep Hien Order of Interbeing. She received ordination from one of the first North American students of Thich Nhat Hanh, Eileen Kiera, Dharmacharya. Lloyd is of Mennonite background and a research faculty member at Dalhousie University, working in the fields of racism, violence and health. She has been practicing Buddhism for many years, beginning in Washington state with Kiera's *sangha* and attending retreats with Thich Nhat Hanh's monastic communities in Plum Village (France), Vermont, and California. Fifteen to twenty practitioners are affiliated with 'Waves and Water' in Halifax, although typically a smaller number meet each week for sitting and walking meditation followed by an hour of audio- and video-taped *dharma* talks by Thich Nhat Hanh, recitation ceremonies for the 'Five and Fourteen Mindfulness Trainings' (Precepts), 'deep relaxation', and other activities common to the tradition. There are also early morning sittings, a monthly silent 'peace walk', and Days of Mindfulness. The group has begun to organize retreats in Halifax and at the Vermont monastic centres. Although Halifax has upwards of fifty Vietnamese families, only one has contact with 'Waves and Water'. They are more likely to practice with one of two Chan temples where Mandarin and Vietnamese are spoken. The Vietnamese Zen tradition of Thich Nhat Hanh has as an ancestor Lin Chi, providing a link with the Japanese Rinzai tradition. But the emphasis is on 'engaged Buddhism', especially practices which focus on peace and putting into action the 'Five Mindfulness Trainings'.

By far the most significant Buddhist phenomenon in Atlantic Canada is Shambhala International, with its world headquarters in Halifax, Nova Scotia. Shambhala has other names that from time to time have been in popular use in Halifax, notably Dharmadhatu ('realm of dharma'), Vajradhatu ('realm of the indestructible') and Karma Dzong ('fortress of Buddhist activity', the latter being the principal temple on Tower Road). This Kagyü/Nyingma guru-focused form of Tibetan Buddhism is associated with one of the faith's most interesting and controversial figures, Chögyam Trungpa, Rinpoche (the Vidyadhara, Vajracarya the Venerable Chökyi Gyatso). Chögyam moved to Halifax from Boulder, Colorado, in 1983, along with one hundred and fifty followers. He died four years later, leaving a rich legacy in the region.

About five hundred members in the Halifax area and three hundred elsewhere continue to make Atlantic Canada their home.

Much has been written both by Chögyam, and about Chögyam, the author of many books on Buddhism (particularly from the perspective of the Vajrayāna tradition). No review of this branch of the Buddhist *sasana* could be complete without some reflection on Chögyam's remarkable life, and the circumstances that drew him to the eastern edge of the North American continent. In this regard, Rick Fields has set down a comprehensive reflection on the pre-Nova Scotia part of Chögyam's biography (Fields 1981: 282). The account notes that in August 1940, at the age of eighteen months, Chögyam was enthroned as the Eleventh Trungpa, abbot of the Surmang group of monasteries in Tibet, by Rangjung Rigpe Dorje, the Sixteenth Gyalwa Karmapa and holder of the Kagyü lineage of Tibetan Buddhism. Chögyam was carefully schooled in Buddhism by his 'root guru' Sechen Kongtrül (in the tradition of the nineteenth-century teacher Jamgon Kongtrul) before fleeing to India in 1959 during the Chinese invasion. He found refuge and studied English in Darjeeling with Freda Bedi and John Driver, remarkable Western figures in their own right. Opportunity to read Comparative Religion at Oxford in 1963 exposed Chogyam to what he sensed was an impressive Western philosophical tradition. Also, somewhat ironically given the location, he was introduced to the culture and art of China and Japan in Britain's great galleries and museums. At the suggestion of the English Sangha Vihara's senior *bhikkhu*, Ananda Bodhi, in 1966 Chögyam established Samye-Linge, a 'contemplation centre' in Dumfriesshire, Scotland. The British Buddhist understanding of the faith was arguably more used to a Theravāda focus or something associated with the scholarly Pali Text Society (which had done so much to preserve the record of the *dharma* in the English language).

Among other events at this critical time, in 1968 Chögyam was involved in an automobile accident that left him with a permanent impairment on one side of his body. According to his account, the mishap also resulted in a kind of revelation that he must take 'daring steps' to teach the *dharma* in the West, reinforcing his commitment to distance himself from specifically Tibetan rituals. These things he now perceived as obstacles which prevented the integration of Buddhism into the West, though in time, appeal to ceremony and Tibetan culture would reappear to strengthen his claim for spiritual legitimacy. He had a son in India before coming to Britain (the Sawang, or Sakyong Mipham Rinpoche, was born in 1962 and is the current spiritual head of Shambala International). Chögyam then married a British woman, Diana Pybos. The Tibetan tradition allowed for lay leadership to wed in some monastic orders (other similar examples include the then head of the Sakya sect, Sakya Tridzin, and Dudjom Rinpoche, head of the Nyingmapa sect), but Chögyam's decision met with general disagreement by English followers whose expectation of monastic leadership was associated in part with celibacy. For this and other reasons, in 1970 Chögyam came first to Toronto, then to Barnet, Vermont, where American supporters provided him with a gracious location ('Tail of the Tiger', now Karme-Choling). It was the beginning of a remarkable outreach.

The 1970s were a time of significant social and religious upheaval in America, following the counterculture movements of the previous decade, and offering many alternative spiritual practices for Westerners (Cox 1977: 13). Tibetan Buddhist Tantric practices held a fascination for many, particularly the notion that *nirvāna* is *samsara*, and that the passions, including sexual ones, could be harnessed for their potent energy and used as a means to advance toward liberation. This kind of pursuit, veiled in such terms as 'twilight language' and 'crazy wisdom' (*vidyadhara*), was ultimately available only to a very few expertly trained gurus, among them Chögyam Trungpa Rinpoche, but enthralment with its focus of 'giving up territory' and rejection of conformity appealed to many Western devotees. As Chögyam ventured further afield in 1970 to Colorado, he first established the Rocky Mountain Dharma Centre and Vajradhatu, the headquarters of his expanding national network of neighbourhood meditation groups, and then in 1974, the Naropa Institute. The latter in turn spawned both a small university and a well regarded Translation Committee dedicated to research and to the preservation of Sanskrit, Tibetan and Chinese Buddhist texts.

Notwithstanding this academic priority, at this point, Chögyam's followers have been described very much in counter-culture terms, and although there was a ritual life available (e.g., in the Vajradhatu Seminary three-month retreat), little emphasis was placed on identifying Chögyam's interpretation of Buddhism with Tibetan culture. This was to change with the visit to America in September 1974 of the head of the Kagyü sect, Ranjang Rigpe Dorje and his retinue of monks and *tulkus* (incarnations of a previous spiritual leaders) with their wondrous instruments, robes and voices. Fields points out the swift turnabout of Vajradhatu from a relatively carefree and nonchalant community to one that duly exhibited the appropriate veneration of the Karmapa and the captivating power of Tibetan ceremony. Hugely impressed by such extraordinary ritual theatre as the Black Crown Ceremony, Vajradhatu followers saw the Karmapa as the Tibetan tradition would see him: a holy monarch of sorts whose every action was justified, no matter how strange. This force flowed over equally into the perception congregants would have of Chögyam after the Karmapa publicly 'empowered' him as 'Vajra Holder and Possessor of the Ultimate Lineage Victory Banner of the Practice Lineage Teachings of the Karma Kagyü' (Chögyam Trungpa 1980: xii; Fields 1981: 330).

In 1976, Chögyam in turn 'empowered' an American disciple as his 'vajra regent' (*dorje gyaltsap*). Thomas F. Rich took on the religious name Ösel Tendzin, and began several years of intensive training with Chögyam. A year later, Chögyam established the Shambala Training Centre in Boulder, thus introducing a crucial element that remains central to the Nova

Scotia-centred organization today. Shambala is the name of a mythical, peaceful, enlightened kingdom, originally said to be of central Asian provenance, though now used more as a metaphor for a state of mind shared by a community freed of conflict. Somewhat ironically, the name is also associated with the image of a warrior (*pawo*). As Fields explains, 'Though meditation is the essential discipline of Shambala Training, it does not teach the way of the monk, yogi or priest, but the way of the warrior, a warrior in this case being someone who is brave enough to face his own tender heart' (Fields 1981: 375). Shambala has the advantage of introducing practitioners to various levels of Buddhist meditational techniques (e.g., *vipassanā*), but not requiring any commitment to become a Buddhist (a claim similarly made by Maharishi Mahesh Yogi's so-called Transcendental Meditation in the context of Hinduism). In time, Shambala was to be the centrepiece of Chögyam's outreach, its very name replacing all others as the organizational identification. It is, however, misleading to suggest that Buddhism is not absolutely central to Shambala International, and those who do commit themselves to Buddhism are also urged to give up identification with secularized Western cultural fixtures (e.g., *The Karma Dzong Sun*, Buddhist Church of Halifax, December 1986, urges replacement of Christmas with a 'Children's Day' marked on the winter solstice).

Chögyam's relocation to Halifax, Nova Scotia, along with key followers over a period of a few years, brought an unusual energy to the small, historic city and largely rural province. There were no doubt many motives for this move, including an awareness that the American government was becoming increasingly wary of Eastern cultic movements such as those associated with Sri Rajneesh or Sun Myung Moon, both in trouble with the law. Chögyam's wife Diana had equestrian contacts in Nova Scotia, and he had made a reconnaissance of the province as early as 1977 and taken a retreat in Mill Village in 1979. As one of Chögyam's early supporters who came with him in the first cohort has remarked, 'Chögyam liked the basic goodness of Nova Scotia, where there was a feeling of humanity without a whole lot of speed'. This is the more likely explanation for the decision to remove the Vajradhatu headquarters and the residence of the spiritual leader from the United States to cool, calm, collected Nova Scotia. To escape any cultic suggestion, Chögyam called his organization the Karma Dzong Buddhist Church of Halifax. The new community was largely comprised of young professionals of Caucasian extraction, who brought with them entrepreneurial skills and a commitment to stay the course in what was otherwise seen to be an economic backwater in an underprivileged part of Canada. They made a major contribution to Halifax in every way, perhaps above all introducing a Westernized form of an exotic branch of Buddhism to a community which had seventy Christian churches and two synagogues, but no established mosques, Hindu temples or Buddhist centres. Further, these new citizens contributed substantially to Nova Scotia's economic and cultural life. Diverse initiatives ranging from high-end provisioners and restauranteurs to bookshops and environmentally sensitive property development have had a positive impact much beyond a community small in number.

The phenomenon of Chögyam's Tantric Tibetan Buddhism in Nova Scotia is made complex by the polarity of religious activity it appeared to endorse, suggesting as it does that the dark aspects of the human psyche are important to enlist in order to see the whole of the human condition and overcome its limitations. On the one hand, there was the ambivalent 'crazy wisdom' of the guru himself, a hard drinking, chain smoking, often intoxicated and promiscuous spiritual leader whose every action, no matter how outrageous, was seen by his devotees to be somehow acceptable – a Tantric lesson deliberately engaging shock designed to help his followers to see beyond the mundane. In her careful research of this period, which involved many interviews with Vajradhatu practitioners, Lynn Eldershaw cites one such incident:

> Many other people were getting really pissed. After he was fully two hours late he comes in drunk and staggers on to the stage and then he sits down and gives this ten minute talk. Then he stops and says, 'Okay, I'll take questions now.' All the questions were about why he made them wait so long. He went along with that for ten minutes and then said, 'Well, it's good for you to wait for me.' Then he walks off . . . People waited two hours for this ten minute talk and an abusive ten minute question period by this drunken Tibetan.
>
> (Eldershaw 1994: 56)

Yet clearly this did not deter the faithful, who saw in this kind of performance a valuable teaching of some kind, no matter how bizarre. Another long-time student of Chögyam's reflected on her relationship with the guru in more empathetic terms:

> My main connection with Chögyam Trungpa Rinpoche is the mind connection of his enormous power and generosity, and [his] ability to open his mind so wide and articulate, so elegantly, that anybody who wanted to tune into his mind could do so. So, I feasted on him. I quenched my thirst and satisfied my hunger and feasted on his wisdom, and his brilliance, and his beauty, and his craziness, and his flare and his outrageousness. His outrageousness most of all.
>
> (Eldershaw 1994: 67)

Chögyam's lifestyle was certainly curious for a spiritual leader from any faith, and likely contributed to his demise in 1987. The regent Ösel Tendzin in turn died of AIDS just three years later. Although this caused not insignificant turmoil within the Buddhist community, remarkably it passed without much commentary by the fairly straightlaced non-Buddhist

159

Halifax public. For example, the Anglican diocesan bishop of the time, knowing that I had met Chögyam twice, asked me if I would kindly explain just what kind of Buddhism was being expressed at Karma Dzong. But there was no hint of righteous opprobrium from this or any other Christian denomination. The Buddhist community seemed to take note of its possible predicament and image, careful new leadership came forward under its Board of Directors, and the organization quickly regained its focus with no suggestion that its headquarters (now known as Shambala International) should leave Halifax for another, more cosmopolitan or central location. His Holiness Dilgokhyentse Rinpoche, a Nyingma prelate and former teacher of both Chögyam and his son, the Sakyong Mipham Rinpoche, advised the latter to then take on the spiritual direction of Shambala and move to Halifax from Britain accordingly. Although a President (Richard Reoch) and considerable administrative staff are responsible for this complex organization (with 160 centres worldwide), its fundamental spiritual focus is nonetheless emphasized in Mipham's leadership role. Unlike his father Chögyam, Mipham has returned to wearing robes, though, like his father, he is not known to be celibate.

On the other hand, Shambala has a remarkable record of quite conventional expressions of Buddhism. Four examples might be given. First, Gampo Abbey, established in Cape Breton in 1984, and associated in many ways with its first leader and presiding figure, the American nun Pema Chödrön, offers well-directed retreats (some up to three years in length), and spiritual direction at the highest professional level. About thirty-five monastics are in residence at any given time. Pema, ordained a full *bhikshuni* in the Chinese lineage in 1981, was an early follower of Chögyam. She writes evocatively of the unconditional relationship that emerged after she began to study with him:

> For the first time in my life I had met a person who was not caught up, a person whose mind was never swept away. I was drawn to him because I couldn't manipulate him; he knew how to cut through people's trips ... The teacher's role is to help the student realize that his awakened mind and the teacher's are the same.
>
> (Chödrön 2001: 114)

Month and week-long retreats (*dathun* and *weekthun*) are also available elsewhere, in Halifax and at a special retreat centre in Tatamagouche on the Northumberland Straight. A second, more academic focus of Shambala International is the Naropa Translation Committee, which has its central office and five full-time staff in Halifax. Shambala promotes Buddhist scholastic activity in many places, but Larry Mermelstein, the Committee's chairman, indicates that work proceeds on up to two dozen texts at any given time, with an enormous amount still waiting to be translated.

A third conventional aspect of Shambala is its gentle propagation of the faith. It is not a missionary Buddhism, like Soka Gakkai. Shambala does, however, have many smaller centres (*deleks*) in Atlantic Canada regularly visited by a teacher (Acharya Moh Hardin). These can be found in St John's and Gander, Newfoundland; Moncton, Fredericton and Saint John, New Brunswick (a small, independent *vipassanā* meditation group meeting at Sackville's Mount Allison University is seeking closer identification with Shambhala); and Sydney, Antigonish, St Margaret's Bay, Wolfville, Mahone Bay, Annapolis Royal and Yarmouth in Nova Scotia. A fourth laudable dimension is Shambala's continuous effort to bring to Halifax outstanding Buddhist teachers and exponents 'to give teachings', which recently have included Dzogchen Ponlop Rinpoche, the Very Venerable Seventh Yongey Mingyur Rinpoche, and Acharya Sulak Sivraksa (the architect of the Network of Engaged Buddhists). Thus Atlantic Canada has close association with one of the modern Buddhist world's most unique forms of Westernized but still traditionally rooted interpretations of the faith. There is every reason to believe that somehow the geography of the region, both physical and geographical, touched the heart of the founding guru – something exemplified, perhaps, at Chögyam's cremation in Vermont where, at a key moment, the mournful bagpipe lament 'Farewell to Nova Scotia' swept down from the hills.

Notes

1 Statistics Canada (2001) *2001 Census*, Selected Regions for Census Metropolitan Areas and Census Agglomerations, Halifax, Fredericton, Saint John, St John's.
2 It is of interest to note that the Dalhousie University Chaplaincy Office, under the informal leadership of Rev. Clement Mehlman, a Lutheran pastor, has put together a brochure, *Buddhist Communities in the Halifax Regional Municipality*. Rev. Mehlman brings spokespersons for the seven different Buddhist groups together on an annual basis, the only time they meet as an organized body.

Bibliography

Chödrön, Pema (2001) *The Places That Scare You: A Guide to Fearlessness in Difficult Times.* Boston, MA: Shambala.
Eldershaw, Lynn (1994) "Refugees in the Dharma: A Study of Revitalization in the Buddhist Church of Halifax," MA thesis (unpublished), Acadia University, Nova Scotia.
Fields, Rick (1981) *How the Swans Came to the Lake: A Narrative History of Buddhism in America.* Boulder, CO: Shambala.
Rinpoche, Chogyam Trungpa (1980) *The Rain of Wisdom: The Essence of the Ocean of True Meaning (The Vajra Songs of the Kagyü Gurus)*, Nalanda Translation Committee. Boulder, CO: Shambala.

APPENDIX

buddhismcanada.com:
a decade in cyber-*samsara*

George Klima

The website buddhismcanada.com consists mainly of a directory of 400 Canadian Buddhist groups. This website exists as a data source on the internet. From this realm of cyber-*samsara*, buddhismcanada.com in one sense reflects the perpetual search and wandering of Buddhist practitioners. In this brief paper I describe our methods for developing up-to-date data of quality for the website. In this regard, William Gibson's notion of 'cyberspace' is helpful. He begins with the idea that there exists a territory inside computer games that, metaphorically at least, is the same realm for all individuals who are playing that game.[1] The term became extended to refer to an inherent virtual reality of computerized networks, such as the internet. But as Gibson himself admits, the term 'cyberspace' is '. . . evocative but essentially meaningless . . . it has no real semantic meaning, even for me'.[2] The notion of cyberspace is itself diffuse, then, and it is recognized that this website-based project connecting so many diverse Buddhist groups in Canada is a novel venture.

In reviewing the history of the website, buddhismcanada.com, we find that the intentions behind the efforts to develop the site all had their roots in our own wanderings as well as the wanderings of our fellow practitioners. Originally, Chris Ng and Michael Kerr were involved with the Toronto Chapter of the Buddhist Council of Canada and, as part of that initiative, they helped organize an annual *Vesak* celebration. (Later, the Toronto Chapter reorganized itself as the Buddhist Communities of Greater Toronto.) This organization needed a contact list for people who were coming to meetings or who needed to be reached for other reasons. Naturally, the list went through various revisions. At every meeting, people were asked to check their information and update it if necessary. Subsequently, K'un Li Shih also attended the *Vesak* planning meetings and argued that the list should be extended so as to be Canada-wide. Inspired by her previous work with Don Morreale's directory, K'un Li Shih designed a questionnaire and a format for a more comprehensive directory, one that would cover all of Canada.[3] This information became available under the name 'Buddhist Women's Network of Toronto.'

In the spring of 1994, I attended one of these *Vesak* celebrations, met Michael Kerr, saw the Toronto version of the list, and offered to publish Kerr's list electronically. My intention at the time was to reduce the 'economic friction' of moving from one group to another. In November I posted Michael Kerr's list on a Bulletin Board System operated by Mike Butler, out of Ajax, Ontario. After a few months, I moved the list to the World Wide Web, then obtained the national list that K'un Li Shih had compiled, and added it to the Web directory.

During 1999–2000, Mathieu Ouellet, who was traveling back and forth between cities in Québec and Nova Scotia for studies and employment, found that information on the website was often out of date. As his relationship with the website developed, Ouellet became most helpful by acting as a local provincial contact for Québec, New Brunswick, and Nova Scotia. It was particularly accommodating that he was able to communicate with personal acquaintances and those in French-speaking groups.

Our Canada-wide web survey is based on the premise that it is of primary importance that the information on each site be accurate and complete. However, many of the identified groups and organizations are in flux, and we find ourselves operating from varying degrees of ignorance. Moreover, there is no one, single Buddhist 'community'. People who associate themselves with one Buddhist group or another constitute a wildly fragmented and polyglot collection. There is no single Buddhist spokesperson, no Buddhist licensing agency, and no Buddhist 'brand manager'. We have found that there is in fact little that Buddhist practitioners have in common except the common goal of seeking refuge in the Triple Gem. Our lack of knowledge about the intimate specifics of the groups whom we contact and list, of our informants, can create a variety of difficulties. We therefore protect ourselves as recorders of reliable information, and the accuracy and completeness of that information, in several ways.

First, our primary aim is to determine which organizations deserve to be set down in a directory of Canadian Buddhist groups. The methodology is straightforward: does a location or site serve one or more of three audiences: practitioners who are moving or otherwise looking for a new group; newcomers to Buddhism who are looking for a group, and academics who are studying Buddhism or Buddhists?

The second method for protecting accuracy and completeness is to be careful about our sources. Every piece of information we publish on the website is tagged with the source of the information and the date on which it was published. The name of the source is often helpful for contacting the group, for sorting out discrepancies and, occasionally, for dealing with groups that are having internal problems. The last-updated tag should give the user an indication of the information credibility, and also serves as a way to prioritize our efforts to stay in touch.

Our sources are nearly always individuals. We rarely take information from websites, for several reasons. Usually, we do not know how 'fresh' the information is because most websites do not use anything like a 'last updated' indicator or tag. As well, we do not know whether the group in question intends that their information should be copied and reposted on our site. Even if we are directed to a group's website, we are not always able to adjudicate how reliable the information is, nor do all the websites necessarily have the information we require. Thus, individual contact remains a priority for identification and verification.

The individuals who serve as our informants are typically 'designated' in some sense. In other words, when I am contacted by a person who offers information about a Buddhist group, I try to determine whether that person is acting in some official capacity. By contrast, sometimes an acquaintance of a temple will send information. We do not publish reports from such helpful friends because such a person is not always conveying the desired information – or even accurate information. In such cases I request that this helpful friend should contact the designated spokesperson for the temple and ask them to send me the update.

Inclusion and exclusion

The buddhismcanada.com website is a privately funded and maintained initiative. We argue that notions of what might be termed equity, transparency, and accountability do not apply. 'Equity' as applied here might be that each group that wishes to be listed should have an equal right. With only the rarest of exceptions we welcome the inclusion of groups; however, no group has any specific right to be included. 'Transparency' might be understood as the obligation to clearly disclose the process by which decisions are made in the operation of the website. Although in this paper we are in fact doing this, it is not out of any specific obligation. 'Accountability' might be defined as an obligation to answer for the content or appearance of a website. Again, we welcome comments and usually reply to questions about the content, but not out of any sense of obligation. Although we make every effort to be true to our objectives, presenting useful information to our extensive audience, and to proceed in a reasonable and fair manner, we do not accept the notion that people who benefit from the website (or who have a complaint against it) should have any reason to moral or legal 'claims' over the site. There is no implicit contract of any sort between the users and the providers because the site is given freely, without the expectation of anything in exchange.

The site is also not a list of recommended groups, such as those found in a 'consumer report' magazine, or in the film review pages of our newspapers.

It would be completely impractical to assess and monitor the hundreds of groups that are listed, and, of course, we do not have the moral authority to do so. Nevertheless, we aver that it is important to impose some simple criteria for what should be included on the site, what should not be included, and what should be removed after it has been included. The inclusion criteria were arrived at after a long period of discussion. Ultimately, these criteria are ones we maintain are appropriate, practical to implement, and that we can live with. Any group that is listed should refer to itself as 'Buddhist'; respect the Triple Gem; have regular contact with ordained *sangha* and hold scheduled events.

Exclusion criteria

Groups of Buddhist practitioners, like any other group of people, sometimes become dysfunctional. For example, we encountered a situation in which a group of Zen students decided that the authoritarian structure of their temple was excessive and so they decided to initiate a '*dharma* experiment', consisting of *ad hoc*, undirected, lay-led meetings. They coined an appealing name for their breakaway group and had one meeting to discuss how to proceed. When I spoke to their contact person a year later, they had not yet had a second meeting. It seemed that, despite their good intentions, the group was likely lacking the diligence and guidance to become a successful independent entity.

We also sometimes hear reports from disaffected ex-members alleging a variety of misdeeds going on at, for example, a temple. Perhaps a monk was caught having an evening snack. Perhaps a nun was doing non-serious work. Perhaps a monk was alleged to have sexual relations with a woman. Perhaps a monk was taking an unusual interest in *dana*, leaving the donor feeling coerced. Or, perhaps, the ex-member is simply indulging in spreading false rumours. It is inappropriate for us to get involved over such matters. Although we do consider self-evident circumstances under which a group's dysfunctional status should lead us to remove them from the directory, because of our limited resources and even more limited moral authority, we realize it would be impractical and inappropriate to be undertaking any sort of investigative role. Thus, we argue that whatever dysfunction exists should be fairly extreme, systemic, and pervasive.

Usage

The directory is frequently used by individuals as an e-mail mailing list, which some will inevitably use to promote their own activities, services, or products. (Because the list is seeded with some non-existent groups, we are able to keep track of who is using the list.) We have no explicit policy of 'reasonable use', and even usage that we consider unreasonable is impossible to prevent. We do attempt to persuade people to refrain from using the directory to create a mailing list for their own purposes. More troubling is the increasing amount of virus-infected e-mails and spam. The only preventive measure we have taken is to list e-mail addresses with an image as, for example, 'bob@domain.com' instead of '<u>bob@domain.com</u>'. We expect that the automatic e-mail harvesters do not yet know how to read images. There has also been a series of attacks that appear to be targeted at us. We receive on average a half dozen targeted virus-infected e-mails daily.

Copyright

There is no copyright protection for the contents of a directory. The information content is public information. Thus we are able to assert our copyright only over the buddhismcanada.com website's format and not its contents. We do assert the copyright because we believe that the format we have developed is a piece of intellectual property that we are unwilling to share. We assert the copyright on behalf of the Buddhist Women's Network of Toronto because we hope that it gives us a greater authority than if we were to make the assertion solely in our own names. We also assert copyright because, at a personal level, we acknowledge that the site is the result of our effort and it should not be republished by other parties who implicitly claim that it is due to their effort. When we discover that the information has been copied by others, we contact the owners of the websites that appeared to have copied our information. Our message is simple: anyone is welcome to copy anything they like; we request only that they acknowledge where they obtained it. This approach has been satisfactory in most, but not all, cases. In the long run, we have decided that the best way to deal with copyright issues is to continue doing our best in providing the directory service. So far none of the imitators have been able to copy our material with sufficient proficiency to endanger our project. At the same time, the traffic to our site continues to climb (presently at 15,000 page views per month). As well, we receive a steady stream of thank-you notes by e-mail from people across the country, which provides us with the confidence that our effort continues to be useful.

Notes

1 Mark Neale (Director) (2000) *No Maps for These Territories* [film]. Great Britain: Mark Neale Productions.
2 *Ibid.*
3 Don Morreale (1988) *Buddhist America: Centers, Retreats, Practices.* Santa Fe, NM: John Muir Publications.

INDEX